IMPOSSIBLE SPEECH

Impossible Speech

*The Politics of Representation in
Contemporary Korean Literature and Film*

Christopher P. Hanscom

Columbia University Press   New York

Columbia University Press
Publishers Since 1893
New York   Chichester, West Sussex
cup.columbia.edu
Copyright © 2024 Columbia University Press
All rights reserved

Library of Congress Cataloging-in-Publication Data
Names: Hanscom, Christopher P., 1972– author.
Title: Impossible speech : the politics of representation in contemporary Korean literature and film / Christopher P. Hanscom.
Description: New York : Columbia University Press, 2024. | Includes bibliographical references and index.
Identifiers: LCCN 2023038252 (print) | LCCN 2023038253 (ebook) | ISBN 9780231208482 (hardback) | ISBN 9780231208499 (trade paperback) | ISBN 9780231557450 (ebook)
Subjects: LCSH: Motion pictures—Political aspects—Korea (South). | Motion pictures—Korea (South)—History—21st century. | Korean literature—Political aspects. | Korean fiction—History and criticism—21st century.
Classification: LCC PN1993.5.K6 H447 2024 (print) | LCC PN1993.5.K6 (ebook) | DDC 791.43095195—dc23/eng/20230927
LC record available at https://lccn.loc.gov/2023038252
LC ebook record available at https://lccn.loc.gov/2023038253

Cover design: Chang Jae Lee
Cover image: © Shutterstock

Contents

Acknowledgments	vii
INTRODUCTION Impossible Speech and the Politics of Literature	1
CHAPTER ONE The Return of the Real in South Korean Fiction	27
CHAPTER TWO Displacing the Common Sense of Trauma: Han Kang's *A Boy Is Coming*	45
CHAPTER THREE Fabricating the Real: Accounting for North Korea in Escapee Narratives and in Fiction	84
CHAPTER FOUR Disturbing Sensibility: Transgressing Generic Norms in *Castaway on the Moon* and *I'm a Cyborg, but That's OK*	123
CONCLUSION	152
Notes	171
Bibliography	207
Index	219

Acknowledgments

My thanks to the organizers and participants at events where I was able to share earlier versions of this work, including the University of British Columbia Centre for Korean Research, the Nam Center for Korean Studies at the University of Michigan, the University of Wisconsin Center for East Asian Studies, the Kyumun Research Institute (Seoul), the Center for Korean Studies at the University of Washington, the Society of Korean Language and Literature (Seoul), the Decolonising East Asian Studies Workshop at the University of Cambridge, and the Korean Studies Institute at the University of Southern California. A 2021 writing retreat in Paso Robles was all-important in providing me the time and space to think together with others about the shape and stakes of the project.

Portions of chapter 1 were previously published in "The Return of the Real in South Korean Fiction," *Acta Koreana* 22, no. 1 (June 2019): 1–16, and are reprinted by permission of the journal.

Christine Dunbar at Columbia University Press has been supportive from the start and, with her team, was instrumental in making it possible for the book to see the light of day. My sincere thanks to the three anonymous readers of the manuscript who gave detailed and constructive remarks that did much to improve the final version. I would also like to gratefully acknowledge the support of the Laboratory Program for Korean Studies through the Ministry of Education of the Republic of

Korea and the Korean Studies Promotion Service of the Academy of Korean Studies (AKS-2015-LAB-2250002).

Finally, thanks and love to my family—Carol, Alice, Stella, and Eugenie—for all the usual reasons, but here especially for reminding me every day of the power that imagination and language have to wondrously and joyously expand the boundaries of the possible.

IMPOSSIBLE SPEECH

Introduction

Impossible Speech and the Politics of Literature

The blockbuster 2013 film *The Attorney* (*Pyŏnhoin*, dir. Yang Usŏk) is most often understood as a fictionalized account of Roh Moo-hyun's work as a human rights lawyer in 1980s Pusan, prior to his term as president of South Korea from 2003 to 2008. The second-highest grossing film in 2013–2014 in South Korea, it is based on the September 1981 "Purim affair," when authorities arrested, tortured, and convicted over twenty people, including students, teachers, and office workers, who had participated in an allegedly "communist" social science reading group and were charged with violating the National Security Law. *The Attorney*'s first half is a comedy, following the exploits of an up-and-coming tax attorney whose primary aim is to gain financially from his practice. Both his greed and his seeming unwillingness to take the practice of law seriously are looked down upon by his peers—snobbish, university-educated lawyers who hold what appears to be the moral high ground in their commitment to justice over profit. The second act is a courtroom drama, during which the main character, Song Usŏk, turns from venal individualist to righteous moralist and defends a young man who has been arrested and tortured as part of the Purim affair.[1]

The remarkable success of the film has led critics to see it as an example of how a historical moment can speak through art, connecting a (long-suppressed) past moment of political resistance to the concerns of the present. The ostensible politics of the film—which came out at the moment when Park Geun-hye, daughter of the former dictator Park Chung Hee, had been elected as the South Korean president—would then be to revive this resistance through the recollection and representation of the past in a deeply divided society still reeling from Roh's suicide in 2009.[2] Delivered in the form of a fictionalized biography, the message of *The Attorney*—so obvious that it comes across as nearly propagandistic—is twofold: that the political ethos of the past must be remembered and narrated, and that the present moment is one in which such a commemorative breaking of silence is itself a political act.

Yet the pivotal moment of the film, the courtroom victory, retains a crucial ambiguity. The attorney Song is questioning a police captain who has been called to the stand as a witness regarding both the legality of the suspected communist's warrantless arrest and detainment and the factuality of the young man's torture. The captain denies that the prisoner was tortured and claims that the arrest was legal, as the suspected thought crime falls under the National Security Law, alleviating the need for an arrest warrant and allowing for detention without charge. "I was simply obeying the law," he tells Song. The attorney responds by asking how the captain had decided that the National Security Law had been violated. "It's not me who judged," the captain tells him. "It's the state [*kukka*] that decides." "The state?" asks Song incredulously, invoking the second clause of the first article of the South Korean constitution: "The sovereign power of the Republic of Korea rests in its people [*kungmin*]; all sovereign authority emerges from the people." Hence, he concludes, "the state is the people [*kukka kungmin ida*]."

The appeal to the rule of law and to patriotism is intended to appeal to the viewer, and the sequence of shots makes it clear that the audience is to adopt Song's perspective as its own.[3] The catharsis of this scene, in which the captain is brought to rhetorical (if not actual) justice, seems a victory for Song and for the liberal democracy that he represents. "The state is the people" can thus be given a populist reading, a reading that the film encourages. Yet as critic Chŏng Pyŏnggi points out, what the film elevates is a model of bourgeois democracy that rests on a broad ideology of human rights while remaining silent on the question of socioeconomic justice.[4] "The state is the people" can then also be read more pessimistically as the total penetration of "the people"

2 *Introduction*

by a way of knowing and feeling that emerges from the interests of an earlier authoritarian government or the present-day neoliberal state in South Korea.

With Chŏng's skepticism in mind, there are three things to notice about this pivotal moment when the resistant politics of the past is brought to bear on the present, each aligned with one of the core chapters of the book: its memorialization of trauma, the logic of the confessional or biographical voice, and the determining force of generic narrative form.

First, the rhetorical and affective power of the courtroom scenes derives in large part from the graphic representation of the tortured bodies of the detainees, who in the narrative present observe the proceedings as defendants. It is through the representation of the past traumatic event of torture that—as a form of documentary evidence and testimony—truth is arrived at and subsequent catharsis is achieved. Yet the traumatic event undergoes no psychoanalytic "working through" in the film. In its graphic and realistic representations of torture, the film instead brings trauma forward in time intact and retraumatizes the invested viewer. The trauma is not so much resolved as shared, a historical wounding that, once forgotten, now makes its way into the present to be experienced by subsequent generations. As such, *The Attorney* victoriously memorializes the affair as a touchstone in the history of resistant politics and democratization by leaving it unchanged. Such memorialization or *memorization* of trauma, as we will see in chapter 2, makes remembering habitual, ties it to regular national ceremonies, and eliminates other possible ways of speaking about an event—in short, it paradoxically makes the event forgettable.

Second, the representation of past trauma is verisimilar, taking on the conventions of biography. The film is quite clearly meant to represent the early career of Roh Moo-hyun, and the early, comedic scenes add to the sense that we are looking at a real person, a fallible human being. The impact of the film comes in his transformation from an ordinary person aiming to support his family to an attorney risking life and limb for the sake of democratization and human rights. The biographical form, which is assumed to be coterminous with personal and historical truth, is structurally amenable to being coopted into the narration of national

Introduction   3

history. Yet, as we will see in chapter 3, literary forms may also resist what Marc Nichanian calls the "historiographic imperative," an injunction that "forbids any consideration of the event outside the coordinates of the fact."[5] Parallel to the presentation of trauma as something that may be fully known and memorialized as the basis for community, under a realist regime, the literary text may also be subjected to the logic of proof, read and evaluated based on evidentiary standards. Yet when a historicist and realist reading method is applied to the work of art, we find a paradoxical torsion: factuality is required of both the expression of traumatic experience (in testimony) and of fictional representation (as biographical confession), both of which are by definition enigmatic and in excess of the strictly knowable.

Third, the film takes advantage of narrative form to establish a logic of salvation tied to the workings of national history. Although the film is billed as a legal drama, it is the law that works to silence testimony while history takes precedence and is presented as coextensive with the facts of the matter. Where photographs of wounds and the physical presence of the victims have failed to produce an admission of guilt (that is, where evidence does not correspond with the facts predetermined by legal authority), it is the last-minute testimony of Lt. Yoon—a medic who witnessed the torture—that turns the tide. This leads to the cathartic moment in the courtroom where, briefly, the facticity of the torture is admitted. "Now, in this way, the truth has been revealed," the attorney Song tells us. "We have a clear incident, a witness, and a testimony."[6] Yet in the next moment, the medic is arrested and taken from the courtroom, and his testimony is ordered struck from the record—he is absent without leave from his post and is hence subject to military, not civilian law. The defendants are charged and jailed.

Mirroring this legal defeat in 1981, the screen then fades to black. What next emerges before the viewer is quite literally a mark of historical time, the text "1987"—immediately recognizable as the year of countrywide uprisings in support of free elections, sparked in part by the death of a university student at the hands of the police. We see Song standing in a fog of tear gas at the head of a group of protestors, exhorting them to "fight for democracy" and to "stand united as citizens" against advancing riot police. He is arrested and charged with promoting illegal gatherings and fomenting anti-government protest. During the final

4 *Introduction*

courtroom scene—in which the attorney Song is now the defendant—we meet with an unexpected strategy. In lieu of any argument whatsoever, his lawyers instead ask the judge to call the roll of all of the assembled attorneys. Song sits in silence as the names of the nearly one hundred lawyers gathered in support are read aloud, an enumeration that is itself silenced as the soundtrack swells and the screen fades to the credits. What is remarkable here is that at the very moment when the main character is given the opportunity to make his case, the film concludes with his silence. What does Song's silence mean, as the final gesture of a film whose intended affective and political impact seems to rest on the act of *breaking* silence?

In the memorializing representation of trauma, the verisimilar mode, which subjects the work of art to a logic of proof, and in the determination of meaning through recourse to a fully known, generic national history, what we see is the foreclosure of possible speech. The silence with which the film concludes is not a silence born of the inability to speak, but rather, from the fact that *nothing remains to be said.* All possible speech is accounted for. The viewer is expected to have a full understanding of the significance of this moment: the line between victim and perpetrator has been drawn; the truth has been exposed in testimony and in the presentation of evidence; the origins of trauma have been located and, in being known, resolved. At the end of the film, the community becomes audible (in the judge's enunciation of the names of those assembled) and visible (in the body of lawyers gathered behind Song) in its unqualified support of Song's character. Consensus is achieved, and all that is left to do is call out one's own name in an acknowledgment of belonging or, more to the point, to have one's named called out by a representative of the state.

The historical narrative presented in the film is what remains in the absence of a legal record or after legal proceedings have failed to produce the truth. History assumes from law the task of demonstrating what counts as a fact, that which is either stricken from or included in "the record." The fictional narrative assigned the task of representing that history in the present moment takes the form of a salvation story, both in 1987 (as we see Song exonerated and beatified in the closing scene) and, crucially, in the context of the rise of conservative politics in the 2010s. The testimonial character of the realist genre, combined with the

Introduction   5

authority of the historical work to arrange evidence in pursuit of the truth, leads to "an almost inescapable providentialism"[7] in the relation of the character to his experience. At the same time, a soteriological logic, moving a character from "a state of deprivation (sin, corruption)" to a "state of release from that deprivation (salvation, liberation)" via a transformative event,[8] not only binds certain sequences in the film together in order (the sin or deprivation of Song's early-career venality, the transformative event of his involvement with the Purim affair in 1981, his liberation on the streets in 1987) but also locates the viewer in a single, larger story[9] structured by the apparently inescapable telos of national history. As we will see in chapter 4, however, the determining force of narrative form may be transgressed and the salvational logic of the nation undermined.

The Attorney conforms to a mode of representation that relies on the verisimilar presentation of trauma, set in a historical narrative that dramatizes the emergence of truth via the (biographical) act of breaking a silence, a truth that in the end not only saves the main character but also acts to proselytize, promising to save those who find themselves in the still-unfolding story of the nation in the mid-2010s. The film takes on the role of the historian, putting an evidentiary logic to work across a network of witness accounts and representing the adjudication of those accounts on the screen as a form of consensual politics ranging from the struggle for democratization in the 1980s through the resurgence of authoritarianism at the moment of the film's release in 2013. Traumatic, biographical, and soteriological narratives work in tandem, all three aiming at a kind of retrospective visibility. The psychological subject of trauma presents a sort of involuntary witness in the form of symptoms or wounds, testifying to the veracity of the historical event and moving toward the salvation of a cure; the biographical subject is understood to speak the truth of experience, a kind of testament to a personal history that finds closure with the writing of the biography itself; meanwhile, a soteriological logic structures both the traumatic and biographical narratives, testifying to not only life events or experiences but also to the meaning of a narrative made up of a "web of storied connections [that] accounts for this and not that occurring," a retelling that is itself understood as redemptive in the present moment.[10]

6 *Introduction*

WHAT IS THE POLITICS OF ART?

Such narrative modes establish a logic that structures a given situation and establishes its intelligibility—what Jacques Rancière describes as the power of the literary work to "integrate [lives] into [a] verisimilar tale of social necessity."[11] I understand these conditions of intelligibility to be the site of politics, conditions "formulated in and by power," yet a "normative exercise of power [that] is rarely acknowledged as an operation of power at all,"[12] taking as its primary focus this relationship between literary form and making sense—a struggle over the propriety of language and the parameters of narrative appropriate to a given event.

Put differently, *Impossible Speech* asks what we mean when we say "the politics of art." The book takes issue with definitions of political art that rely on the representation of subject matter already understood as "political" in order to make their claims to value or relevance. Examples drawn from literature and film demonstrate how such "political art"— while striving for empathy or understanding with victims or marginalized subjects, or aiming to "break the silence" about heretofore underexamined historical events—in fact often silences those subjects, excluding them from the realm of the "sayable" in their drive to expose, make visible, and achieve understanding of personal or historical truth.

Against this pervasive realism and the idea that politics is coextensive with the nation, an alternative treatment of political art examines the operations that establish the limits of what can be said, seen, or heard, focusing on texts that expose and push against those limits. In close readings of literary and film works, I find that it is at those moments when speech is relegated to nonsense that we can in fact find the political gesture of art. The following chapters thus aim to explore both the ways in which the work of art can undermine this demand for consensual meaning in its presentation of the limits of representation—in the "impossible speech" of those who are not asked, expected, or allowed to put forward their thoughts in discourse—and the grounds of legitimacy upon which a given statement or representation of speech is understood (or not understood) as "political."

I focus on four figures central to recent fiction and film—the migrant laborer, the witness to or survivor of state violence, the North Korean refugee, and the socially excluded urban precariat. It is tempting to read

Introduction   7

these works of fiction and film as verisimilar representations of historical events and thus as documents with probative value, conforming to the pre-given common sense of a situation. Indeed, the narrative modes that the core chapters reexamine—the traumatic, the confessional, and the soteriological—are most prone to being coopted by narratives of national consensus. Yet the book is not interested in "political art" in the sense of works that exploit their proximity to the real in order to take sides in a particular issue or debate—an approach to literature that values the work of art to the extent that it provides evidence of sociohistorical truth. *Impossible Speech* challenges the seeming inevitability of national context and an interpretive schema that assigns meaning based on culture and place. In that declaring something nonpolitical may be seen as the political gesture par excellence,[13] the book refocuses our attention on "nonpolitical" art as the very site of politics.

In order to think the politics of literature outside of the common sense of what typically constitutes political art, the book makes the question of the limits of speakability coterminous with the question of politics, here understood not as the organization of consensus but more fundamentally as the determination of the limits of speech—who is allowed to speak and what is allowed to be spoken. Political resistance is not necessarily the "call to action" addressed to a predefined community, those who would occupy already-existing positions of power following a rearrangement of elements within that community. It comes rather from the "individual without a proper place in the social edifice,"[14] an "excess . . . lived as the outside of intelligibility,"[15] from those unauthorized to speak in the name of a given community.

Throughout, I rely heavily on Rancière's definition of politics as a speech situation, a struggle over the decision on what may be said, seen, or heard that is at the same time linked to the configuration of subjects in a given situation or community. Politics is generally understood as "the set of procedures whereby the aggregation and consent of collectivities is achieved, the organization of powers, the distribution of places and roles, and the systems for legitimizing this distribution."[16] Against this definition, which Rancière renames "police," he poses a clash of "police" and "egalitarian" logics opposed to the clear and instrumentalist identification of subjects and their places in a given community. Politics is "whatever breaks with the tangible configuration whereby parties and

8   *Introduction*

parts or lack of them are defined by a presupposition that, by definition, has no place in that configuration—that part of those who have no part."[17] Elsewhere, he writes that politics occurs when that part that has no part in the community appears as "inhabitants of a common space and demonstrate that their mouths really do emit speech capable of making pronouncements on the common which cannot be reduced to voices signaling pain."[18] The question is thus who is qualified to speak, and what is to be made of that speech: "Political activity is whatever shifts a body from the place assigned to it or changes a place's destination. It makes visible what had no business being seen, and makes heard a discourse where once there was only place for noise; it makes understood as discourse what was once only heard as noise."[19]

At the risk of oversimplifying Rancière's thought, for the purposes of this study, there are two basic assumptions that follow from this, and that run throughout the book: that the site of politics is not at the level of the statement of the text but the set of operations that work to establish the domain of the sayable or the visible; and that this domain is, in some sense, coextensive with the definition and boundaries of community. If "for all time, the refusal to consider certain categories of people as political beings has proceeded by means of a refusal to hear the words exiting their mouths as discourse,"[20] then *Impossible Speech* chooses to focus on the representation of those who are ordinarily outside the boundaries of discourse but whose entry onto the stage signals not only a struggle to speak or be heard, but "a fight for the ownership—the propriety, the property—of speaking."[21]

IMPOSSIBLE SPEECH

This focus comes, however, with a special qualification. The idea here is not to identify and simply put forward subjects who are not usually given the opportunity to speak. The four figures on which the book focuses align with particular sociopolitical phenomena: the influx of migrant labor into South Korea in the 2000s and 2010s; the Kwangju uprising and massacre in 1980; the slow collapse of social support systems in North Korea from the 1990s onward; and the post-IMF neoliberalization of the South Korean state and a consequent rise in the precarity of economic and social existence. Given these coincidences, it is tempting to read

Introduction 9

these works of literature and film as realistic representations of historical events and thus as documents with probative value. But rather than focusing on the overt statement made by the text or a particular "politics" advocated for by the artist, *Impossible Speech* addresses the capacity of the work of art to confront the boundaries of what is sayable or visible in a given situation, and how that boundary itself reflects (and expands) the normative limits of common sense and speech.

"Impossible speech" takes on a different valence in each chapter, but at base signals a language that is *understood to be unsayable*, a contradiction in terms that points to the way in which the unsayable is necessarily seen as such in advance. This operation establishing the limits on what can be said—what Nancy Fraser calls "framing"[22] or what Judith Butler terms "foreclosure"[23]—regulates the social domain of speakable discourse. "Impossible speech" is not out there somewhere, waiting to be discovered—it is the rules of speakability that actively produce such impossibility.

The point here is thus not to simply place minor characters on the stage, to provide them with the opportunity for speech. This itself would present a troubling politics of representation, assuming the authority to speak for the subject or to decide whose speech is to mean what. *Impossible Speech* makes no moral claim to "give voice" to the unheard; nor do I aim to provide an ultimate meaning of the speech of these subjects in the context of a given culture. Rather, I point to moments in which a subject begins to come into being outside of the police regime, a subjectification that resists the singularity of identity and "operates in the interval between several nominations," localizing "what has its being only in the gap of places and identities."[24]

"Between several nominations" suggests that a singular meaning of a word has not yet been attained, that a one-to-one relation between word and thing is not yet established. There is a kind of radical potential here, when something appears as *real* (in the world, possible) but not yet *actual* (fully realized, spent of potential),[25] not yet linked to a specific place or status. A pre-given place (whether geographical or social) has not yet been fixed into a consensual meaning. This "violent inclusion in a form of sensible community of . . . a language which escapes this language," the "transgression of the ordered division of voices and idioms, that transgression which attains its ultimate point with the inclusion in language

10   *Introduction*

of the impossibility itself of speaking,"[26] *breaks the law* of the police order in which one's place, job, function, body, etc., are fixed and where language functions to identify, to reproduce orderly relations between subjects without exceeding the field of possible description.[27]

By focusing on texts that treat the "violent inclusion" of utterances as if they precede any such consensual determination, my argument resists the typical idea of realism as the verisimilar representation of what exists and is available to sense perception. Such an idea of realism insists that points of correspondence be found between the text and the world, and that the truth of narrative is guaranteed by the plausibility produced by an arrangement of such points of connection. The reception of (especially non-Western) texts tends, however, to hide any potential of the artwork to exceed the given by arranging such correspondences under the explanatory concept of "culture," an idea that "has the sole effect of effacing this movement of subjectification," naming as it does a preexisting identity that puts subjects *in their place.*[28]

The narrative modes with which the book is concerned typically locate the politics of the text at its surface and the action of subjectivization in the performance of a pre-given identity. Each of these modes conventionally establishes a logic of "the only possible" speech: the involuntary expressions (symptomatic or otherwise) of the traumatized subject, the authentic statements of the historical individual, or the spontaneous cries of those in love, or in pain. Such a generic logic conforms to a generic consensus, what could be called—awkwardly—the impossibilization of impossible speech. When all possible speech is identified, what emerges is a kind of silencing. "The question is not what it is I will be able to say," Butler writes, "but what will constitute the domain of the sayable within which I begin to speak at all." Speech falling outside of the common sense of established discourse, which might include "asocial ramblings" or "psychotic ranting," points to a kind of impossibility itself produced by the establishment of a realm of speakability and, further, haunts that normative realm.[29]

Two opening examples serve to set the stage by describing how texts that seem to engage with the "political," whether in terms of current or past events, may work instead to reproduce the normative. In the "migrant labor fiction" of the first chapter, we see literary works most often deemed "political" in their representation of the marginalized foreigner

Introduction   11

functioning, at the level of form, to reinforce a politics of exclusion rooted in monolingual national identity. The speech of the foreigner is silenced, put in its place under the logic of the existing political order, an act disguised by the seemingly progressive politics of the literary text.[30] The second chapter points to a similarly conservative gesture, hidden under the guise of progressive politics, through a critical analysis of Moon Jae-in's speeches on the anniversary of the Kwangju uprising and massacre. In both cases, what we can say is that speech is rendered all too possible: a fullness of language is established that silences or excludes language not intelligible on its terms. In this way, the book opens by showing that the nonpolitical can be produced in the very proliferation of statements of a given subject's politicity, removing that subject from the scene of political decision into the realm of foregone conclusion.

To speak outside of this domain is to question the very status of the subject, and the subsequent chapters of the book focus on such moments when the attempt is made to move outside of "the domain of speakability" that "consummate[s] one's status as a subject of speech."[31] Each core chapter in the book deals with a different form of speech, with each mode of speech "impossible" in its own way. Each thus addresses texts that appear to challenge the boundaries of the speakable or the visible, an archival system that "governs the appearance of statements and generates social meaning,"[32] a set of norms that "precede the possibility of description" or produce descriptions that "are themselves normatively structured in advance, through a foreclosure that establishes the domain of the speakable."[33]

The book thus calls the consensus signaled in the opening examples into question, in part through a critique of conventional narrative forms of trauma, confession, and salvation. The second chapter, dealing with the Kwangju massacre of May 1980, addresses the impossibility of testimony—or, the resistance to compulsory testimony—in relation to traumatic catastrophic events. The third chapter stages two versions of the impossibility of "telling the truth" about North Korea through parallel analyses of fiction and North Korean escapee narratives, pointing to the limits of confessional and biographical genres. The fourth chapter looks at nonsensical speech in two recent South Korean films. The conclusion returns to the question of testimony by investigating examples of film and fiction that attempt to narrate the experience of comfort women, and

12 *Introduction*

focuses on the "compulsory discursivity" required of the witness in a context where the past bears directly on the politics of the present. Here too, an evidentiary logic is leveled against the imaginative text, depriving it of the capacity to exceed or adjust the normative sense of the situation and subjecting it to the interpretative frame of either the consensual national community or the international human rights regime.

These modes of speech are not all impossible in the same way. Trauma presents us with a situation in which the victim is rendered unable to speak by the psychologically overwhelming nature of the event itself. North Korean refugees are compelled to narrate their life stories—whether under preliminary questioning by agents of the National Intelligence Service, upon intake at the Hanawŏn resettlement center, or for a foreign audience in interviews, books, or public talks—according to predefined parameters of verisimilitude outside of which their language may be judged to be beyond the truth.[34] Those excluded from the social (through unemployment and homelessness, self-isolation, or diagnoses of mental illness) are depicted as not authorized to speak within a system of social or medical paternalism—they are subjects whose speech is understood in advance as nonsensical rambling. Language is constrained in each case by generic limits molded by expectations of the normative. It is at these moments of the representation of inauthentic, inappropriate, or inarticulate speech that we find a clash between the established logic of a situation and what it deems unintelligible, a struggle for the right to speak or the standing to enter into discourse, and a "storming" of language[35] and expansion of the boundaries of the sayable.

In a certain way, *Impossible Speech* is itself structured to challenge conventional approaches to literature, which tend to be organized by the assumptions that literary works are formed by their historical context, that change in literary history takes place developmentally, and that this change represents the unfolding of an idea or principle. Often, perhaps especially in the case of non-Western literatures, this last one is assumed to be the character of a region, people, or nation as reflected in the work.[36] Under such conventions, the assembly of migrant labor fiction, Kwangju literature, American fiction, North Korean defector narratives, and film comedies under a single analytical framework might strike the reader as unusual. Further, it should be apparent there has been no attempt to provide a chronological ordering of the texts.

Introduction   13

Rather than any attempt to explain or justify a set of texts by their belonging to a preexisting area or culture or to a (national) literary history—both of which would immediately limit the possible meanings to be derived from the texts—I have brought together figures that in their exteriority to common sense draw attention to the boundaries of discourse and to what Chow called above the struggle over the "propriety of speaking." It is this exteriority, a "transgression of the ordered division of voices and idioms,"[37] rather than any necessary logic of cultural, linguistic, or national belonging that provisionally binds the diverse texts under analysis together and allows a challenge to the reductive categorization of literary and film texts by national, cultural, or linguistic origin. Bringing these diverse works together under a more expansive definition of literature may disorder usual ways of thinking about fiction and film and allow for new or interesting readings of these important contemporary texts.

CHAPTER SUMMARIES

Chapter 1, "The Return of the Real in South Korean Fiction," takes "migrant labor fiction" in South Korea as an opportunity to think about the long-standing question of the politics of representation. Over the first decade of the twenty-first century, fiction written in South Korea dealt increasingly with transnational migration: migrant marriages, transnational labor and migrant workers, the multiculturalization of the cities and countryside in Korea, cross-border movements from North to South, and the return of out-migrated ethnic Korean populations including the so-called Chosŏnjok from Northeast China or Central Asia. This fiction considers the place of such migrants in the context of a systematic enforcement of mobility and immobility, exploring ideas of community made intelligible in a globalized present still governed by or distributed across boundaries of nation, ethnos, and class. While such efforts have often been received positively as a sign of multiculturalization and the weakening of ethnic nationalism, I argue that the politics of representation in migrant labor fiction is less transparent than this dominant reading suggests.

Rereading recent fiction from Kim Insuk, Kim Chaeyŏng, and Kang Yŏngsuk, I find that each of these now-canonical examples of migrant labor fiction proposes to cross geopolitical borders through the fantastic representation of speech outside of linguistic difference, where characters are able to communicate seamlessly across language barriers. Such a fantasy, I argue, does not diminish the need to think through such representations in terms of the problem of realism; and indeed, while the surface politics of migrant labor fiction in South Korea appears to present a transcultural ideal of postnational community, these representations of speech instead retain a culturalist impulse for which the "tie of language" remains linked to the "tie of blood." Beyond an empathetic politics that aims to persuade the reader of the humanity of the foreign laborer, culture remains linked to an economy of human types signaled by monolingual belonging, and the fantasy of linguistic sameness conceals a deeper fantasy, that of the "mother tongue." It is the silent image of the laborer across these stories, stubbornly unintelligible to the reader, that resists the weak multiculturalism shared by much migrant labor fiction.

If politics is the determination of the field of speech itself—what can be said and by whom—then it would seem possible to read migrant labor fiction as political precisely in its fantastic expansion of linguistic intelligibility. Literature would take on the role of imagining forms of community that exceed the immobilities that structure the idea and practice of the nation. Such literature might also be thought to regain its political commitment, lost in the "postmodern turn" of the 1990s, in the figure of the dispossessed laborer. Yet what this chapter finds in its close readings of recent examples of migrant labor fiction is that national identities continue to be established along linguistic lines that can only be overcome through mystical experience. The affective expression of these stories reveals quite the opposite of their surface politics—namely, an anxiety regarding language and community and a nostalgic longing for pre-traumatic wholeness bound to a raced and classed hierarchy of human types. The subject is never at risk in this fiction; the status of speech is never threatened. The chapter suggests that impossible speech cannot take place under the ideology of the mother tongue, a belief in the positivity of originary language. The supposedly "impossible" speech of the migrant laborer is possible only in the embrace of a fantastic, radical communicability, outside of which the "stubborn silence" of unintelligibility is consequently located.

Introduction   15

Chapter 2, "Displacing the Common Sense of Trauma: Han Kang's *A Boy Is Coming*," aims to examine the ways in which catastrophic historical events may be shaped into a common sense of the national community, and how the fictional text may intervene in this common sense. Focusing on the literary representation of the May 1980 Kwangju uprising and massacre, the chapter engages with the logic of trauma, a discourse that has significantly determined both aesthetic and political responses to Kwangju into the present. Dominick LaCapra's "traumatropism"[38] establishes the traumatic historical event as both a myth of national origins and as a multigenerational experience of victimhood, making the commemoration and repeated performance of trauma mandatory and establishing the state-sponsored narrative of the event as historical (and legal) truth. This chapter seeks an alternate model of trauma that expands the meaning of the traumatic event both geographically and temporally in a way that undermines the capacity of state culture to appropriate and consolidate that event as the basis of national belonging. Intervening in the debates surrounding the representation of historical disaster, such an alternate model does not deny the historical reality of the event, but strongly questions the bias toward realist (mimetic) representation of trauma.

The main text under analysis in the chapter is Han Kang's novel *A Boy Is Coming*, published in 2014 on the anniversary of the uprising and appearing in English translation as *Human Acts* in 2016.[39] I find that this novel resists traumatropism and its "making sense" of Kwangju—a sense making that confirms the boundaries of possible speech about Kwangju—by rejecting the imperative to speak intelligibly of an event the experience of which defies description and presenting the reader with the speech of those outside the normative boundaries of political community. *A Boy Is Coming* can thus be read as an introspective consideration of what "properly" representing an event of horrifying violence and mass death would mean. Han rejects all of the major premises of traumatropism: that of a pre-traumatic idyllic world to be returned to, tropes of heroism or victimhood, the placement of the event into a coherent narrative of national development, and the very possibility of testimony and witness. Against the neoliberal state's appropriation of Kwangju as a coherent symbol of national unity and economic progress, this chapter finds that *A Boy Is Coming* refuses the idea that Kwangju is a historical object fully known and "over and done with." At its ethical core, the novel rejects the idea that the disaster can be made sense of and fully grasped either in testimony or in the historiography that rests on such witness accounts. Instead, "Kwangju" is understood as an "unstable sign" that can be brought into the present as an enigmatic message that demands repeated attempts at interpretation.

I argue that Han's novel is able to strike a position that retains the historical reality of the horrific, catastrophic violence of the state mobilized against its own citizens while retaining the radical and future-oriented question of the event in the present. Against the demand for speech or compulsory testimony in a situation where sense cannot and must not be made, *A Boy Is Coming* pushes back against the set of generic norms that "precede the possibility of description" and foreclose what is speakable of the event.

Chapter 3, "Fabricating the Real: Accounting for North Korea in Escapee Narratives and in Fiction," focuses on the representation of North Korea in both fictional and testimonial forms. The turn from Kwangju to North Korea pivots on the way in which both *A Boy Is Coming* and Adam Johnson's 2012 *The Orphan Master's Son* utilize confessional forms and tropes that are usually understood to yield truth, including witness testimony, interrogation, police reports, documentation, photography, confession, and biography. Johnson's Pulitzer Prize–winning novel, a fictional representation of life in North Korea, is divided into two major sections: the first a biography, the second a confession. These modes of storytelling, structured by a kind of contract with the reader that guarantees their truth,[40] presents the subject as veracious either in the objective, chronological retelling of a life or because the confession is understood to be a spoken or written truth.

However, like *A Boy Is Coming*, Johnson's novel rejects the objectivity of these tropes even as the author exploits them for the appearance of truth that they give. *The Orphan Master's Son* approaches situations and events the representation of which have been proscribed or declared impossible, either in terms of the prohibition against the representation of atrocity, or in terms of the practical inaccessibility of the event (either to the past occurrence, or, in Johnson's case, to the "reality" of present-day North Korea). I argue that the heightened, almost hallucinatory realism of Johnson's prose works to challenge the idea that biography and

Introduction 17

confession yield truth as they are conventionally understood to do, and pushes back against the demand that texts dealing with the non-West present the truth of the matter to an audience comprised of Western "civilized humanity."

The novel reveals the fundamental illogic or arbitrariness at the base of the production of systematic knowledge about North Korea. This operation is strikingly close to Said's description of the ontological realism of Orientalism—the creative power of discourse to name, to classify, and to hierarchize—in short, to determine reality in its establishment of the terms of the discussion according to the logic "it is what it is because it is what it is."[41] The chapter's analysis turns on the parallel between the Orientalist logic that fixes the reality of the non-Western other in a process of knowledge production and the totalitarian logic of the novelistic representation of North Korea, a logic for which "all stories are real." Johnson's use of fantasy reportage transgresses the boundary between truth and unreality in a way that forces the reader to confront how, and why, a "reality" considered intelligible is ordinarily represented on the page.

Reception of Johnson's fiction has tended to ignore this critical aspect of his writing, seeing it instead as a "window on the mysterious kingdom of North Korea,"[42] a "carefully documented story" of "how people lived and died inside a cult of personality that committed unspeakable crimes against its citizens."[43] This tendency to receive Johnson's novel *as fact* presents an inverse to the tendency to read the testimony of North Korean escapees *as fiction*. Thus, whereas journalist and author Barbara Demick was surprised to learn that, given the accuracy of its details, *The Orphan Master's Son* was not a memoir written by a North Korean,[44] North Korean escapee narratives have been discredited either for their stereotypical qualities or for errors in testimony (the most prominent example is Shin Dong-hyuk's 2012 *Escape from Camp 14*), with the refugees themselves derided for seeking payment in exchange for sharing witness accounts.

Perversely, the rejection of North Korean escapee accounts stems from the very demand for speech that coincides perfectly with fact in a situation where observed reality is absent and factuality itself is constantly in question. In the case of escapee narratives, such communication is assumed to be inevitable, obligatory, or involuntary. As language is assumed to be a veracious (biographical, confessional) extension of the historical existence of the escapee, it is no wonder that scandal arises when errors, falsehoods, or exaggerations are discovered in their accounts. Escapees are thus subject to a dual humiliation: first, the demand for realistic representation of the most horrifying violations in the most conventional language; and second, the recrimination that comes when this narrative is either uninteresting ("like all the other ones") or inaccurate, violating both literary and evidentiary codes of coherence and correspondence, respectively. The probative value of biography and confession that Johnson's novel explodes—a disavowal that enables speech in a situation where veracious representation is shown to be strictly impossible—returns as expectation and demand in the case of escapee narratives, forcing speech to become both obscene and pornographic, available to voyeuristic enjoyment.[45]

Chapter 4, "Disturbing Sensibility: Transgressing Generic Norms in *Castaway on the Moon* and *I'm a Cyborg, but That's OK*," looks at *Kimssi p'yoryugi* (*Castaway on the Moon*), a 2009 film by Yi Haejun, and *Ssaibogŭjiman kwaench'ana* (*I'm a Cyborg, but That's OK*), a 2006 film by Pak Ch'anuk. These films are understood to be similar in three ways. First, each is populated by subjects who are partitioned off from society: the suicidal castaway and the *hikikomori* in the first, the occupants of a mental asylum in the second. Second, both films are framed by what appear to be normatively soteriological genres, tracing narrative arcs expected to result in the salvation of characters either through romantic love (rescue from loneliness and isolation) or medical cure (rescue from illness and death). Third, neither film contains what we could call proper dialogue. In *Castaway*, the two protagonists only speak to one another in the very last sequence of the film; in *Cyborg*, language is constantly in the process of becoming something else, and characters communicate primarily through miscommunication and through the sharing of symptoms.

I read both films as "making visible what has no business being seen, and making heard a discourse where once there was only place for noise," staging a situation the logic of which requires that pronouncements by those who "don't count" seize both intelligence and intelligibility.[46] The characters in *Cyborg* and *Castaway* are consequently characters that *transgress*, violating norms by exceeding the limits of the acceptable or

Introduction   19

probable. Such transgressions are not iconoclastic expressions of alternative subjectivities but are rather operations by which the subject is fundamentally at risk even as disciplinary control persists. Such subjects are not only criminalized—penalized, incarcerated, isolated by the state and the medical establishment—but are often invisible to those around them. They move and act with a strange freedom through an unseeing social space (the city, the online community, the asylum and network of doctors), a system that does not register their presence or registers their presence only as that which must be managed, isolated, or expunged from the social body. The characters are thus not only alienated or incarcerated but also finally exceed what Rancière calls the sensible itself, the law that separates those who "count" and who take part in the community, and those who are excluded—a law that presupposes a division between the visible and invisible, the audible and inaudible, and the sayable and unsayable.[47]

The partitioning of *space* in both films is thus aligned with the capacity for *speech* and the *sensibility* that makes that speech intelligible or unintelligible to others. This chapter argues that space and speech are indices of belonging, defining the sensible limits of a community consisting of political subjects. I begin by looking at the establishment of distinct spaces in the two films—from an abandoned island in the middle of hyperurban Seoul to the cramped isolation of a high-rise apartment in *Castaway*, and from the fantastic space of the asylum in *Cyborg* to the isolation cells that separate the characters. How do the efforts made to cross these spaces critique discourses that establish categorizing space itself? In *Castaway*, the city space is disrupted by the primitive, a disruption that puts into motion a questioning of stable identities and the imagination of a postnational, post-consumer relationality between the two protagonists of the film. In *Cyborg*, within the partitioned space of the asylum, it is the space of the human body that is transgressed, first in the fantasy of the patient who believes that she is nonhuman (or more precisely, a human supplemented by the nonhuman), and then in the equally fantastic surgery performed on her body to ensure that she can both retain her identity as cyborg and survive (be healthy) as a human. If *Castaway* critiques urban, capitalized, and legal or evidentiary identities, *Cyborg* exceeds the limits of the medicalized

20 *Introduction*

patient and calls into question psychiatry's compulsorily somatic understanding of health.

It is the violation of genre norms and the promise of salvation—the explosion of conventions of the Robinsonade and the romantic comedy—that lay down the basis for moving beyond supposed universals of the national and the medicalized human body. Both *Cyborg* and *Castaway* refuse the narrative closure of redemption, evading a cure in the case of the former and rescue in the case of the latter, allowing a remnant of transgression to remain in each case that leaves the characters in crisis—"rescued" but still outside the norm. If the characters remain different, then the films themselves also reject generic sameness at the narrative level, formally mirroring their content and enabling an interpretive method to develop that attempts to map a space beyond established sensibilities of what constitutes the human and its belonging with others.

Both *Cyborg* and *Castaway* thus dramatize the situation of subjects rendered or judged incapable of occupying "the space-time of political things" and reject the prohibition against considering "certain categories of people as political beings" and allowing them voice.[48] Rather than understanding these "light" films as apolitical, approaching from this angle allows us to see art as political in how it configures material and symbolic space. If politics is "the configuration of a specific space, the framing of a particular sphere of experience, of objects posited as common and . . . of subjects recognized as capable of designating those objects and putting forward arguments about them,"[49] then these films are political precisely in their reframing of space and speech.

Each of the chapters also addresses some significant aspect of literary history. Chapter 1 looks at the "return of the real" in Korean literature, particularly the way that migrant labor fiction has filled the gap left by the evacuation of political polarity following the fall of military authoritarianism. With the migrant laborer as the new figure of the oppressed poor or *minjung*, literature seemed poised to regain its significance as a political force. But in borrowing the language of *minjung*, migrant labor fiction also inherited the ethnic nationalism that accompanied that politicized term from the 1970s and 1980s—an ethnic nationalism that is a poor fit in the context of international labor

Introduction 21

migration. Realism returns, but through the screen of a fantasy that hides its race-based monolingualism.

Chapter 2 finds Han Kang's novel confronting the gap between the demand for documentary realism and the impossibility of testimony in the face of historical atrocity. The novel chooses a mode akin to Michael Rothberg's "traumatic realism" that resists both the idea of a founding trauma that can be fully known and narrated and a mode of governance built on consensus around shared victimhood. Through the use of multiple perspectives and voices and of fragmented narration, and by taking as a central theme the impossibility of testimony, the novel is able to reject the idea of making historical sense of the catastrophe while at the same time "making Kwangju present" in a way that expands, rather than limits, its significance.[50]

Chapter 3 works at the intersection of hyperrealistic fantasy and first-person witness accounts to bring to light the ontological realism demanded of non-Western texts. A strange inversion between Johnson's novel (the "window" onto North Korean reality) and the testimony of North Korean escapees (considered unreliable and/or stereotypical) reveals the power of normative discourse to prefigure the shape of the real, as generic forms of biography and confession are shown to work differently depending on their position in relation to the sayable.

Finally, Chapter 4 analyzes narratives that dramatize the transgression of normative space and speech by excluded subjects, while at the same time performing a kind of solidarity with its characters by violating genre norms that demand meaning and closure. Genre is especially appropriate as an object of consideration here for two reasons: first, because "it supposes that questions of meaning and truth are always questions of form and of the situation of utterance";[51] and second, because genre sets the common sense of a given community of discourse and the "rhetorical behavior" appropriate to the situation.[52] In these senses, we can think of genre as a potential site of politics. Both *Cyborg* and *Castaway* mark moments where genre dislocates itself,[53] pushing back against the easy location of meaning in a familiar and recognizable form—that regulative frame within which a generically specific world is constructed.[54] Here, and in chapter 3 as well, genre is treated as a mechanism of foreclosure, restricting the capacity of a subject of representation to speak or behave and establishing the norm or convention that stipulates the

22   *Introduction*

boundaries of intelligible language.[55] As a regulative frame, genre operates "at the thresholds of communities of discourse, patrolling or controlling individuals' participation in the collective . . . differentiating, initiating, restricting, inducing forms of activity, rationalising and representing the relations of the genre to the community that uses it."[56] At the same time, as Todorov notes, genre is also a point at which we can observe the capacity of the work of art to exceed a classificatory given, to itself both indicate (in generic belonging) and exceed the norm established in the generic convention.[57] Texts modify genres in using them,[58] and both films analyzed in chapter 4 resist the common sense of their genres, which in turn become sites of challenge where the decision on what may be said by whom and in what situation is brought to the fore.

In each case, the capacity of the subject to speak about something comes up against a limit. Monolingualism, trauma, generic norms, and radical marginalization and precarity work to prohibit or disqualify speakers who are nonetheless made heard on the page or on the screen in ways that resist the foreclosure that regulates the domain of the speakable. Forms of literary or film narrative are put forward that push against the consensual bounding of possible speech, allowing the emergence of political subjects (in Rancière's sense) "between nominations" and prior to the mutual determination of identity and space or place. Such texts object in both form and content to the declaration that all speech is possible, a declaration that denies the capacity of language to exceed both the expected (future) and the remembered (past) or to have any effects beyond common sense (present).

Given this central concern, the conclusion returns to the discussion of testimony, opening the question of so-called comfort-women narratives in which the concerns of previous chapters intersect in the demand for identity in suffering, the location of possible speech, and the compulsory discursivity required of witnesses whose testimony provides not only the facts of personal experience but also the grounds for deciding on facticity itself. These aspects all come together on the stage of international human rights politics introduced in chapter 3, where the realist demand of "civilized humanity" again silences the voice and obscures, under the blinding light of total visibility, the capacity of language to intervene in the very definition of possible speech and, in so doing, to engage with the problem of the politics of art.

Introduction   23

AGAINST "COMPULSORY DISCURSIVITY"

The central chapters of the book present examples of what I am calling "impossible speech." An array of characters are called upon to speak impossibly, to address events and experiences that are for various reasons not available to speech. The speech of such subjects is thus "discounted, and the viability of the subject [is] called into question." As Butler writes, "the consequences of such an irruption of the unspeakable" may range from "a sense that one is 'falling apart' to the intervention of the state to secure criminal or psychiatric incarceration."[59] The witnesses to the massacre at Kwangju, whether dead or traumatized into silence; those who have survived the North Korean death camps; those who have been cast out from society and are institutionalized and incarcerated—these are the subjects who assume the position of the speaker in these works of literature and film. Each chapter indicates a politics of art adequate to a given historical or literary-historical moment, evident both in the placement of subjects who have no standing to speak and in the representation of the speech that emerges from their mouths *as speech* despite its seeming unintelligibility. Such a politics makes visible "what had no business being seen," and makes heard a "discourse where once there was only place for noise."[60]

The emergence of impossible speech does not, however, necessarily mean that we observe the *truth* of this or that event or subject. As Wendy Brown points out, it is possible to make a fetish of breaking silence, an operation that takes for granted the belief that silence and speech are opposites. Such a conceit "enables both the assumption that censorship converts the truth of speech to the lie of silence and the assumption that when an enforced silence is broken, what emerges is truth borne by the vessel of authenticity or experience." What emerges in impossible speech is not some "presumed authenticity of 'voice.'"[61] Such authenticity assumes that identification has already taken place—that an identifiable subject is speaking from an identifiable (geographical, cultural) place. This way of thinking opens the literary text up to judgment based on evidentiary standards and strips the work of its capacity to enact radical change to language or thought. As with Song's character in *The Attorney*, whether spoken or in silence, the "authenticity of 'voice'" means that consensual meaning has been achieved—that all possible speech has

24   *Introduction*

been accounted for, which is itself a form of silencing. Thus speech is not necessarily equivalent to freedom;[62] the opposite is just as possible.

Impossible Speech proposes an approach to literary works that undermines assumptions about the relationship between politics and art that rely on the melancholic reproduction of trauma, the privileging of realism and the evaluation of texts via evidentiary standards (or, inversely, the assignment of probative value to fictional statements), and the inevitability of national context and an interpretive schema that assigns meaning based on culture and place. In thinking anew about the politics of literature, the book follows Rancière in holding that politics is a speech situation and finds that the representation of political subjectivization takes place when the normative boundaries of speech are exceeded or adjusted.[63]

The subjects of these narrative works—the migrant laborer, the victim of state violence, the refugee, the homeless, the abandoned and suicidal, the mentally ill, the dispossessed precariat—may appear as somehow naturally "political" in their *being*. But such a designation would rob the text of its capacity to exceed the norms that determine what is sayable or visible under a consensual political regime by demanding that the characters speak the truth of their beings, a truth given in advance by the language that they speak or the position they occupy in space or in history. I reject this "compulsory discursivity"[64] attached to texts ordinarily considered political, based as it is in the sense that all possible speech is known in advance and in stripping texts of any potential to exceed norms in what Lecercle calls a "storming" of language.[65] Against contemporary approaches to literary texts that demand an authenticity rooted in status or place, I aim to reserve for art the capacity to delineate the *possible* in advance of its ossification into the *known*, and the power—from within the bounds of the sayable or a given collection of identities—to introduce gaps or breaks into the real.

"Impossible" does not, in the end, refer to speech that is strictly not possible or to the representation of fantastic or impossible content. Impossibility signals, rather, the introduction of a break between a perfect agreement between the real and the possible, the verisimilar and the necessary.[66] The impossibilization of impossible speech amounts to an assertion that all speech is knowable, that the boundaries of the sayable are set in advance and encompass all possible speech. The politics of the

Introduction 25

literary text is not only to represent the unintelligible that exceeds such boundaries, but to adjust the limits on the sayable, and in so doing to propose new configurations of community, for "there is no opposition to the lines drawn by foreclosure except through the redrawing of those very lines."[67] Within the newly drawn configuration, we see new subjects appear, removed from the naturalness of identity, those whose "noise" is now understood as "speech." Beyond both the ostensible message of the text or the supposed intention of the author, this study aims to register the emergence of such moments of impossible speech and to carry the force of these moments over into how literary works are read and classified as political.

CHAPTER ONE

The Return of the Real in South Korean Fiction

This chapter takes so-called migrant labor fiction in South Korea as an opportunity to think about the long-standing question of the politics of representation. Looking at recent fiction from Kim Insuk, Kim Chaeyŏng, and Kang Yŏngsuk, we see that the experience of crossing geopolitical borders, figured in these stories through the fantastic representation of "impossible" speech outside of linguistic difference, does not diminish the need to think through such representations in terms of the problem of realism, for which fiction is comprehended and valued to the extent that it expresses the actuality of the subject. In these stories, this actuality comes to the reader in two linked forms: the mundanity of the everyday, particularly the trope of urban poverty and the figure of the common people; and the imagined divorce of speech from ethnic-national or cultural context. What the chapter finds is that rather than presenting a transcultural ideal of postnational community, representations of speech in these stories instead retain a culturalist impulse for which the "tie of language" remains linked to the "tie of blood." Beyond the interpretation of an empathetic surface politics that aims to persuade the reader of the humanity of the laborer, culture remains linked to an economy of human types signaled by linguistic belonging.

Kim Insuk's prize-winning "Sea and Butterfly" (Pada wa nabi) tells the story of a mother taking her daughter from Korea to China to obtain an "international education"—the key, the mother tells us, to becoming a global citizen.[1] While her daughter is expected to attain this ideal, which is at base a linguistic achievement, the narrator is completely unable to make herself understood in the Chinese language and relies on the services of Chaegŭm, described to the reader as an ethnically Korean young Chinese woman. Chaegŭm plays a triple role (or bears a triple burden) in the story: a "native" guide for the narrator in China; the daughter of an undocumented migrant who works at the narrator's mother's restaurant in South Korea; and a "foreign bride," headed to Korea to marry an aging bachelor whom she has never met. Having assumed a common ethnic bond and a concomitant fluidity of affect and language with Chaegŭm, the narrator finds herself unexpectedly alienated by a sense of strangeness, an incommensurability figured in the story through Chaegŭm's struggles with Korean as she "stammers" and gropes for the right words in an "unfamiliar" language.[2]

In the penultimate scene of the story, the problem of language arrives at a strange resolution. The narrator has been drawn into a tattoo parlor. "I had only been in the country for ten days," she tells us, and "couldn't buy a bag of salt . . . by myself, let alone navigate a tattoo parlor, but my feet led me through the door."[3] At the same time that the proprietor addresses her in speech that she cannot comprehend, she sees a butterfly tattoo on the wall behind him. As she moves toward it, the old man rises from his chair, "first muttering something unintelligible, then shouting." Curiously, the narrator suddenly gains the ability to understand the man's subsequent extended discourse on the dangers of butterfly tattoos, particularly for (Korean) migrants. What is important here is not the content of the speech, but the fact of its comprehensibility. "Somehow," she tells us, "I'd managed to catch every word."[4] This is presented as an empathetic communication, one that appears to violate the rules of speakability in transcending linguistic difference.

Over the first decade of the twenty-first century, fiction written in South Korea dealt increasingly with transnational migration: migrant marriages, transnational labor and migrant workers (*ijumin nodongja*), the multiculturalization of the cities and the countryside in Korea, cross-border movement from North to South, and the return of out-migrated ethnic Korean populations, for instance the so-called Chosŏnjok from Northeast China or Central Asia. This fiction considers the place of such outsiders in

28   *The Return of the Real in South Korean Fiction*

the context of a systematic enforcement of mobility and immobility and explores ideas of community made intelligible within a globalized present still governed by or distributed across boundaries of nation, ethnos, and class.[5] As we will see below in an analysis of two oft-examined examples of "migrant labor fiction," Kim Chaeyŏng's "Elephant" (K'okkiri) and Kang Yŏngsuk's "Brown Tears" (Kalsaek nunmul pangul), this intelligibility arrives through the fantasy of linguistic sameness, a transcultural communication that figures the crossing of geopolitical borders through speech that functions outside of linguistic difference.

Such efforts have frequently been received positively as a sign of multiculturalization and the weakening of a vigorous ethnic nationalism that posits linguistic and racial homogeneity as the basis of national belonging. The argument below holds that the politics of representation in migrant labor fiction is less transparent than this reading suggests. The fantasy of fluency that appears to enable understanding both conceals and reinforces a more primary fantasy, namely, the fantasy of the "mother tongue." Rather than adopting the surface message of these works as a sufficient politics, I follow critic Kang Chingu in considering the racialized image of the migrant as distinct from this fantastical communion, an image intelligible through its silence or its unintelligibility. While the fantasy of translingual communication in unknown languages seems to remove language from the pseudobiological status of the ethnic-national mother tongue, the presentation of such images underwrites the homolingual address that "assumes the normalcy of reciprocal and transparent communication in a homogeneous medium"[6] and the silence or unintelligibility that is assumed to lie without. Despite the apparently effortless fluency that marks the crucial moment in "Sea and Butterfly" and in each of the stories below—the moment of "impossible" speech made possible—an authenticity of voice remains that reinforces a system of consensual meaning under which neither the limits of the sayable nor the status of the subject come into question.

THE LIMITS OF TRANSNATIONAL MIGRANT LABOR FICTION IN SOUTH KOREA

Critics have been wary of the representational schema by which figures such as migrant laborers, marriage migrants, or political refugees appear

The Return of the Real in South Korean Fiction   29

in fiction. As Kang Chingu points out, there is a diversity of approaches to such representation: from fiction that actively reproduces difference (of the foreign other) to that which criticizes racist or class-based forms of discrimination and exclusion and imagines a future solidarity across cultural difference. Regardless of the particular politics of the text, Kang argues that authors have primarily tended to represent the migrant subject in three ways: as the perpetual other; as infantilized and in need of protection; and, less frequently, as a threat to society, in particular to a monolithic state ideology and the myths that support it. Each representative mode, he argues—no matter how critical it seems of the systematic exclusion of migrants—cannot but reproduce the self/other dichotomy in that the *image* of the migrant laborer functions independently of the critical message of the fiction in question.[7]

Yŏn Namgyŏng refers to this zone of gradated representation in terms of what she calls a "borderland" (*chŏpgyŏng chidae*) of racialized cultural difference where self and other, citizens and migrants, come into contact and conflict. Focusing partly on the links between fictional settings and concrete sites (industrial neighborhoods, military camptowns)— spaces marginal to both the city and to perceived Korean identity—Yŏn points to a contradiction between a discourse of inclusive multiculturalism and South Korea's status as a subempire. This status compels a nationalist rhetoric against its own peripheral status to the U.S. empire even as it depends on the periphery for its labor force. It is a colonial mode that leverages the threat of external domination to enforce an internal economy of inclusion and exclusion, a schema that establishes identity based in ethnic-national belonging against the constructed difference of other groups. As Hwang Hodŏk writes, "between the compulsion of capital without borders and the compulsion of the state to register [to identify, document, record], something is born—and that something is the colonial."[8] Thus in "multicultural" fiction we can observe what Yŏn calls an internal colonization, a racialized difference operating within state borders that is nonetheless consistent with the boundless reach of transnational capital. Difficulties in representing the situation of migrant labor in Korea emerge and play out across these marginal spaces in recent fiction, where the very extension of sympathy to the migrant laborer takes part in a strategy that creates and maintains the racial hierarchy of the internal colony.[9]

While Kang focuses on the independence of the image of the migrant from the politics of the text—a way of privileging formal and affective effects over discourse—Yŏn subordinates the overt politics of the text to its overall position in a hierarchy of racialized imperial relations. Continuing these lines of critique, which resist the surface politics of "multicultural" fiction and its (overt or implicit) claim of postnationality, Yi Kyŏngjae reviews four ways in which migrants have typically been treated in recent works. First, he writes, there are works of fiction that portray immigrants as "pŏlgŏ pŏsŭn cha"—subjects "stripped naked"—representing the reality (*hyŏnsil*) of absolute exclusion from society. Short fiction such as Kim Chaeyŏng's "Elephant," Yi Sibaek's "Dirt Cheap" (Kae kap), Sŏ Sŏngnan's "Paprika," (P'ap'ŭrik'a), or Kang Hŭijin's "Ghost" (Yuryŏng) fall into this category; these texts deal with migrant laborers, marriage migrants, and North Korean refugees, representing the suffering of those without recourse to law or empathy in the South Korean context. The risk, writes Yi, is that in representing an insurmountable barrier between (national) self and (migrant) other, such fiction may reinforce the total alienation of migrants from Korean society.

Second, there are works of fiction that attempt to traverse or overcome the very otherness of the migrant by assimilating them as Koreans, such as Kim Ryŏryŏng's "Wandŭki," Pak Pŏmsin's "Namaste" (Namasŭt'e), or Pak Ch'ansun's "Karibong Mutton Kebobs" (Karibong yangggoch'i). Here the pendulum, Yi writes, tends to swing too far in the opposite direction, ignoring difference and cultural specificity (*koyusŏng*) in the attempt to imagine the migrant laborer without their otherness.[10]

A third type points to fiction that presents the universal humanity of the migrant laborer and the Korean subject. Works such as Kim Yŏnsu's "New Year's Blessings for All" (Moduege pokdoen saehae) or Han Chasu's "A Rainbow on a Tropical Night" (Yŏldaeyaesŏ on mujigae) treat laborers as humans "without the need for a modifier" (*susigŏ*), while works by Son Honggyu or Kong Sŏnok aim to find the potential for solidarity between immigrants and Koreans on the basis of a socioeconomic communality. Here, as an "unmodified" humanity conceals the socioeconomic reality of migrants, Yi sees a failure to consider particularity in the attempt to find a universal basis for community.

Yi advocates instead an ethical stance that recognizes difference at the same time that it imagines universality, an approach that takes into

The Return of the Real in South Korean Fiction   31

account a common "human dignity" while also remaining attentive to particularity.[11] His position echoes a common sense that extends across the work of the three critics here briefly reviewed: that the subject/object split is basic to any definition of migrant labor fiction; that the same split is closely tied to the political ideology of the ethnic nation within the larger context of global capital, and can be negotiated depending on the relationship between the local and the global in a given situation; that literary form can produce effects independently of the politics of a given text; and that a logic of verisimilitude determines both the fitness of texts for analysis and their status in a hierarchy of literary value.

The politics of the literary text is assumed to arrive in its message, in the presentation of what Hayden White calls a "verbal image of 'reality'" that is achieved "by registering a series of propositions which are supposed to correspond points by point to some extra-textual domain of occurrence or happening," a "real" domain of human experience.[12] In terms of both form and content, the category of "migrant labor fiction" depends on such a presupposition of representational veracity. Yet while a work may attempt to represent most fully the suffering of the disposable migrant subject for the reader, drawing the alien into empathetic understanding, it may just as easily and at the same time represent that subject in a way that reinforces stereotypes of the foreigner, constructing difference by reifying the racialized other. Both rely on proximity to the real, whether for critical effect or for analytical purchase.

The politics of the text does not reside precisely in its verisimilitude, then, but rather in the assumption of the *possibility* of that verisimilitude, here in the image of the migrant laborer—the assumption that makes proximity to the real appear attainable in the first place. In his analysis of the transition from representational to aesthetic regimes, Rancière points to a shift in sensibility wherein the image is no longer a "codified expression of a thought or a feeling" but is rather "a way in which things themselves speak and are silent," bearer of a "silent speech."[13] Such images can be silent, for Rancière, in two ways. First, there is "the meaning of things inscribed directly on their bodies, their visible language to be decoded. . . . the capacity to exhibit signs written on a body, the marks directly imprinted by its history, which are more truthful than any discourse proffered by a mouth." These are "silent witnesses of a condition inscribed directly on their features, their clothes, their life

32 *The Return of the Real in South Korean Fiction*

setting." Second is an "obstinate silence," the appearance of a "naked, non-signifying presence" in possession of a "secret we shall never know," a secret "veiled by the very image that delivers them to us."[14]

In the stories below, reality comes to the reader in two linked forms: in the mundanity of the everyday, via the inscription of foreignness and poverty on the bodies of the migrant laborers represented; and in the imagined divorce of speech from ethnic-national or cultural context. In the latter case, we see the spontaneous ability to understand an unknown language, the uncanny fluency in the voice of the migrant laborer narrator, or, as with the narrator of "Sea and Butterfly," the fantasy of communication outside of linguistic difference. The characters in each of these stories find themselves with the unexpected ability to make meaning in completely unknown languages, or with a fluency that throws into question the limitation of mother tongue to mono-ethnic national community. Communication is at once freed from the pseudo-biological status of the ethnic-national, "a political category that has been disguised as a biological one,"[15] and reintroduced as a figure for transcultural community.

Yet this fantastical fluency or hyperintelligibility constitutes the other side of the silent image, an image both inscribed as a "cipher of history"[16] and obstinately silent in its unknowability. This occurs partly because the concept of the mother tongue, in positing a transparent communication between members of the same ethnic-national community, establishes at the same time a surrounding unintelligibility or silence, and partly because such fluency—both the representation of fluency in the speech of the characters and in terms of the fluency of the narrative language (Korean) itself—masks a continued reliance on a mother-tongue ideology necessary for the fiction to achieve its surface effects. Despite the appearance of transculturality and a focus on a shared horizon of experience, a culturalism—that "fatal junction of the concept of nationality with the concept of culture"[17]—remains, for which group and culture overlap and where cultural difference occurs only between the interior and exterior of an ethnic-national community based in a mother tongue.[18]

Behind the linguistic fluencies and cross-language communications made possible in these stories as the apparent basis for the construction of both understanding and community, there is another fantasy at work.

The Return of the Real in South Korean Fiction　　33

This fantasy holds that borders are eliminated as they are crossed, and that language is consequently freed from its correspondence with an ethnic-national community, "the tie of language" no longer representing the "tie of blood."[19] Whether the fantasy is defending against an impermissible wish the fulfillment of which would violate social taboos or whether it is functioning in the narrative past tense as a sort of screen memory, disguising a conscious or unconscious mental content through the innocuous presentation of a past moment,[20] it establishes a boundary that crops up precisely when another boundary's elimination or transgression is imagined or represented. It thus emerges invisibly under the guise of a fantasy that expresses just the opposite—the elimination of borders and boundaries.

FANTASIES OF FLUENCY: "ELEPHANT" AND "BROWN TEARS"

In Kim Chaeyŏng's 2005 "Elephant," language plays the role of a marker of difference but it also holds out the possibility of community.[21] The protagonist, Akkas, is the twelve-year-old child of a Chinese Korean mother and a Nepalese father. "Of course, as an ethnic Korean from China she could get by anywhere in this country," he tells us of his mother. "At least she'd have a quick comeback in Korean if anyone tried to shame or mistreat her."[22] His father, on the other hand, reminds him of a clown "when he speaks his garbled Korean . . . Everyone looks like an idiot when their words are unclear."[23] Outside of a local convenience store, Akkas "can hear the racket" that the laborers make as they talk together. "They speak a mixture of Korean, Russian, English, even Nepalese, and I convert it all into Korean the instant their words reach my eardrums and slip inside my head."[24] Language is a barrier, but at the same time it holds out a certain hope for a common sense.

The common sense of migrant labor is figured in Kim's story through the "timeless trope of urban poverty."[25] The category of the poor is represented as community oriented, embodying an ethos of mutual suffering. At the same time, this shared experience or ethics of the community of the poor is broken when poverty is represented as the experience of the marginalized individual.[26] Leaving aside the question of whether or not this itself undermines the incorporation of migrant

34 *The Return of the Real in South Korean Fiction*

laborers into the political category of the *minjung* (common people) and the imagination of new forms of community, this entire dynamic is masked by the uncanny fluency of the narrator, the fantasy of seamless communication across ethnic-national and class boundaries. While the *minjung* is strategically claimed in public discourse by migrant laborers as a political identity,[27] how does cultural representation of *ijumin nodongja* forego the politics of the *minjung* in representing such laborers as both atomized individuals and as unproblematically fluent "native speakers"?

Naoki Sakai defines the native speaker as "one who bears the mother tongue or national mother tongue as the ground of personal authenticity."[28] In this sense, the narrator's discourse reinforces both the individuation of the laborers (he is the universality to their linguistic particularity) and the qualifying relationship between language figured as ethnic-national and the capacity to narrate the real. Language is racialized, giving us a perspective on the "enormous gap between classism of the preceding mono-ethnic context and the racialized class system in the fast-multiracializing context of contemporary South Korea." While the migrant laborers have in a sense become or joined the *minjung* of the present, the status of "laborer" has not been conferred upon migrant workers by the racially discriminatory state.[29] Further, as Rey Chow writes, that racial identification is reinforced through attention to language, where it is the "(foreign) accent" that both marks one as a non-native speaker and defines, in its failure, the "uncorrupted origination point" of a pure language embodied by the native speaker.[30] The fantasy of fluency here hides but reinforces the primary fantasy that there is a pure language in the first place.

For Kang Chingu, beneath the surface of this narrative voice—that of the mixed-race Akkas, who exists on the border of "them" and "us"—what we ultimately see are resolutely stereotypical images of migrant laborers living in squalid conditions, dreaming of their hometowns in foreign countries, stealing from "us" and from one another in the extremities of their poverty.[31] In Yŏn's analysis, this image at the same time displays conditions of internal colonization and racial hierarchy. The migrant laborers are completely marginalized, yet are simultaneously subject to a social hierarchy based on the identity of race and class.[32] The representation of a link between national belonging and race is made

The Return of the Real in South Korean Fiction   35

clear in the story as one of the characters, Koon, passes as white, or when Akkas attempts to bleach his skin.

As Yŏn points out, the Korean character P'iryong's diatribe outside the small store where the laborers congregate reveals the identification of migrant laborers in terms of both class and historical development. In response to the multilingual banter among the drinking laborers, he slurs:

> Damn it, quit it with the jibber jabber. I'm starting to feel like I'm in some other country. Do you guys have any idea how this country got to be the way it is now? When I worked in a factory way back when, losing fingers was nothing. Whole forearms flew off and even necks got sliced. . . . You won't catch any Koreans working in such places nowadays, though . . . to be blunt, it's backbreaking work and they know it firsthand. That's why they leave it to all of you—they didn't bring you over here for a joy ride. . . . They didn't even [treat their own] nationals [as human beings]—what makes you think they'll [treat you any differently]?[33]

The status of the suffering laborer, the proletariat, is here passed to the migrant worker, in the temporal shift from "way back when" to "nowadays." Falling into Yi Kyŏngjae's third type, the picture of "unmodified" humanity bound through socioeconomic commonality, the workers here become the same, "treated no differently." That is, though in terms of their social status or their ethnic identity they are marked as different, in terms of their labor and their value to the market, they are identical.

Akkas's father is a key figure for this in the story. Trained in Nepal as an astronomer, he works making light bulbs at a factory in Seoul, moving from the celestial to the industrial, the cosmic to the man-made. Handling the hot glass every day has stripped his fingers of their skin, leaving him without fingerprints. Labor deprives him of the mark of his identity. Without a birth certificate, his son Akkas, unknown to any state or nationality, inherits this lack. This intergenerational sameness remains located within an exclusionary hierarchy figured in terms of morphological difference. Even as "socioeconomic commonality" is offered through the politicized category of the *minjung*, the "sameness" of labor is made different through the familiar colonial gesture of consigning the other

36　*The Return of the Real in South Korean Fiction*

to a past moment. Foreign labor here is relegated to the "imaginary waiting-room of history"[34] even as it joins the ranks of the common.

The anxiety of sameness/difference appears here as well in terms of language. Whereas in "Sea and Butterfly" the characters are removed from the ethnic-national context of Korea and Korean becomes a misleading sign of familiarity in a strange territory, in "Elephant," language appears to move across ethnic-national identities through the "mixing" (*twisŏkkim*) of language and through the "mixed-race" character of Akkas. In both stories, language appears delinked from racial identity, yet both rely on a fantasy of fluency—of immediate and seamless communication—in order to establish an idea of community outside the ethno-nation. In this sense, in both stories, a mystical communion across languages takes place, with the protagonists either suddenly comprehending a language completely unknown, or comprehending all spoken languages and translating them into the narrative language of the story.[35]

In "Brown Tears" too, questions of sameness and belonging appear through an anxiety regarding language. Written by Kang Yŏngsuk and first published in 2004, the story presents a young female narrator living in a dilapidated Park Chung Hee–era apartment building "covered with moss and rust" and "looking like an abandoned temple," managed by an elderly man and his wheelchair-bound wife and passed over by urban redevelopment.[36] We learn that the narrator is somehow "lumped together" with the "losers who live in that villa"[37] on the second floor, which she shares with a trio of migrant laborers—a Sri Lankan woman and two men—who live together in an apartment down the hall from the protagonist. The narrator is careful to point out, however, that there is no basis for this so-called community—though they live across the hallway from one another, "there hadn't been the slightest hint of camaraderie based on our shared social status not to mention any actual communication between us."[38]

The narrator has suffered a heartbreak as the story opens, and, after a failed suicide attempt, somewhat whimsically decides that she needs a hobby and enrolls in an English language course. "It wouldn't really have mattered if they were teaching the international language of Esperanto," the narrator tells us, "or the revered but long forgotten language of a Chinese minority that had disappeared a thousand years ago, or even sign language."[39] In the English class, however, she is unable to speak: "Out

The Return of the Real in South Korean Fiction   37

of the blue, I'd developed a severe stutter, and it quickly devolved into a kind of aphasia. . . . The moment my name was called, my whole body stiffened . . . I began to stutter, it was so bad that I couldn't breathe."[40]

The anxiety about language here is not simply due to the narrator's unfamiliarity with English. "Forget English," she tells us. "The words that I already knew in my mother tongue [*maŭm sok e itnŭn mal*] would barely leave my mouth."[41] The narrator longs to speak again but cannot. Further, her neighbors do not speak Korean. When they walk in the yard together, they mumble in their mutually unintelligible languages;[42] she cannot understand the "mother tongue" (*mogugŏ*) of the Sri Lankan woman;[43] and the narrator is also gradually estranged from her English classmates, who ask her why she insists on making an outcast of herself in her apparent refusal to speak.[44]

The narrator is thus in a relation of incommensurability with both those inside and those outside of her sphere of "natural" or "primary" language. Having lost the power of speech, she is considered "one of the losers who live on the second floor" by the building manager or as an "outcast" by her classmates; on the other hand, not knowing their language, she has no way of communicating with her neighbors.

It is only when the narrator aids the Sri Lankan woman through a health crisis (she comes across her neighbor half-dead from an acute case of hemorrhoids in her apartment) that she finds herself in the company of the migrant laborers, "chatting together in languages that the other couldn't possibly understand."[45] Here, Kang Chingu notes, the story shows a relation of compassion or sympathy between "us" and "them," aiming at a kind of patronizing solidarity, while at the same time putting forward an image of the foreigner as distinct from this fantastical communion, an image embodying the poverty, criminality, and filth of the migrant, her "unintelligible sounds" and her smell marking her as irretrievably and silently other.[46]

The story closes with a fantasy of renewed community when the narrator opens her mouth and begins to speak in her English class. She reports to them, in English, what her neighbor has told her prior to her departure for Sri Lanka: about her home in Sri Lanka, about growing up with her little sister, and about how she was brought to Korea. That is, the narrator reports the speech of the Sri Lankan migrant, spoken to her in a language that the narrator doesn't understand (presumably

38 *The Return of the Real in South Korean Fiction*

Singhalese or Tamil), to her Korean classmates, in a language that she doesn't know (English). "My friend lives in Sri Lanka," she tells them. "Sri Lanka is a beautiful place, my friend told me that night."[47]

The narrator then shifts into the first person, voicing the Sri Lanka woman's enunciative position in their previous conversation: "I don't know how I got here. I fell asleep after I'd eaten candy that a stranger gave me, and when I woke up, I was in a strange place. Every night I dreamed a dream that I was looking back."[48] Her breakthrough in the English class is followed by another at the apartment building when the manager's wife stands up from her wheelchair. "Apparently," the story closes, "a miracle was upon us."[49]

For Yi Kyŏngjae, "Brown Tears" is an example of fiction that moves beyond either a focus on the otherness of the migrant or an unproblematic assimilation of the other into Korean identity. The story does this by representing a communal bond between the Korean narrator and the Southeast Asian woman, a shared feeling (*kyogam*) that emerges not through a common language but through a common understanding of suffering. It is at this moment, when the narrator can relate to the suffering of a "disposable human," that she sheds her aphasia and "confesses what the Southeast Asian woman has been through." "What is more important than the content of the speech," Yi writes, "is the form of the speech itself, in that it demonstrates the need to communicate, in whatever way possible."[50] The narrator becomes, for a moment, the Southeast Asian woman, communicating in English, and it is here, Yi holds, that a true, ethical communication may emerge—at the point where it is no longer possible to distinguish who is the same and who is other, which is self (*tongilcha*) and which is other (*t'ajain*).

Yet here too, the recovery of speech in the shift from aphasia to fluency both within and across ethnic-national lines—"putting oneself in the place of the other" through the apparent erasure of boundaries of inclusion and exclusion marked out by language communities—masks the relationship between discourse and image. Speech remains the fundamental criterion of belonging. It is through the recovery of speech that the narrator also recovers her sense of belonging. As well, the speech that returns is figuratively or (so to speak) diegetically a foreign language but is rendered in Korean. The author can hardly be faulted for writing in Korean for a Korean-speaking audience, but at the same time, this too

The Return of the Real in South Korean Fiction   39

signals a fundamental limit to the fantasy scene with which the story ends. All language comes to us as Korean. Finally, the miraculous shift from aphasia to fluency occurs too late—the immigrant has been returned to her country, and only her story remains to be told to and understood by a community of Korean listeners.

Su Kyŏng has pointed out that there are two dynamics to the closing scenes: *the thing that was missing returns*, and *the thing that was present disappears*.[51] In the first case, we have both the return of speech and also the miraculous return of mobility to the elderly woman living on the first floor of the narrator's apartment building, who stands up from her wheelchair in the final moments of the story. In the second case, we have the removal of the hemorrhoids by a leading South Korean proctologist, and also the disappearance of the woman and the two men who had lived with her at the end of the story, as they have (been) returned to their home countries. Behind the dramatic and parallel physical returns (of mobility, of speech) and in the return to health marked by disappearance or removal, we find screened a secret wish: that the thing that was here return to where it had come from. Only then will the return to fluency and belonging be possible.

The silence of the Sri Lankan woman, broken only by unintelligible noise, goes hand in hand with the unexpected translingual fluency of the narrator, who, like Akkas in "Elephant" and the narrator of "Sea and Butterfly," achieves a perfect transparency of communication across languages. This fluency appears to exceed the failures of language that mark a speaker as foreign. Yet this transparency masks both the primary fantasy of the mother tongue as the basis of community and the opacity of the unnamed woman, the "reality" of migrancy inscribed on her mute body. This image is not permitted to interrupt the narrative with its sheer material presence—even as the fact (*facere*) of the woman is obscured behind the flood of speech, the "naked, non-signifying presence"[52] is compelled into sayability, the secret of a real made known to us in the unlikely and fantastic presentation of the narrator.

THE RETURN OF THE REAL

Wherever intelligibility is posited, assumed, or demanded, there is something relegated to unintelligibility. Where a particular discourse is put forward as having maximum or universal intelligibility, something is relegated to nonspeech, to invisibility, to the unsayable or unrepresentable. In this sense, politics is not the exercise of or struggle for power, but—as Rancière holds—"the configuration of a specific space, the framing of a particular sphere of experience, of objects posited as common . . . of subjects recognized as capable of designating those objects and putting forward arguments about them."[53] This is a conflict over what he calls the "distribution of the sensible"—that which allows something to appear sensible or reasonable, held in common, and that at the same time prohibits something else from appearing as such. This sensibility is the definition of the limits of a community consisting of political subjects, an index of belonging and of the limits of intelligibility, where intelligibility is understood not as something *given to*, but as something *given in*: the capacity to be understood, a competency given in an object, person, or statement, prior to, or simultaneous with, the appearance of understanding. "For all time," Rancière writes, "the refusal to consider certain categories of people as political beings has proceeded by means of a refusal to hear the words exiting their mouths as discourse." The political act, in this sense, would consist in "reconfiguring the distribution of the sensible which defines the common of a community, to introduce into it new subjects and objects, to render visible what had not been, and to make heard as speakers those who had been perceived as mere noisy animals."[54]

If politics is the delineation of the field of speech itself, of what can be said and argued and the determination of those who may make those arguments, then it would seem possible to read these stories as political precisely in their representation of the strange expansion of linguistic intelligibility, the appearance of commensurability in the rendering of what had heretofore not been heard. Literature would take on the role of imagining forms of community that exceed the immobilities or forced mobilities that structure the idea and practice of the ethnic nation. If the 1990s and early 2000s were characterized by what critic Hwang Chongyŏn called a "postmodern turn," marked by unreliable narrators who no longer speak for all Koreans, the supersession of a literature of political commitment by fiction focused on the minutiae of everyday life, and the disappearance of national culture into the uncertainty of individual identity,[55] then we could say that the real had in fact returned in migrant

The Return of the Real in South Korean Fiction   41

labor fiction. Literature would have regained its political commitment with the figure of the dispossessed laborer at its center, even if national culture reappears as a problem rather than a given, and even though the narrator lacks the confident authority as a representative of that national culture. Language, on the surface of these stories, seems a plurality rather than the univocal enunciation of ethnic-national sameness.

But what we have found is that hidden behind the fantastic linguistic fluencies and cross-language communications seemingly made possible in these three stories is a return of the real in the form of a boundary or border that reestablishes itself at the very moment of its apparent dissolution. It is in the relationship between the voice of the narrator and the fiction's representation of national culture that we find the structuring principle of these stories: in "Elephant," the making fluent of the voice of the child Akkas; in "Sea and Butterfly," national identities that continue to be established along linguistic lines and which can be overcome only in a moment of mystical experience; and in "Brown Tears," where speech remains the fundamental criterion of belonging in a story that represents multiple languages under the umbrella of a Korean tongue itself missing from the thematics of language presented to us in the narrative. These fantasies form a kind of screen memory that defends against the wish that "what was missing would return, and what was present would disappear," an object of desire that would violate the globalist multicultural discourse of the present era.

Where a new reality seems to appear before our eyes, a reality that would authorize new ways of thinking about community, we see a memory of the present that exposes more of a longing to return to pretraumatic wholeness than a revolutionary attack on culturalism. At the moment when the ideology of the mother tongue seems to disappear, the identity of speech and (ethnic-national) community reasserts itself along newly formed lines of transcultural incommensurabilities that arise not at the level of content but at the level of form. The "real" of the stories appears not only in the representation of the reality and struggles of migrant labor and a changing socioeconomic situation. The fantasy of communication across linguistic barriers emerges as much a sign of anxiety regarding language and community as of a utopian impulse toward seamless multicultural belonging. Behind the silent image of the migrant laborer and the fantastic disavowal of difference, race—the "tie of blood"

42   *The Return of the Real in South Korean Fiction*

signaled by the "tie of language"—continues to structure the social, providing avenues by which sameness and difference are imagined.

Rather than disturbing language at either the level of speech or the level of fictional representation, the fantastical situations put forward in the three stories analyzed above render incomprehension representable in a way that undermines the potential for fiction to serve as a site for challenging and rethinking the boundaries of sensibility in a way precisely the opposite of what we will see in chapter 4. Fantasy instead works to hide the raced and classed hierarchies of human types, representing a particular way of seeing, an *identification* "in which the parties are presupposed as already given, their community established and the count of their speech identical to their linguistic performance."[56]

The impossible speech of the migrant laborer becomes possible in the embrace of a radical communicability by which all speech is knowable, a system of compulsory discursivity that aligns what is said with the already given in a "verisimilar tale of social necessity."[57] In a sense, silence itself is silenced in the supernatural fluency of the characters across these stories, an impossibilization of impossible speech in the demonstration that all speech is knowable. As we will see in the chapter 2, this gesture of establishing the boundaries of the sayable in advance, bringing the possible into agreement with the real,[58] is especially pronounced in political speeches memorializing historical events designated as national. South Korean president Moon Jae-in's annual addresses on the anniversary of the May 1980 Kwangju uprising and massacre also work to foreclose the traumatic event and the national subject in a way that, as Butler writes, establishes the domain of the speakable[59]—aiming to account for all possible speech and to put in place a kind of archival system that fixes in advance the possibility and the sensibility of statements and their social meaning.

With migrant labor fiction, the celebratory language of "border crossing" gives the sense that we have entered into a period in which national boundaries are being broken down and the naturalized links between language, culture, nationality, and ethnicity are being dismantled. As a consequence, a focus on works representing migration, cross-border labor, emigration and diaspora, and subjects "stripped naked" are understood to have become topics with a particular political valence. Yet in the works of fiction most closely associated with this turn,

The Return of the Real in South Korean Fiction   43

the possible is not disturbed and "native" speech remains the criterion of belonging. That the crossing of geopolitical borders is figured in the specific examples above through the fantastic representation of speech outside of linguistic difference does not diminish the need to think through such representations in terms of the problem of realism, for which fiction is comprehended and valued to the extent that it expresses the actuality of the subject. If the real returns in migrant labor fiction, it returns in a way that is normative, and leaves open the question of whether or not there is a literary language adequate to the experience of the unrepresentable.

CHAPTER TWO

Displacing the Common Sense of Trauma

Han Kang's A Boy Is Coming

When violence takes extreme forms,
forms of knowledge are also implicated.
—MICHAEL ROTHBERG, *TRAUMATIC REALISM*

It is, after all, the revisionist historians who say:
Establish the facts. Prove them, go on and prove them!
—MARC NICHANIAN, *THE HISTORIOGRAPHIC PERVERSION*

This chapter aims to examine the ways in which catastrophic historical events may be shaped into a common sense of the community, and the intervention that the literary text may make in this common sense, expanding (rather than verifying) the sense of the traumatic event. I argue that Han Kang's 2014 novel *A Boy Is Coming* retains the idea of the unrepresentability of trauma while rejecting its singularity and hence its capacity for endless repetition in the search for a lost absolute community. The chapter proposes instead a model of trauma as an unverifiable, enigmatic message that makes its effects felt in the "piercing" of the present by the past rather than in the endlessly melancholic repetitions that characterize a traumatropical regime.

On May 18, 2019—the thirty-ninth anniversary of what is now known as the Kwangju Democratization Movement—South Korean President Moon Jae-in delivered an address as part of the annual events memorializing the uprising and the massacre that followed. The speech relied on affects of shared grief and shame, calling attention to the brutal violence visited by the state upon its own citizens in 1980, and was motivated in part as a response to a wave of Kwangju deniers, with Moon rebutting the "illogical statements that both insult and deny" the events of May 1980. Yet, the president told his audience, the uprising had also given subsequent generations a common identity rooted in a sense of shared victimhood. In part due to the ongoing collective debt to those who died in the massacre, Kwangju is also something that "we have all experienced together. Wherever we were at that time, whether we learned early or late about Kwangju's May, does not matter—we all experienced, together, the pain of Kwangju."[1] Moon revisits this theme in his 2020 address—standing directly in front of the Provincial Office building that had served as a makeshift headquarters for the civilian militia during the uprising—by referencing the "spirit of May" (*Owŏl ŭi chŏngsin*), an inherited ethical imperative to "respond to the pain of others" that "permeates the hearts and minds of each and every one of our citizens."[2]

Taken together, the speeches present a concise example of the way in which historical trauma may become part of a narrative of national identity. As Cho Yŏnjŏng writes, when historical tragedy is re-created in narrative, those narratives tend to take on one of three general forms: narratives of accusation that confirm a system of good and evil, narratives of record or testimony that both establish the truth of the traumatic event and resist its forgetting, or narratives of cure that address the trauma through a repetition meant to heal.[3] Moon's addresses achieve all three narrative modes.

First, a systematic (and hereditary) evil is established. Moon references not only the authoritarian governments of the past, but also—in a slightly more oblique reference to the "heirs of dictators"—Moon's immediate predecessor in office, the impeached and then imprisoned ex-president Park Geun-hye, herself the daughter of Park Chung Hee, the military ruler who led South Korea from 1961 until his assassination in 1979. The good of those citizens of Kwangju who resisted the intervention of the authoritarian state's military forces in May 1980 then becomes a transgenerational moral imperative. In the 2019 speech, Kwangju is named the origin of the struggle for democratization that culminated in the 1987 protests and South Korea's first postwar free election. In the

46 *Displacing the Common Sense of Trauma*

2020 speech, the uprising is placed in a longer genealogy of national history, from the April 19, 1960, protests against Syngman Rhee through the 1979 Pusan-Masan protests against Park Chung Hee's Yushin regime, the 1987 struggle for democratic elections, and the 2016–2017 Candlelight Revolution calling for the impeachment and prosecution of Park Geun-hye.

Second, Moon both upholds the event of Kwangju as a long-established historical truth and at the same time points to the need for further investigation and fact finding. Against the "distortions and denigrations" of those who deny the historical fact of the uprising, the president is unequivocal: consensus was reached on the factuality of the event more than twenty years ago, when the South Korean government passed legislation to replace the original designation "Kwangju Incident" (Kwangju sat'ae) with "Kwangju Democratization Movement" (Kwangju minjuhwa undong) and when the court ruled that the suppression of the uprising constituted military rebellion and treason. At the same time, as he did in his 2017 comments at the May 18 memorial ceremony, Moon continued to call for renewed investigations into the atrocities committed by the military in its suppression of the uprising, demanding the "illumination of the truth" and laying bare the "facts of state violence" through the investigatory activities of the May 18 Democratization Movement Truth Commission.[4]

Third, such laying bare aims not at punishment of the guilty but toward "the work of properly recording history" and correctly remembering truths that form a healing "basis of national harmony and unity." It is only by properly remembering and narrating the past that forgiveness and reconciliation can be achieved, Moon told his audience. The work of determining historical truth is to be supplemented by practices of remembrance, such as the long-promised amendment to the constitution to include mention of Kwangju, or through other memorialization like the reconstruction of the Provincial Office building in Kwangju or the repurposing of the former police torture facility in Seoul's Namyŏngdong neighborhood as a museum devoted to human rights and democracy. Yet these are not mere acts of remembrance—they work on the grounds of both history and law to constitute a permissible definition of the event and to delineate a proper way of speaking about political dissent. The fact is literally brought into alignment with the law as

Displacing the Common Sense of Trauma 47

both historically and legally incontrovertible; or, in the case of the torture museum, what had long stood as a symbol of state violence—a literal black mark on the urban landscape—is written into a state-sponsored narrative of democratization and progress.

I begin this chapter with Moon's anniversary addresses because they so successfully present the conventional parameters for making meaning out of a traumatic historical event marked as national. His speeches memorialize the uprising as fully known, its significance established once and for all; confirm historical factuality and legal decision as the basis for that knowledge; universalize the experience of Kwangju to "each and every citizen"; uphold a transmissible, transgenerational victimhood and a "debt owed by all," defining trauma and its effects as hereditary phenomena; and place the traumatic event within a coherent narrative of national history and at the foundation of national identity across political lines (excepting those "heirs of dictators").

Moon's speeches thus reproduce a conventional understanding of trauma, even as they claim to move beyond it. The "catastrophic event," too overwhelming in its initial moment to comprehend, is experienced again and again after the fact, repetitions that "seem not to be initiated by the individual's own acts but rather . . . as the possession of some people by a sort of fate, a series of painful events to which they are subjected, and which seem to be entirely outside their wish or control."[5] What is crucial is that the *unknowing* acts of the haunted survivors, who against their will reenact trauma as per Cathy Caruth's canonical account, are reclaimed here as *knowing*, willed acts of remembrance and reenactment that carry on the work of representing the traumatic moment. The enigmatic voice of the traumatic wound that bears witness to a truth that cannot be fully known[6] is captured, in nationalist discourse, in a net of historical truth supported by legal decision and the state-sponsored performance of remembrance and mourning. Any unknowing is entirely due to deficits in the reach of historical methods or to the "distortions and denigrations" of Kwangju deniers.

Historical trauma is thus understood as both "over and done with"— fully known and established as fact—and at the same time as an identity to which fidelity is demanded. Dominick LaCapra refers to this as "traumatropism," the tendency to convert trauma into a "legitimating myth of origins,"[7] transvaluing trauma into "a test of the self or the group and

48 *Displacing the Common Sense of Trauma*

an entry into the extraordinary." Such a "founding trauma" can become the "valorized or intensely cathected basis of identity for an individual or a group" and as such can produce the desire to remain within the trauma, making its "reliving a painful but necessary commemoration or memorial to which one remains dedicated or at least bound"[8] and which demands "endless melancholy or grieving."[9] Trauma thus becomes the basis of solidarity among the national community as an inherited historical fact but also as a moral sense (the "spirit of May") linked to the present and future goals of the community. The traumatic event is to be constantly and correctly remembered through memorialization, commemoration, and repeated performance,[10] and, to the extent possible, reenacted in the material, legal, and historical fabric of the nation.

In such a model, there is no question of how or whether Kwangju should be represented. It is either represented properly (by the state), or improperly (by Kwangju deniers). Further, at no point is representation *im*possible. The parameters of speech—which is not only understood as entirely possible, but legislated as being such—are clearly set, and moral positions are attached to any given instance of speech along a defined spectrum of possibility. There is good speech and there is bad speech, but there is never no speech. All speech about Kwangju is accounted for, even when it is impermissible (an impermissibility that is itself intelligible within the moral system of speech and sensibility about Kwangju), and the areas in which or from which speech is impossible are apparently eliminated.[11]

This chapter takes issue with the effort to establish the total visibility of Kwangju (the impossibilization of impossible speech) that seemingly takes place through the very expansion of speech to "one and all," a domain of the sayable that, perhaps counterintuitively, results in forgetting and silence. I focus on the 2014 Han Kang novel *A Boy Is Coming*, which at first seems to share much with conventional retellings of Kwangju. First published on May 19, 2014—the date immediately giving the publication itself the sense of a commemoration—*Boy* is a fictional recounting of the events immediately following the violence of the first days of the uprising. Critics have understood the novel as a form of testimony that aims to present the "true memory" of Kwangju[12] against the distortions and denials of Kwangju by the right wing in South Korea that were prevalent in 2013 as Park Geun-hye came into office, a "true

Displacing the Common Sense of Trauma 49

reconstitution [*chaegusŏng*] of the past . . . based in the subjective memory of the individual."[13]

Against these readings, I hold that *Boy* adheres neither to an expectation that the proper response to trauma is a historically valid "reconstitution" nor to the all too prevalent assumption that an alignment between the voice of the literary text and the witness to the disaster is necessary to bring such a truth into being.[14] Instead, as we will see, the novel holds to both the impossibility of testimony and to the possibility of representation, working against the demand that the text correspond to the historical or empirical reality by putting forward a model of trauma distinct from traumatropical common sense and adhering to a figural language that always announces itself as not being the thing represented. A core ethical message of the novel is that sense must *not* be made of the extreme violence of Kwanjgu, but that we must not leave off trying to make sense of the enigmatic voice and its unintelligibility, "the silences, throat clearings and coughs, hesitations, stitched loosely together with dry, stiff words."[15]

The novel thus addresses the thing that is made impossible in the contemporary discourse on Kwangju, which is the impossibility of speech itself. *Boy* restores the capacity of speech to exceed the possible against the (historiographical, realist) demand for total clarity; the singularity of Kwangju commemorated as "over and done with" (and hence forgotten) is discarded, and the name itself is extended as a present and future signifier for "all places, all times, where dignity and violence coexist,"[16] detached from its status as a name the full meaning of which has been agreed upon in advance. Against the idea of political art that claims identity or overlap with the event and on that basis arrogates to itself the ability to "tell the truth" of that event, the novel hangs on to its status as literature, calling attention to the gap between language and the event in both its form and its content. In this sense, *Boy* probes the limits of what is sayable about Kwanjgu and raises the question of the politics of art beyond the realist contract that values the work of literature to the extent that it corresponds with the supposed real of the event. The novel acknowledges but firmly resists the singular nomination of Kwangju as a founding trauma about which everything can be articulated and pushes back against the compulsion to testify to what is already known. It is the work of art, not the archival document, that stands at the

50 *Displacing the Common Sense of Trauma*

juncture of the imperative to remember and the prohibition against making sense of the inexplicable.

DISPLACING THE COMMON SENSE OF TRAUMA

Divided into six chapters and an epilogue, Han Kang's novel incorporates multiple perspectives in multiple narrative presents, from Kwangju in 1980 through the 2010s. Decomposing bodies and survivors alike speak in Han's prose. The thread running through each chapter is Tongho, the title "boy" who narrates his own death in the opening chapter. He tells his story in the second person, and continues to occupy the position of "you" in each subsequent chapter as both the subject of (direct) address and the object of narration in depictions of both the past and present. When the dead are finished with their stories—the second chapter is narrated from atop a pile of putrefying corpses by another child killed on the street in the first days of the uprising—those who had appeared in the boys' retellings reappear as survivors who live with the "shame of not dying."[17] Two young women who volunteered with Tongho at the Provincial Office narrate the third and fifth chapters; the fourth chapter consists of the testimony of a participant who was imprisoned and tortured after the event; and the sixth chapter is a reminiscence narrated by Tongho's mother.

The novel immediately disavows two essential aspects of a trauma-tropical *making sense* of Kwangju: the very possibility of return itself, and the constitution of national community on the basis of founding trauma. Tongho raises the first impossibility early in the opening chapter. Walking out of the gymnasium where he has been part of a team working to identify corpses and toward a memorial service being held in front of the Provincial Office, he thinks: "If that other world [*tarŭn sesang*] continued, you would have taken your midterm examinations last week. Today, the Sunday after exams, you would have slept late and gotten up to play badminton with Chŏngdae in the yard. Just as the past week hasn't felt real, the time of that other world feels [just as] unreal."[18]

It is a specific event that has split the "other world" from the present, an event witnessed the week before. Frightened by the appearance of soldiers on the street, Tongho had veered into an alley leading down to a streamside, where he falls into step behind a young couple. Tongho

Displacing the Common Sense of Trauma 51

hears the man protest, presumably to a soldier, that they are merely headed to church.

> Before the man in the Western suit had finished speaking, you saw something happen to a person's arm. A person's hand, the small of a person's back, a person's leg—you saw something that it was possible to do [ŏttŏn il ŭl hal su ittnŭnji poatta]. Save me. The man shouted, gasping. They brought the clubs down on him, not stopping until the man's twitching legs had grown still. You don't know what became of the woman who had been standing next to him and who hadn't stopped screaming, after they grabbed her hair. Because, your chin trembling, you had clambered up the incline of the bank of a stream only to enter into an even more unfamiliar scene unfolding on the street.[19]

Here Tongho sees *something that had not been possible but had become possible*—something becomes possible through the performance of (what had been) an impossible act. The passage of reminiscence is immediately followed by an ellipsis, the mark of an omission of language appearing as a blank space on the page; the narrative resumes abruptly with a return to Tongho's present moment, outside the Provincial Office building. There are two indications of conventional trauma in the passage: Tongho does not fully grasp what he is seeing ("*il ŭl hal su ittnŭnji poattda*"), he sees that some act has become possible, but the concrete act itself escapes him; and he is unable to narrate those experiences clearly to himself after a passage of time. The experience is figured as the passage from an incomprehensible scene into an "even more unfamiliar scene [*kwanggyŏng*]" after which the retelling ceases.

The fifth chapter is told through the perspective of Kwangju survivor Im Sŏnju, one of the young women with Tongho in the Provincial Office building in May 1980. Sŏnju is also narrated primarily in the second person. "About 20 years have passed since that summer. *We've got to dry up your seed, you Commie fuckers*. You have gotten here, turning your back on the moment when they dashed water on your body, spitting curses. Any path by which to return to a time before that summer has been cut off. There is no way to return to the world [*segye*] before the massacre, before the torture."[20] For both Tongho and Sŏnju, there is

52 *Displacing the Common Sense of Trauma*

no return to the "before" of the traumatic event—an impassable divide exists between the "then" and each of the narrative "nows" of the novel. At the same time that a conventional model of trauma is appealed to in the representation of overwhelming experiences that are incomprehensible in the moment of their occurrence, the narrative also rejects two "returns" that characterize a traumatropical model: the idea of a return to an ideal, pre-traumatic past and the obsessive return to the moment of trauma as a path toward healing. In other words, what is rejected is the continuity of a world that extends both before and after the traumatic event.

Continuity between a world that exists prior to and after the massacre is also rejected in the frequent and incoherent appearance of the national anthem, from the first pages of the novel forward. We may return to the first chapter and the central figure of the young student Tongho, presented by an unknown and heterologous narrator in the second person—a position occupied by Tongho throughout the entire novel, and a narrative strategy that works to both make the "boy" an object of knowledge and to implicate the reader in the story being told.[21] Volunteering at the Provincial Office in Kwangju under the direction of militia leader Kim Chinsu, Tongho presents the events of May 1980 in the precise and almost clinical language allowed by the distance of the second-person voice. Working alongside others, including Im Sŏnju and Kim Ŭnsuk, another young woman who narrates a later chapter, his job is to "process" the corpses, recording in a ledger their gender, a rough estimate of age, the clothes and type of shoes they were wearing, and assigning each a number, which he also jots down on a slip of coarse paper and attaches to the chest of each body with a pin. This information records the details of the deaths and identifies the dead for family members who come to mourn and to dress the bodies for funeral rites. It is here that markers of national identity first appear to confuse Tongho. "There was a part of this process that you had not been able to understand—the bereaved families singing the national anthem at the short, informal memorial service held after the caskets had been prepared. Spreading the national flag out on the coffin and tying it tightly in place with cord was also strange. Why would one sing the national anthem for people who had been killed by soldiers? Why wrap their coffin with the national flag? As if they hadn't been killed by the nation."[22] The national anthem and the well-known

Displacing the Common Sense of Trauma 53

traditional song "Arirang" appear repeatedly in the narrative, observed from various characters' perspectives. Tongho, for instance, recalls the crowds in the streets around the Provincial Office: "They sang the national anthem, voices piled indistinctly upon voices into a tower tens of thousands of storeys high."[23] Crucially, Tongho takes a distanced perspective on this—though he joins in the singing at one point, he pauses at the phrase "Roses of Sharon, three thousand *ri* of splendid rivers and mountains" and loses himself in consideration of both the Sinographic characters (無窮花 三千里 華麗 江山, especially the character for "splendid") and the ambiguous meaning of the spare language of the verse. "Is it that these are beautiful rivers and mountains where there are flowers? Or, are the rivers and mountains beautiful *like* the flowers?"[24]

Others also encounter the anthem in a variety of situations. In a later chapter, a survivor and interviewee—who had spent time in prison with the militia leader Kim Chinsu—recalls that "it was around one o'clock in the afternoon when the soldiers opened fire [on the crowds of civilians], *in tune with* the national anthem flowing from the speakers in front of the Provincial Office."[25] The anthem here provides a rhythmic soundtrack to the massacre of civilians. At the same time, the interviewee also recalls singing the anthem together with other protestors marching on the street: "It was like a miracle," he reports. "Like we had all stepped outside of the shells of our selves" and joined together into a single entity, "the most enormous and sublime heart [*simjang*] in the world."[26] The national anthem also marks the moment of the death of Tongho's friend Chŏngdae, who narrates the second chapter as a decaying body stacked on top of others in an open grave. "Had I been together with . . . those many people, together raising their voices and together singing songs?" he asks. Chŏngdae had joined in, "singing along with the national anthem, my throat bursting" at the moment he is shot in the side.[27]

While Tongho is not in a position to witness these other encounters with the national anthem, he is aware of it being sung in various modalities: as an expression of grief by the families mourning the dead in the gymnasium of the Provincial Office, as a marching tune sung by soldiers, and as a song sung by the protestors in the streets. He questions the young woman Kim Ŭnsuk about this. "Why would one sing the national anthem for people who had been killed by soldiers?" She responds that the soldiers are rebelling, that they have seized power, beating and stabbing and

54   *Displacing the Common Sense of Trauma*

shooting people—"How can you call such people 'the nation'?" Tongho's internal response to this is in keeping with the unsolved ambiguity of nationalist symbolism in the novel. He thinks: "You are confused: it's as if you've gotten an answer to a totally different question [than the one you'd asked]."[28] This confusion is again figured in the narrative, almost immediately following this exchange. "That afternoon, there were particularly large numbers of positive identifications, with [funeral rites] held at caskets up and down the hallways, all at the same time. You caught your breath, inclining your ear at the subtle discordance that arose as, through the sounds of weeping, the national anthem was being sung, like a round, passage after passage running against one another. As if in such a way you could manage to understand what this thing called a nation was."[29] Tongho's confusion (*hollan*) is mirrored in the discord (*pulhyŏphwa*) of the multiple iterations of the anthem. Neither the content of the anthem nor its significance as a symbol of community belonging are clear. The *ordinariness* of the anthem is violated as the *order* that it typically represents is collapsed into discordance.

At minimum, this discordance could be called counterhegemonic, a "de-officializing" of language, an "expropriation" of language (here, the anthem) "for non-ordinary means."[30] Working as it does against consensual meaning, it might also be thought of as a moment of what Rancière calls "dissensus," which is "not a conflict of interests, opinions, or value" but rather "a division put in the 'common sense': a dispute about what is given, about the frame within which we see something as given."[31] If Kwangju is an event, "that rare historical occurrence that shatters a situation," then its dissensus also "demands a new language."[32] What the novel achieves in presenting Tongho as the voice of Kwangju is akin to what Lecercle calls the "storming" of language in his analysis of Michel de Certeau's recounting of the "capture" of speech during the events of May 1968.[33] It is not simply that *Boy* gives voices to speech that often goes unheard in dominant discourse, including the speech of the young, of women, and of laborers.[34] What we witness in the discord of the anthem in *Boy* is a violent process, a rejection of interpellation (here, as either a national subject *or* a protestor—the heroism of both identities is rejected by the novel) and a displacement, "the emergence of the rare historical event that makes the language of the situation obsolete and anachronic." But it is not that a new or more sufficient language comes into being. "The

Displacing the Common Sense of Trauma   55

same words have to be used, and the same syntax," continues Lecercle, "only the general tone and the nuances of meaning are not the same—an apparently innocuous shift which, because it affects the whole of the established language, amounts to subversion." He names this operation an inversion, language taken against its common sense, "forcing the usual words to mean what they cannot or will not mean"—a remaking that extends to "an inversion of hierarchical positions, in both knowledge and authority."[35]

The language in *A Boy Is Coming* is inevitably "the same language"— the narrative is intelligible to the reader, the lyrics of the anthem are unchanged. No new lyrics are proposed. Yet at the same time, as we will see below, the novel displaces the "common sense" of Kwangju, resisting the enactment of state power and its legitimizing language (the anthem as the soundtrack to the event's state-sponsored memorialization). Yet at the same time we do not see the "anthem of the revolution" appear in the "wooden language of rebellion [that] merely parroted the wooden language of authority."[36] That is, the anthem or "Arirang" are not simply appropriated by the forces of resistance, which would show the "frailty of the purely negative posture,"[37] an appropriation (rather than a displacement) of common sense. Instead, the novel performs parallel operations: undermining, controverting, or inverting language in its radical nonidentity with the common sense of the (national) community; and raising questions about the capacity of any language at all to make (common) sense of traumatic disaster.

THE NON-SENSE OF KWANGJU

We have seen that traumatic events, when converted into a "legitimating myth of origins," can produce "an endlessly melancholic impossible mourning,"[38] a desire to stay within the trauma and to repeat or "act it out" rather than working through it toward a "more desirable future."[39] The trauma, whether experienced directly or inherited in discourse, becomes an entry point into community belonging for which its "reliving" serves as a ritual of renewed identification and consensus. This is partly, LaCapra writes, to do with a confusion between absence and loss. When absence (which does not necessarily imply a lack) is converted into loss, nostalgia and a continual seeking after the lost object may result.

56 *Displacing the Common Sense of Trauma*

What is posited to have been lost in Kwangju is "absolute community" (*chŏltae kongdongch'e*), described by Jung-woon Choi as "sheer collectivity" formed by citizens "who autonomously overcame their fears, risked their lives in struggle, and came together freely to reaffirm and celebrate their humanity, their true citizenship."[40]

The mistaking of absence for loss here is masked effectively both by the performative regeneration of the past, where it is "relived as if it were fully present rather than represented in memory and inscription,"[41] and by the closely related reliance on historical work and fact finding to bolster the reality of that past in the present and to achieve consensus on its content and its meaning. There is an odd mingling of the sure knowability of the past in the present and the conviction that this lost reality is as-yet unrealized, an uncertainty that then drives the repeated return to that same past object. Thus works such as Im Ch'ŏru's *Spring Day* (*Pomnal*), written by a survivor of the massacre and aiming to testify to the truth of the violence and the event—its "really real-ness" (*chŏngmallo silchae haessŭm*)—"fossilize Kwangju as a completed, past event. . . . an event that must be commemorated and is hence gradually forgotten."[42]

Yet it is only in recognizing the impossibility of settling upon a final definition of Kwangju and "undertaking the task of continually making present [*hyŏnjaehwa*] the already happened as an event impossible to [fix with a] name" that a revictimization of the victims of tragedy can be avoided. "Rather than 'remembering' Kwangju as a historical event and in the end, then, 'forgetting' its present potentiality, it is necessary to maintain a stance of 'disavowed mourning' [*puintoen aedo*] toward Kwangju and to draw new political possibilities from it."[43]

Mourning in this sense is not a transformation of absence into transhistorical loss and a "retrospective consciousness of the lost community and its identity,"[44] but is rather an ongoing avowal of the unknowability of the traumatic event. Rather than aiming at absolute historical veracity and a corresponding realistic representation of the event, mourning admits that the original loss may transform the subject in unknown ways. "Freud reminds us that when we lose someone, we do not always know what it is *in* that person that has been lost," Butler writes. "So when one loses, one is also faced with something enigmatic: something is hiding in the loss, something is lost within the recesses of the loss." Mourning may thus be "maintained by its enigmatic dimension, by the

Displacing the Common Sense of Trauma   57

experience of not knowing incited by losing what we cannot fully fathom."[45]

Boy does not simply dispense with trauma. Rather, two modes of unintelligibility are put forward: the unintelligibility of the thing that was lost, and the unintelligibility of what remains. There are no archetypical victims or heroes in Han's narrative. Tongho himself is perfectly nondescript, with "a face so ordinary that you could easily mix it up with someone else's, a face the characteristics of which one would forget as soon as one took one's eyes off it."[46] It is so ordinary that the ethnographic narrator of the novel's epilogue cannot be certain of it in video footage taken near the Provincial Office in 1980. Tongho is not historically verifiable. Neither are the members of the civilian militia heroes. "It's no good if we become victims. It's no good for us to let it lie at being called victims," Sŏnju remembers a fellow activist saying.[47] Or, the narrator of the epilogue tells us, "when [those in the civilian militia] were asked why they stayed behind, even though they knew they would be defeated, the survivors and witnesses all gave the same answer. *I don't know. It just seemed like something I had to do.*" This leads her to conclude: "I was mistaken to think of them as 'victims.'"[48]

Conventional narrative modalities of trauma—as we have seen clearly in the case of Moon's annual addresses—demand the intelligibility of the past in order to guarantee the intelligibility of a community in the present. The historical truth of the traumatic event must be made known and commemorated again and again, brought into the present as a seeming expedience against trauma that both retains the figure of the traumatized subject in the citizen, "obliged to repeat the repressed material as a contemporary experience, instead of, as the physician would prefer to, remembering it as something belonging to the past,"[49] and makes that citizen fully accountable and fully visible within the perceptual grid of a normative national identity. Han's novel—a work filled with agonizing suffering, both past and present—rejects this logic of a pervasive founding trauma that would present that hereditary suffering as "the humane content that unfreedom counterfeits as positivity,"[50] refusing to give suffering *sense* or the trappings of glory. The ethical core of the novel insists that the massacre remain senseless, that it must not be made sense of in the narrative. The massacre can be made "sensible" neither as something "wise" or "prudent" or "practical," nor as "readily perceived," easily

58 *Displacing the Common Sense of Trauma*

made available to the senses. Against the traumatropical pairing of full knowledge and visibility with the melancholic compulsion to return to a past in which the identity of the community is based, in *Boy* the enigmatic non-sense of Kwangju is maintained.

Here then is a path to admitting the reality of trauma and loss without succumbing to the impulse to erect trauma at the base of contemporary political expediency and the policing of the borders of community, a "founding trauma" that stands as both an "interminable aporia"[51] and an event that is "over and done with," the meaning of which is made clear through perpetual return to the past and the excavation of its facts. This pretense, that we can fully know the past event—as if it were not mediated by memory and language—is rejected in Han's novel, which understands Kwangju as an *ongoing* event and as a name with expansive meaning, contained neither temporally nor spatially. "The experience of that violence cannot be limited to the short, ten-day-long period of the uprising," Sŏnju thinks. "It's like the exposure to radiation at Chernobyl, not something that [simply] passes by but something that continues, ranging over decades."[52] Torture, the narrator tells us in the epilogue, is like that radiation—it permeates the body, remaining for decades, deforming chromosomes, lingering in the bones long after death.[53] Kwangju names a tendency to brutal violence not confined to May 1980: "in Cheju, in Kwangtung and Nanjing, in Bosnia, and all across the New World, a uniform cruelty, as if it is impressed upon our genes."[54] In the end, "Kwangju" loses its sense of historical specificity, its rootedness in the singularity of a traumatic event: "When I saw images of the tower on the roof of the apartment building ablaze at dawn in January 2009, I remember muttering without even realizing: *That's Kwangju.* Kwangju was a different name for those things that are isolated and helpless, trampled upon by power, those things that must not come to harm that are harmed nonetheless. The exposure to radiation still hasn't ended. Countless times, Kwangju has been reborn and slaughtered."[55] The singularity of Kwangju is disavowed, even as its meaning attaches to instances of organized violence across time and space. In this sense, Kwangju fails as a containable, intelligible historical event. The task of fiction is not to confirm Kwangju as such an event, forcing a retraumatization of the reader through an encounter with obscene violence. Rather, the novel first presents Kwangju as "an event the meaning of which and perhaps

Displacing the Common Sense of Trauma   59

the historicization of which is, from the first, impossible"; the rupture of the event cannot be "solved," it cannot be fully grasped in testimony.[56] *A Boy Is Coming* is not a novel written to sustain an originary traumatic wound, an experience of one extended to all as a condition of community. The perpetual second person signals others, rather than drawing attention to the experiences of a single victim; and, as Ji-Eun Lee points out, the present tense in Korean implies a future tense that "could describe an action from any time (past, present, future) for a realistic effect"[57]—the name of Kwangju signals an ongoing event in which others are implicated. Outside of a state historiography that aims to fully capture the event and to set the parameters of speech within which Kwangju will be intelligible, the novel is "preoccupied with those points remaining after the meaning making of other discourses—that is, those points that have broken away from or are 'beside the point' of signification."[58] Against the logic of "over and done with"—the logic of explanation or a full accounting—*Boy* breaks out of the trope of trauma, putting "Kwangju" forward as a name without singular referent, a repetition with difference that expands the political capacity of the memory of atrocity beyond the commonsensical strictures of the apparently possible.

"THERE ARE ONLY CORPSES": REPRESENTING THE ABSENT WITNESS

We have seen various moments from Han's novel that are "beside the point" of codes of representation by which sense is usually made of Kwangju. While *Boy* hardly dispenses with the historical actuality of Kwangju or with the continual demand to acknowledge the event and to call for an accounting, neither does it accept a transparency of representation or an unproblematic reproduction of testimony and the consequent arrival of a truer truth or a realer real. It is not a "true reconstitution [*chaegusŏng*] of the past . . . based in subjective memory of the individual."[59] Rather, the text accepts and even promotes Kwangju as what Sŏ Yŏngch'ae calls an "unstable sign," for which memorialization has not led to stable symbolization of the event.[60] It is an "unfinished event,"[61] an event the meaning and historicization of which are impossible. As Cho writes, "it is because the tragedy of Kwangju and, at the

60 *Displacing the Common Sense of Trauma*

center of this, Tongho's death, cannot be fully explained that the fiction aims less for a complete narration and focuses more on various characters' voices, enumerating those characters' voices as fragments."[62] The novel, she writes, "resists the work of historicizing and giving meaning to Kwangju as an anonymous collective tragedy" by continually *making present* (*hyŏnjaehwa*) the already happened. Symbolization and ritualization are rejected, and Kwangju appears as a *"presence that refuses a name,"*[63] both through the rejection of its singularity and through the proliferation of possible referents.

It is not that Tongho's death is a mystery that cannot be explained. Rather, authorized, verifiable speech is undermined from the first chapter forward. As we have seen, the narrative steadfastly refuses to acknowledge the participants in the uprising as either heroes or victims. Tongho's face is unverifiable; his participation in the uprising is not documented in the exhibition. He is not authorized to speak on the basis of his status as a "hero"; we are not authorized to label him a passive "victim" of the massacre and to speak for him. At the same time, neither is his silence established as a "site of political resistance" to a politics figured as coterminous with the totality of available speech, that is, the discursive regime of power and its "normalizing effects."[64] His "silence" is not the silence that can be read in the "marks directly imprinted" on his body by history in his "features . . . clothes . . . life setting";[65] rather, his is an *enigmatic* silence, an unverifiability that demands continual attempts at interpretation. The enigma of Tongho springs primarily from the fact that the novel begins with, and is organized around, his death and absence—that is, with "the autobiographical moment of the witness's death."[66] He is not only not authorized to speak, but is not *available* to speak. The second-person voice used in the opening chapter to implicate the reader and to produce a distance between Tongho and the event of Kwangju—a gap that precludes the capture of Tongho's witness in a narrative of heroism or victimhood—continues in subsequent chapters to recall Tongho not as a witness but as an absent cause.

In the aftermath of the violence at Kwangju, "there are only corpses lying there, silent";[67] speech is thus either fantastically represented as coming to us after death, as in the opening two chapters, or witnesses are called forward to speak in a kind of dual address, both in the stead of the missing and as interlocutors with the ghostly "you" that remains into

Displacing the Common Sense of Trauma 61

the present. The survivor Sŏnju hears the voice of Tongho in the night, for instance, but even when the direct speech of the (absent) witness is represented, the voice is uncertain of what it wants to say: "I don't know what I would want to say if I met you," she hears him say. "What would it be possible to say?"[68]

Given its thematic focus on death and silence, it is no surprise that *Boy* has frequently been read as a performance of the problem of testimony and as a meditation on the possibility (or impossibility) of representing that testimony in the work of art. For Kim Yosŏp, the remains of Tongho persist in the lives of those who survived, and their representation presents a "restoration of lost testimony," realizing the sacrificed life that cannot speak for itself in the multiple perspectives of the novel—a kind of network of memories.[69] For Hwang Chŏnga as well, the central work of the novel is to "testify to the impossibility of testifying",[70] the focus of the novel, writes Cho Sŏnghŭi, is not testimony itself but "the impossibility of testimony" (*chŭngŏn ŭi pulkanŭngsŏng*).[71] This impossibility in *Boy* is often discussed through Agamben's "lacuna of testimony," in which survivors cannot testify to the experiences of the dead and can thus only produce "a discourse 'on behalf of third parties,' the story of things seen close at hand, not experienced personally."[72]

Yet testimony is not precisely impossible in Han Kang's work. As Cho writes, "*A Boy Is Coming* is not a work that simply confirms the 'impossibility of testimony' regarding the tragedy of Kwangju. It can [rather] be read as a piece of fiction that overcomes that 'impossibility of testimony' with the 'possibility of representation.'"[73] The question then is how this impossibility is represented. For Cho Sŏnghŭi, *Boy* is a novel in which the author lends her voice to those who have lost their voices in death (Tongho and his friend Chŏngdae, or Chinsu, the militia leader who commits suicide following his torture). Thus, she writes, *Boy* is a work that "bridges the gap of testimony."[74] Kim Yŏngch'an writes that Han Kang's fiction "suggests the impossibility of finding a starting point with regard to the representation of the other's suffering through sympathy [*yŏnmin*] or pity [*konggam*]"[75] and extends Cho's idea, holding that the author's goal was to "become the voice [of the other] to the extent possible."[76] Here fictional representation disappears—the author seems to take on the voice of the other, becoming, precisely, a witness who stands in where another cannot testify.

62 *Displacing the Common Sense of Trauma*

As we saw clearly in the case of migrant labor fiction, such critical perspectives ignore the literariness of the voice—that is, the question of representation itself. One of the most oft-cited lines in the novel comes when, in the epilogue, the narrator seeks out Tongho's older brother, a survivor still living in Kwangju, and asks for permission to tell Tongho's story. "Consent?" he replies. "Of course I consent. But in return, you must write it well. By all means, you must write *properly* [*chedaero ssŏya hamnida*]. Write it so that my brother can be desecrated [profaned] no longer."[77] The novel signals its status as literature, as a story, as communicable, precisely by pointing to the absence that must be written,[78] and written properly. This is not the case of an erasure or the pure replacement of the victim's voice with that of the author's; it is the *representation* of an erasure.

The appearance of a silent play at the center of the novel is just such a representation of the erasure of speech, as opposed to the actual erasure of that speech. We encounter the survivor Kim Ŭnsuk, who narrates herself as "that woman" in the third chapter, roughly five years after the massacre. Ŭnsuk works for a small publishing house. She has retrieved the manuscript of a collection of plays from the censorship office; the volume has been so thoroughly redacted that it is "as if burned,"[79] so saturated with the ink of the censor that it is swollen and deformed—the figure of what remains after the violent policing of language. In addition to a few scattered words "stitched together"—you, I, that, how, look, your eyes—only a few sentences remain intact:

> After you were lost, our time became evening.
> Our houses and streets became evening.
> In this evening, which brightens or darkens no longer, we eat
> and walk and sleep.[80]

The sentences reference the perpetual evening in which the survivors live; the "you" suggests that the boy will play a central role in the play. The censorial deauthorization and destruction of language here produces an "incomplete" text that may no longer attain the status of the document or stand as evidence. It is compelled to speak *as literature*—a kind of language that announces its incompletion and the necessity of interpretation in advance—by the very regulation of speech that mars it.

Displacing the Common Sense of Trauma 63

Boy suggests that the only way to speak about Kwangju from the present is in the work of art.

The eventual staging of the manuscript illustrates both the necessity of interpretation and the impossibility of testimony. Ŭnsuk is surprised to receive an invitation to a performance of the play, which is undertaken in near-total silence. At the opening of the performance, "the woman began to speak. No, it was as if she began to speak. No, the woman was not saying anything. She was only making shapes [*talssak*] with her lips, without a sound. That woman [Ŭnsuk] could clearly read the shape [*moyang*] of those lips. Because she herself had typed up the third proofs of the play from the manuscript paper that [the playwright] had written on in pen." The words formed by the woman on stage are: "After your death, [we] could not hold a funeral. / My life became a funeral." A man on the stage then "speaks": "His lips are shaped like those of a thirsty fish. At that portion where [the tone of] his voice must get higher, the sound *kkiik, kkik*, like a groan, comes out. That woman reads the shape of his lips as well."[81] The audience becomes aware of the ruse, and begins trying to read the lips of the actors; watching, Ŭnsuk "shapes her own lips, without herself knowing it. As if imitating the actors, calling out without employing her throat. *Tongho*."[82] A boy appears and mounts the stage, facing the audience; Ŭnsuk "glares fiercely, staring as if to pierce the boy's face, on which his silent lips are moving."[83]

It is possible to understand Ŭnsuk here as a figure for the author, as imagined by Kim Yŏngch'an. We see an "impossible dialogue" and hear "the voice of the other that cannot be heard."[84] Ŭnsuk's facility as an editor, a proofreader—one who *works with the words of others*—allows us to understand what the actors on stage are saying. She recalls the words that have been erased; her narration delivers them to us. "In this unrealistic scene, in which an 'I' replaces an 'I' and the other speaks—hidden here, [we see] how in order to depict such suffering, one must entirely erase oneself, one's own grammar, style—and must lend oneself to the voice of the other."[85] This is one understanding of testimony: that the one testifying erases themselves and assumes the voice of the other, the absent witness in whose stead the one testifying speaks.

Yet there are three things that we cannot ignore that mitigate against this reading of the play as figuring witness as an empathetic "standing in" for the other. First, as the boy turns to face the audience, Ŭnsuk closes

64 *Displacing the Common Sense of Trauma*

her eyes. What fills the space on the page that would have been occupied by the boy's speech is a soliloquy in which Ŭnsuk repeats almost verbatim the lines spoken by the woman on stage: "After your death, [we] could not hold a funeral. / My life became a funeral." Here, Ŭnsuk's words, mimicking those spoken by the woman, obscure the boy's speech; we are given access to her "unspoken" thoughts in the gap left by the erasure of the boy's speech. Second, this is delivered in explicitly figurative language. As with the lines of the play that had remained uncensored ("After you were lost, our time became evening"), the text signals its communicability *as literature* in its very style. Third, at the close of the chapter, the narrator overtly prevents us from hearing what the boy is saying (we only know that "his silent lips are moving") and shows us Ŭnsuk's "piercing" gaze upon his face.[86] The boy's message remains enigmatic—like the ghost of Tongho, we do not know what he would want to say if he were able to speak; and we see the *piercing* of his speech by Ŭnsuk's gaze. I will return to both points momentarily. For now, it is clear that this is not an erasure but the representation of an erasure (the reader can perfectly well understand the silent play through Ŭnsuk's mediation), and that we are left, in the end, with the image of silent speech rather than its translation into a speech that would *make sense*. At the very least, we are not seeing Tongho "endlessly summoned into the present" in the memories of the survivors[87]—something more complex is taking place.

PSYCHOLOGICAL AUTOPSY AND THE LIMITS OF TESTIMONY

Perhaps the most obvious way in which Han's novel raises the question of the impossibility of testimony is in its apparent rejection of witnessing. Sŏnju, the former labor activist, works as an archivist in the early 2000s; she is someone through whom others' testimony and evidence pass, a kind of amanuensis.[88] Crisis arises with the receipt of a tape recorder by mail, along with a blank cassette—a call to testify, to present her own experiences in language. She has rejected such calls in the past (a volume of such testimony lies, unread, at the back of a cabinet in her office). "Try to remember," the accompanying message instructs her, "and add your testimony" to the compilation of witnesses.[89]

Displacing the Common Sense of Trauma 65

Testimony. Meaning. Memory. For the future. . . . He asked you to confront [those memories] and to testify. But how is that possible? *Is it possible to testify that a 30 cm wooden ruler was shoved into you tens of times, all the way to the back of your uterus? Is it possible to testify to the butt of a rifle mashing, splitting your cervix? . . . Is it possible to testify to being permanently unable to bear children? Is it possible to testify that I've become unable to bear the touch of others, especially men? . . . Is it possible to testify that I have been made to loathe my own body . . . ?*[90]

There is a triple shame at work in the novel: the shame of the body; the shame of surviving; and what Nichanian calls "realist shame," the shame that comes of being compelled to express the inexpressible and the assignment of probative value to that testimony. Each character in the novel, save Tongho, expresses some form of shame. Chŏngdae, speaking from a mass grave, wants only to be free of his shameful, rotting flesh.[91] Ŭnsuk feels the shame of hunger: "Within the familiar shame, the shameful thing that eating is, she thought of the dead. That those people would never be hungry again, because they were dead. But for her, she was alive, and felt hunger. It was precisely this that had persistently caused [her] distress over the past five years. That she felt hunger, that she had an appetite."[92] The survivor who had been imprisoned with the militia leader Chinsu recalls that the point of the torture was not the inevitably false confession (from one with nothing to confess) but to "prove to us that the thing called 'you' is a filthy, stinking body, a wounded, decaying body, the whole body [nothing but] a starving beast."[93] The shame of the body and the shame of survival come together: "What is repeated in the cases of Ŭnsuk, Chinsu, and Sŏnju," writes Cho Yŏnjŏng, "is not so much the 'guilt of the survivor,' but rather the shame of 'flesh that cannot die.'"[94]

Upon receipt of the demand for witness testimony—a "psychological autopsy" (*simni pugŏm*)[95]—Sŏnju endures all three forms of shame. Her narration reminds us of all the ways in which the body can be despised.[96] She lives under a constant sense of guilt that her survival is unjustified and suffers haunting reminders of the deaths of others. *"I don't know whose footsteps they are,"* she tells us in the night. *"Is it always the same person, or is it a different person every time? I don't know."*[97] Finally, Sŏnju cannot reconcile the facts of the matter with what she is asked to say about them. She tries to imagine the inadequate physical form that the recorded testimony would take: "You think about the world of quick deaths, guns and knives and clubs, sweat and blood and flesh, wet towels and drill bits and metal pipes, that come into being through the voices in the cramped confines of that cassette, along its glossy, brown tape."[98] This is not simply a matter of condensation. As Cho Sŏnghŭi (citing Jean Améry) points out, suffering is incommunicable because it is subjective. What emerges from such a representation can only be an expression of the limit of the power to communicate in language.[99]

It is not only the limited power of communication but the *right* to compel any such attempt that drives Sŏnju's rejection of the demand for testimony. "By what right," she asks the absent interlocutor, "will you tell my story to others?"[100] This question is mirrored in the previous chapter by the prisoner, whom the same "scholar" of Kwangju has contacted with a similar demand. The prisoner's first response is to point out the inadequacy of his testimony in the face of the inevitable absence of the witness, Kim Chinsu, the militia leader who has committed suicide in the aftermath of his imprisonment and torture. "I don't understand. Can we restore Kim Chinsu to life now, through the recording of my words? Perhaps our experiences had been similar, but they were by no means identical. To the extent that we cannot hear from him, himself, the things that he alone experienced, how can you conduct an autopsy on his death?"[101] Or later, a photograph is found lying next to Chinsu's suicide note, and the scholar wishes the prisoner to explain. "Must I explain?" the prisoner asks, in the one-sided conversation that concludes his chapter. "Must I guess for what reason Kim Chinsu had this photograph with him, until the end? Speculate as to why it was placed next to the suicide note? Must I speak to you about the children here who fell in straight lines, dead? *By what right do you make this demand of me?*"[102] As an autopsy explains the cause of death and thus determines the facts of that death for the legal and historical record, the witness here is being burdened not only with the demand to tell but also the demand to explain and to establish causality. It is this demand that the character of the prisoner rejects.

Here the prisoner's conversation with the scholar ends, and there is an ellipsis in the text. The connection between the photographic image and the suicide note goes unexplained, remaining enigmatic and in need

Displacing the Common Sense of Trauma 67

of interpretation. The demand leveled at the witness has been refused, just as the cassette sent to Sŏnju remains blank. It seems that testimony remains impossible, and silence is maintained. Yet, as with the silent play, here too what we have is not simply a refusal and the representation of a silence (in place of the erasure itself), but the production of testimony in order to make evident the silence. The final pages of the prisoner's chapter consist precisely of his testimony—his retelling of the events that led to the image captured in the photograph, of the corpses of children lying where they fell, bizarrely, in a straight line. "It's not that they were arranged neatly [after the fact], laid side by side like this. It's that they had come out walking in a line. They had come out in a line, both hands in the air, like we had told them to."[103] Likewise, we cannot help noticing that Sŏnju's very refusal to testify also *contains her testimony* (she has been raped, rendered barren, psychologically damaged, and so on).

This demonstrates very well what Rancière writes on prohibitions against representation, namely that the "extreme experience of the inhuman confronts no impossibility of representation"—that catastrophe is not "'unrepresentable' in the sense that the language for conveying it does not exist. The language exists and the syntax exists."[104] Han's novel bears this out. Everything is available to representation: the thoughts of the dead, the incomprehensibility of the national anthem sung over the coffins at the Provincial Office, the brutality of the massacre, the erasure of the witness, the censored manuscript and the voices of actors silently shaping their lips to lost lines, the horrors of torture and rape. What we have here is exactly the "impossibility of testimony" overcome by the "possibility of representation." But we have seen as well the novel's refusal to submit to the singular name of Kwangju, to fit its testimony into neatly constructed narratives of victimhood or heroism. *Boy* instead aims at a "form of investigation that reconstructs the materiality of an event, while leaving its cause on hold," speaking of an event "without cancelling its enigma."[105] The prisoner, in the end, *describes* the scene in the photograph with perfect accuracy; yet he will not *explain* what is seen in the photograph. The novel thus undertakes "the continual present-ing [*hyŏnjaehwa*] of the already-happened situation" as an event impossible to name. This," writes Cho Yŏnjŏng, "is the sole method that does not make of the victims of tragedy victims once again."[106]

68 *Displacing the Common Sense of Trauma*

This is precisely the opposite of what we see in a classic example of a "Kwangju film," Yi Ch'angdong's 1999 *Peppermint Candy* (*Pakha sat'ang*). As is well known, the film uses a reverse chronology to maintain a state of unknowing in the viewer. We do not reach the mysterious event that lies behind the film's odd behaviors, inexplicable symptoms, and so on, until the penultimate sequence, in which the main character—a soldier fulfilling his mandatory military service—mistakenly fires upon and kills an innocent student in Kwangju in May 1980. This structure, a kind of detective story in which the viewer gradually discovers the past trauma behind the main character's downfall and eventual suicide (the event with which the film begins), not only mirrors the conventional understanding of trauma in which the subject is "obliged to repeat the repressed material as a contemporary experience, instead of . . . remembering it as something belonging to the past,"[107] but also subjects the viewer to the same experience of return. Even as the film reaches an explanation for the behavior of its protagonist-analysand in returning to and reenacting the scene of the trauma, we remain locked in a cycle of unending, melancholic return, as visual overlaps between the opening and closing scenes clearly indicate. In a way, the film expresses the paradox of Moon's annual May addresses—the event is explained, fully known, and "over and done with," but must nonetheless be experienced again and again. Trauma produces and reproduces its effects, transmitted through the reenactment of the traumatic event—a willed act of remembrance—within a narrative of national history. The traumatic event is not unknown or enigmatic in any way, but it must nonetheless be horribly repeated again and again, without difference.

BEYOND THE HISTORIOGRAPHIC IMPERATIVE

How then can Kwangju be written *properly*—in a way that will work against the ongoing denigration or perversion of the memory of the uprising and massacre—and what is the role of literary language in such a writing?

The first thing to notice about this entreaty to proper writing is that it contains the ethical core of the novel: the imperative to continue trying to write Kwangju, an act that should be undertaken "even if what is communicated is the very failure or limit of communication."[108] Second,

Displacing the Common Sense of Trauma   69

it is not only the refutations of Kwangju deniers that pervert the memory of Kwangju, but as well the reduction of the event to a narrative of victims and heroes, a story that feeds neatly into the discourse of absolute (national) community. The reiteration of "Kwangju" through continual performance not only works to fossilize it as a completed past event, an event that in its commemoration is gradually forgotten,[109] but also serves to mask the lack of resolution that marks the event. As Sŏ Yŏngch'ae points out, there has been no public justice as a result of the sacralization of the event (in the establishment of the May 18 National Cemetery, for instance) or of the formalization of the name of Kwangju in various laws that have been passed (the Kwangju Compensation Act in 1990, the Special 5.18 Law in 1995, etc.). The place of justice has been established, he writes, but it is filled with expedient political power.[110]

Boy's refusal of the conventional narrative mode of trauma comes in two forms, both of which have an impact on its "proper" narration of the disaster in a specifically literary register. One is the rejection of consensual historiographic discourse and what Nichanian calls the "realist shame" that comes with the idea of testimony (and its accumulation into an archive) as having probative value. The other, closely related, is an insistence on the enigmatic nature of the catastrophe itself, and its use of literary language to *pierce* the present with a Kwangju that cannot be fully known and that, as we have seen above, shifts from a past-directed orientation to one focused on bringing Kwangju to bear on the "expedient political power" that fills the place of justice in the present moment. I turn to the epilogue of the novel to review these two rejections, suggesting a model of trauma that abandons neither the overwhelming, unknowable nature nor the material reality of the massacre, but that at the same time declines to fix a single, incontrovertible meaning to the event.

The final section of Han's novel, titled "A Lamp Covered with Snow," is narrated by an author, adding a seventh voice to what is already a diversity of perspectives. Temporally, the epilogue takes place in 2013, and details an almost ethnographic process of researching the massacre and the writing of, presumably, the novel at hand. This "author" has traveled to Kwangju, visiting key sites—the gymnasium where corpses of murdered citizens were laid out, the Provincial Office, the May 18 Institute at Chŏnnam National University, the 5.18 Cultural Foundation, the

70 *Displacing the Common Sense of Trauma*

security headquarters where residents were tortured during and in the aftermath of the uprising,[111] and the middle school of the titular boy, Kang Tongho. The narrator has also visited the site of her childhood house in Kwangju, which had been sold when her family moved to Seoul when she was nine. She inquires at the business that now occupies the site and is able to locate the previous owner, Tongho's older brother, who then delivers the injunction that she write her novel properly.

The very raising of this question prevents us from understanding the epilogue as autobiographical. There are certainly biographical overlaps with Han Kang's life—from her family's move from Kwangju to Seoul in her childhood to the fact that she is the named author of the novel that is apparently being researched in the epilogue. Critic Hwang Chŏnga goes so far as to make the case that the only successful testimony in the novel comes in the epilogue as the narrator reveals the process by which the novel was written.[112] The voice of the epilogue's narrator also comes from the near past, situated in the year just prior to the novel's 2014 publication. But, in a novel that has so clearly made a problem of testimony and witnessing, we can hardly understand these statements as baldly autobiographical, arriving as they do within the boundaries of the fictional work.

The epilogue in fact raises almost every limit faced by testimony in the preceding six chapters. The author-narrator finds it impossible to return to what was a different world ("I thought, I had started too late"), as the physical landscape has radically changed over the intervening thirty-four years, though the national flag still hangs over the scene.[113] The past and present come into even starker contrast as she attends a wedding in January 2013: "the people were gorgeous, composed—it seemed incongruous, strange," she writes. "I couldn't believe it. That so many people had died. My senior, who wrote literary criticism, complained laughingly that I had not send him my collection of stories. I couldn't believe it. That so many people had died."[114] The novelist is confronted with an impossible amount of documentation ("My ground rule was to read all the documents that I could find," she writes, until she could not continue).[115] It is in the epilogue that the narrator states that the characters populating the preceding chapters were neither heroes nor victims, resisting the generalization of both categories; that the name of Kwangju is expanded into the present moment; and that the narrator is

Displacing the Common Sense of Trauma   71

faced with the demand for speech (from Tongho's brother) and the impossibility of that speech ("I had started too late").

That impossibility is viscerally represented in the form of three dreams. In the first, she is running from soldiers, falls, and is stabbed in the chest with a bayonet. In the second, she learns that some of those arrested in 1980 had been held in underground cells into the present day and would secretly, tomorrow at three p.m., be executed. In the third dream,

> I had received a small radio from someone, as a gift. I was told that it had the function of setting back time—I just had to enter the year and day on a digital instrument panel. Upon receiving it, I entered "1980.5.18." Because, if I intend to write about it, I have to be there. Because that would be the best way. But in the next moment, I was standing alone at the deserted Kwanghwamun intersection. *Right. Because only the time changes. Because this is Seoul.* If it was May, it should be spring, but the street was as cold and desolate as a day in November. It was so quiet that it was frightening.[116]

It is possible to read the three dreams as attestations of experience, lending the author an authenticity that comes from her "experience [of] the deaths as events in the present"[117] and allowing her to present to the reader the "true memory" of the event.[118] However, such an interpretation not only flies in the face of the thematic prevalence of the indeterminacy of testimony throughout the preceding six chapters, but also defies the substance of the dream at hand—the time machine fails, the author is too late, the experience of the event is inaccessible.

The dream is rather a device that allows the semblance of the past breaking into the present. We are not given access to a singular, knowable past. Instead, the dreams establish a relationship between past and narrative present through an avowedly figural language. The narrator is neither a survivor "who attempts to document an undocumentable experience" nor a bystander "who feels impelled to bear an impossible witness to the extreme from a place of relative safety."[119] She instead occupies that "uncertain boundary" between report and invention,[120] working in a literary language that signals its literariness in advance, a communicability located in the constitutive tendency to speak figurally or allusively,

72 *Displacing the Common Sense of Trauma*

to put in place an avowed noncoincidence "between facts and truth, between verification and comprehension."[121] What makes fiction the *proper* mode of representing Kwangju, over and against "the work of properly recording history" and correctly remembering truths that in Moon's speeches form a healing "basis of national harmony and unity"?

The idea of profaning or desecrating (*modok*) the memory of the dead brother clearly references the context in which the novel was written, a period during which South Korea saw right-wing denials, "distortions," and "denigrations" of the event.[122] In the state memorialization and remembrance of Kwangju, proper speech is guaranteed by "proper recording of history," a fidelity to facts that results both in the truth of the matter and in the unity of the community. At the base of the "fully unified community"[123] lies a historiographical tendency to approach past traumas through an empirical lens, for which truths, unmediated by language, are not subject to distortion over time and space. Under a traumatropical regime, "one is inclined to privilege survivor testimonies as bearing witness to the past or even as conveying unmediated truth,"[124] and writing is "subordinated to content in the form of facts, their narration, or their analysis." Representation is in this context simply a "medium for expressing a content, and its ideal goal is to be transparent to content or an open window on the past—with figures of rhetoric serving only an instrumental role in illustrating what could be expressed without loss in literal terms."[125]

The reference to documentation in *Boy* is nearly continual: ledgers (in which the characteristics of the dead are clinically noted), interviews, police reports, notes, collections of testimony, translations, recorded confessions, the suicide note, the photograph. But the confessions produced under torture are false, "scripts prepared in advance, with our names filling in the blank spaces";[126] the suicide note remains unseen; the collection of plays remains censored, and the stage play wordless; the collection of testimonies remains discarded and silent; the recorder goes unused, and the cassette remains blank. Documentation—testimony put to probative use—is represented but is rejected. "I do not want to talk about what happened next," the prisoner testifies. "No longer does anyone have the authority to tell me to remember."[127] Both the prisoner and Sŏnju absolutely reject the demand for testimony, asking: *By what right do you make this demand of me?*

Displacing the Common Sense of Trauma 73

In this way, even as it represents the shame of the body and the shame of the survivor, the novel rejects what Nichanian calls "realist shame," that shame that emerges when testimony is documented, archived, put to probative use, and inserted into a "discourse of proofs." This is the "realist insult" that comes from the logic of refutation and the archive, that which "seizes testimony at the very moment it is uttered and instantly puts it at the service of historiographic refutation."[128] Echoing Blanchot ("We will bring no proofs"), Nichanian's astonishing work details the "historiographic stranglehold," that which "forbids any consideration of the event outside the coordinates of the fact."[129] "Testimony," he writes, "does not constitute a proof of the facts. If one must prove the facts, testimony has no probative value at all."[130] Instead, testimony must be liberated "from its realist and documentary function," drawn out of "the sphere of refutation."[131] The scandal is that revisionist historians or deniers of genocide "claim to uphold precisely the same values of objectivity and of scientificity, the same rigorous methods of historical research, the same reference to documents, and the same coherent use of archives."[132] So long as testimony is made to serve a historiographical function, so long as the adjudication of the disaster is placed on the field of history, the event may not be assigned the status of irrefutable fact—the event is endlessly up for debate.

Is there then no difference between historical truth and the negationist lie, Nichanian asks? Of course there is: "it is only that this difference *is not of a historical or historiographical nature*."[133] It is this subsumption of testimony to the logic of facts and to its probative value that *Boy* rejects. As opposed to the moment when "the nonsensical is seized by sense, in which it makes sense and even makes historical sense,"[134] Han's novel insists that Kwangju *not make sense*, that there is no making sense of the massacre, that it is senseless and must remain so. The purported totality of testimony is an aim that is, from the first pages of the novel, clearly impossible, when it is not openly rejected. Yet at the same time, the novel's intervention is not that representation is impossible, as we have seen above. Rather, the novel resists the idea that sense can be made of Kwangju in the production of full visibility or in the assemblance of a totality of testimony—it is a case in which "the causes that render the event resistant to any explanation by a principle of sufficient reason, be it fictional or documentary, must be left on hold."[135] It is not that

74 *Displacing the Common Sense of Trauma*

representation is impossible; it is rather an ethical adherence to the unintelligibility of the event and a resistance to a coherence of representability and intelligibility, the very coherence that underlies both the realist contract and the traumatropical regime of nationalism.

As with the prisoner's refusal to testify to the connection between the photograph of the murdered children "who fell in straight lines, dead" and the suicide note, the epilogue centers on a photograph of Tongho, located among the student records at the elementary school he attended. "It was a face so ordinary that you could easily mix it up with someone else's," the narrator writes. "A face the characteristics of which one would forget as soon as one took one's eyes off it." It is unverifiable—she "cannot be certain" (*hwaksin hal su ŏpnŭn*) of the face.[136] This treatment of the photograph quietly resists a "commonsensical empiricism"[137] that tells us that "photographs transmit immutable truths" and that little is lost in the "translation" and reproduction of the real in the photographic image.[138] In the case of the photograph, Allan Sekula tells us, our awareness that "history is an *interpretation* of the past succumbs to a faith in history as *representation*," with the photograph manifesting the very "appearance of *history itself.*" Historical narration, he continues, "becomes a matter of appealing to the silent authority of the archive, of unobtrusively linking incontestable documents in a seamless account. (The very term 'document' entails a notion of legal or official truth, as well as a notion of *proximity to* and verification of an original event.)"[139]

In its refusal to succumb to such a positivist, historicist injunction that "forbids any consideration of the event outside the coordinates of the fact" and demands that the speech of the witness take on a probative value, Han's novel maintains the *enigmatic* nature of the traumatic event, submitting neither to a historical nor to an aesthetic determination of the account of the past. As we see in the epilogue, the traumatic effects arise neither from the past event itself nor purely from the present encounter with the detritus of that event.

THE AFTERWARD-NESS OF KWANGJU

Against the total visibility demanded in dominant Kwangju discourse, both of the historical event itself and of the community rooted in the hereditary trauma of its experience, *Boy* maintains a principled

Displacing the Common Sense of Trauma 75

adherence to the question of the representation of "that which had no business being seen."[140] The novel refuses the idea of "Kwangju" as something that is "over and done," fully knowable and fully speakable and hence susceptible to the sort of melancholic reiterations we see in films like *Peppermint Candy* or in Moon's public addresses above, which aim to present the truth of Kwangju even as they rely on the repetition that is constitutive of conventional ideas of trauma. Instead, the novel addresses the thing that is made impossible in the contemporary discourse of Kwangju, which is the impossibility of speech itself. In this way, Han makes two important moves: her novel resists the notion that testimony or witness gives an unproblematic access to the truth of the recalled event, and it also resists the construction of an "archive" of Kwangju, in Foucault's sense of an archive as "a system that governs the appearance of statements and generates social meaning,"[141] a set of norms that "precede the possibility of description" or produce descriptions that "are themselves normatively structured in advance, through a foreclosure that establishes the domain of the speakable."[142]

Han's novel is able to strike a position that retains the historical fact of the horrific, catastrophic violence of the state mobilized against its own citizens while retaining the radical and future-oriented question of the event. *Boy* does this not by rejecting trauma but by operating under a different idea of it. As we have seen, trauma may be conceptualized as a mode of understanding an event and its effects in the present (including its representation in language) and as a source of identity to which one must remain faithful in perpetual and melancholic repetition. Such an understanding puts trauma into the service of nationalist discourse and makes the event and trauma coincide, setting in place a formation that perpetually returns to the past in a circular action that leaves the trauma unchanged. Historical method and the realistic mode of presentation that it demands become crucial to maintaining the traumatic event as a known fact and as a source of identification, experienced again and again by subsequent generations through performative reiteration.

A strikingly different idea of trauma operates in Han's novel. First, the event and meaning of trauma are constructed, before our very eyes in the epilogue, as they are worked through (*Durcharbeitung*) by the narrator. The traumatic effects emerge from the very establishment of a

76 *Displacing the Common Sense of Trauma*

relation between the present and the past, a linkage that is part and parcel of the novel's structure and its operation. As with Blanchot, trauma does not stem solely from the original scene or from the retelling of that scene, but "in the sequence of the two scenes and their linkage," a linkage by which the past is actively constructed as traumatic.[143] Such a perspective admits neither the sense that the past is unknowable (and open to absolute relativism), nor that the past is fully knowable (and subject to the "silent authority of the archive" and its "seamless account"). Rather, meaning is produced through the interpretation of enigmatic messages generated by the catastrophic traumatic event, an event that is *no less real* for the enigma that it presents to the experiencing subject, who herself had no proper context for understanding the message delivered at the moment of the traumatic occurrence.[144]

Boy does not "act out" the traumatic event, repeating it in an effort to both fix Kwangju as an immutable, eternally commemorable fact (and thus to effectively forget it) and to retraumatize the present through an ideal of transhistorical wounding that guarantees the continuity of expedient political power. It should be clear from the above that the novel does not equate culture with trauma; the boundaries of a community are not established in the repetition of traumatic symptoms stemming from the *actual experience and witness* of the singular event. Rather, Kwangju appears via what Laplanche calls an "afterward-ness," as the maturing subject is allowed to "gain access to a new level of meaning and to rework his earlier experiences."[145] Here, the traumatic experience is understood as a "failure of translation,"[146] a communication that was not adequately understood in the moment of its occurrence—the "enigmatic message" that both "poses a question and elicits various attempts at a solution."[147] Unprepared to properly interpret the event at its moment of occurrence, to translate its message, the subject nonetheless returns again and again to the "non-translated remnants" until a fuller meaning of the event is attained.[148] It is here, Laplanche argues, that we find the point of trauma, with "afterward-ness" (Laplanche's rendering of *Nachträglichkeit*) not equivalent to a "deferred action" but rather signaling a complex point of memory, knowledge, and representation, through which a link is formed to the past in the present moment. It is not only for the receiver that such messages are enigmatic, but for the sender of the message as well, who "*says* more than he consciously means."[149]

Displacing the Common Sense of Trauma 77

This "afterward-ness" disturbs a discourse of trauma that seeks for the matter to be over and done. The character of the scholar arrives in *Boy* to perform a (psychological) autopsy, a forensic procedure carried out on a corpse, for the legal and historical record. In the novel, however, the enigmatic messages of the dead remain with us—"a scandal for a realist for whom the dead are really dead."[150] Rather than an "endless melancholy or grieving" for which "the past returns and the future is blocked or fatalistically caught up in a melancholic feedback loop,"[151] mourning in the novel is a continual asking: "What would he be saying now?" Though long dead, the boy is always arriving, a "message laden with meanings in need of translation."[152] The residue of the enigmatic message demands a response in the form of an active reconstruction of the past "restricted from the perspective of the present,"[153] a continual response to that which has "been impossible . . . to incorporate fully into a meaningful context,"[154] a message in need of continual translation because "the codes eliciting its translation or the formulation of its meaning are missing."[155]

Here is a model of trauma, not as repetition without difference but as *repetition with change*, a present-ification of the event through a multiplication of its referents (Nanjing, Yongsan, Bosnia, and so on). An expansion rather than a verification, mourning rather than melancholy, such an idea of trauma resists both a fixing of the singularity of the past event and the limitation of possible speech to an archive within which the sayable of Kwangju—those "preexisting discourses that mediate and circumscribe experience"[156]—is established. As such, trauma admits the unintelligibility of the original event/message for both the "speaker" and the "recipient," and the traumatic is constructed in the present through the interpretation of that meaning generated by an event that is no less real for its unintelligibility. At the same time, this model admits the ethical imperative of the novel—to *write properly*, to return to the enigmatic voice of Kwangju again and again in order to pierce the veil of common sense and allow that which "has no business being seen" or heard to emerge.

The word "trauma" is most often understood as coming from the Greek for "wound," but can also be derived from *tetrainein*, one of the senses of which is "to pierce."[157] It is in this sense that trauma functions in *Boy*—not as a constant return to the past, immutable "wound," but through the *piercing* of the present moment by the enigmatic message from the past. Such trauma is not "over and done with," nor is it easily narrated. Trauma that emerges to pierce the familiar, consensual images of the past and the boundaries that guard what can be said about it also admits a kind of layering of translations over time through evolving attempts to interpret the enigma of the traumatic event. This is how the two photographs of Tongho function in the novel. The final image, that innocent, bland school photo—which is also plastered onto his new gravestone, following exhumation from the original burial site (the Mangwŏldong Cemetery) and reburial at the new May 18th National Cemetery, built by the government in 1997—is *pierced* by the photographic image of the murdered children.[158] The trauma stems not from the original scene or from its retelling, but from the "afterward-ness" of the images and the logic of the linkage between the two scenes actively constructed by the novel. It is the relationship between the absolutely normal, everyday school photograph and the image of the corpses that "pierces" our present and invites the working through of the trauma that resides in that relation.

Locating trauma in the relation between present and past rather than in a sacred, originary event allows the novel to perform its critique of traumatropical narrative modes that demand both the sublime unrepresentability of the event and, paradoxically, at the same time, a mimetic representation faithful to the facts and itself carrying documentary, probative value. Earlier attempts to address the events of Kwangju in literary form have taken either path. Among the best known of these is Ch'oe Yun's *There a Petal Silently Falls*, which presents Kwangju and its aftermath through the figure of an orphaned girl who wanders the countryside, unable to conceptualize or express the loss of her family in the massacre, and subject to repeated physical abuse.[159] "As you pass by the grave sites scattered throughout the city," the story opens, "you may encounter her, a girl whose maroon velvet dress barely covers her, a girl who lingers near the burial mounds. Please don't stop if she approaches you, and don't look back once she's passed you by. If your eye should be drawn to the flesh showing between the folds of that torn, soiled dress, or drawn to something resembling a wound, walk away with downcast eyes as if you hadn't seen a thing."[160] Here we are instructed to look away from "something resembling a wound," the trauma at the origin of the

Displacing the Common Sense of Trauma 79

girl's wandering. Though the wound is the source of all symptoms in the novella and the referent for all symbolic violence endured by the girl in her wandering, the reader is prohibited from looking, as the author is prohibited from representing. Im Ch'ŏru's monumental *Spring Day* takes an opposite route, displaying a compulsive need for full visibility aimed at a historical reconstruction of the ten-day uprising—"a record faithful to the facts"[161] that would do justice to the "absolute community" of citizens banded together to resist the military intrusion of the authoritarian state.

Han's novel resists both the possibility of such a record and the idea of an essential community based on the common experience of the traumatic event. *Boy* rejects all three narratives common to the re-creation of historical tragedy: narratives of accusation, which establish an inside and an outside, victim and perpetrator; narratives of testimony, which take on the documentary function of proving the facts; and narratives of cure, which aim at collective healing through the repetition of the trauma.[162] The struggle between "good" and "bad" speech in contemporary discourse about Kwangju, the compulsive desire for the wholeness of the archive and hence for a totality of testimony that stands in for historical truth, and the logic of the absolute community that demands singularity of affect based in repetitive fidelity to an originary event all signify "politics" as understood in its usual sense of "the exercise of, or struggle for, power,"[163] that "set of procedures whereby the aggregation and consent of collectivities is achieved, the organization of powers, the distribution of places and roles, and the systems for legitimizing this distribution."[164] Rancière has renamed this conventional understanding of the function of politics the "police." It is, he writes, "an order of bodies that defines the allocation of ways of doing, ways of being, and ways of saying, and sees that those bodies are assigned by name to a particular place and task: it is an order of the visible and the sayable that sees that a particular activity is visible and another is not, that this speech is understood as discourse and another as noise."[165] This ordered assignation or distribution suggests both an ontology and an epistemology, ways of being and knowing that give a police-politics its subject matter and at the same time function to legitimize its exercise of power.

In Moon Jae-in's public addresses on the anniversary of the uprising and massacre, knowing (the establishment of a factual historical

80 *Displacing the Common Sense of Trauma*

reality) and being (the common "spirit" of the nation) are closely linked in establishing a unified, homogeneous community of memory and experience. In this context, speech about Kwangju is at once restricted and universalized. On the one hand, as we have seen above, there is impermissible speech about Kwangju, namely its denial as a historical fact—"illogical statements that both insult and deny." On the other hand, in his 2020 speech, Moon quotes a "youngster" as having said that, *"If there is a specific qualification [needed] to speak about Kwangju,* then the spirit of May has not yet fully bloomed."[166] Kwangju, Moon continues, is "not something that belongs to someone, but is something that belongs to us all."

The speech thus performs a paradox: it universalizes the capacity to speak about Kwangju as a qualification or a right at the same time that it partitions speech into the permissible and impermissible. A particular way of speaking is normalized under the guise of universality and becomes the criterion for inclusion in the national community. Here the political question of language comes to the fore, where "the issue is the distribution of the word as a mode of establishing a certain community."[167] In Moon's speeches, words and knowledge are made to coincide in a way that appears to eliminate the possibility of "no speech," as the enigmatic messages emanating from the traumatic event are understood to have been fully interpreted, their meaning decided upon and presentable in a transparent, communicative language.

In this sense, the dominant discourse of Kwangju presents the already-evident: the "regime of the all-visible," the "police figure of the population exactly identical to the counting of its parts," a count that is "always even and with nothing left over," a people "absolutely equal to itself" and that can subsequently "always be broken down into its reality."[168] The *radical potential* of Kwangju—the uprising or movement of people outside of their established places and the leveling of hierarchies of speech—is co-opted into a normative picture of community, and narrative modes of accusation, historical truth, and hereditary trauma serve to cement the "absolute community" of the nation.

It is worth noting that the second half of Moon Jae-in's 2019 speech on the anniversary of the uprising is devoted largely to holding Kwangju up as a model of economic progress, and both the 2019 and the 2020 speeches push the centrality of the democratizing ethos of the uprising

Displacing the Common Sense of Trauma 81

into the future, where they not only bind the national community into a unified, harmonious whole as a bulwark against authoritarianism but also promote what he names in the 2019 speech "economic democracy" (*kyŏngje minju chuŭi*). Moon closes the 2020 speech with a remarkable call to "go beyond the democratization of our society and our politics and achieve democracy in our homes, our workplaces, and in our economy." We must remember Kwangju, he concludes, "for the sake of a cooperative world system." In this way, an ethics of (national) resistance and democratization is cynically turned to the purposes of a neoliberalizing (global) economy.[169] Resistance to this consensus is referred to in the 2019 speech with the interesting phrase "meaningless waste" (*ŭimi ŏpnŭn somo*), where "waste" can also be read as "consumption."[170]

This logic of economic common sense and a "return to normal" is inverted in *Boy* through the character of Ŭnsuk, who has witnessed the silent play. Her own memories of Kwangju center involuntarily on the fountain in Kwangju's central square. The image of the fountain first comes to her under interrogation in her narrative present, as she receives bruising blows to the face. "She is not sure why she recalled the fountain, at that moment. Behind her eyelids, briefly closed, the June fountain spurted a dazzling spout of water."[171] Ŭnsuk recalls how the city-operated fountain had stopped during the uprising[172] and recounts her outrage that the city had turned the water back on following the massacre and suppression of the movement. The appearance of the cheerful, sparkling water streaming from the fountain prompted the younger Ŭnsuk into action: "Until the beginning of school break, that woman called the Public Service Center [Civil Complaints Office] every day, from the public phone booth next to the bus stop. I think it is not right for there to be water coming out of the fountain. Please turn it off."[173]

Here "meaningless waste" is translated precisely into the "progress" that so disturbed Ŭnsuk when the city began to beautify itself in the wake of the massacre. Like Ŭnsuk, the novel rejects the return to normal and the pressing into service of images of catastrophe toward an "economically viable" community—the construction of "the innocent prosperity of an economic miracle" on "the buried ruins of a will to destruction."[174] This will to destruction is buried not through forgetting but through memorialization, the corruption of the monument by the document.[175]

82 *Displacing the Common Sense of Trauma*

Boy does not submit to a traumatropical logic that aims to wound by presenting testimony, veracious statements the probative value of which aims to prove again and again, in endless melancholic repetition, the facts of the horror of the event to whoever will listen. When trauma is subject to the historiographic imperative, even the dead are not safe from the logic of trauma that submits them to the power of a conformism that would overpower them once and for all.[176] *Boy* presents instead the scandal of the impossible voice of the dead, keeping alive the enigma of the event. Against the realist imperative and far from a forensic autopsy, the event is given to us in a literary language that by definition announces itself in advance as not-the-thing—a fable, not a document—making the unstable symbol of Kwangju "a different name for that which was harmed, that must not have been harmed."[177] The verb tense here is awkward— that which must not have been, yet which was—and it is perhaps rendered best in the imperfect tense, as a damage that continues in different forms and in different places, that must not be but is.

Thus *Boy* gives us a double scandal: resurrecting the silent from their documentary grave against the realist for whom the dead must remain dead, and stubbornly representing the impossibility of witness against the historian who would fix the meaning of Kwangju through an accumulation of testimony and fact. "Must I explain?" asks the prisoner, to which the moral regime of the traumatropical, in its endless and melancholic pursuit of historical truth of the founding trauma, answers "Yes." "Who has the right to compel my speech?" the survivor asks, and the nation answers "We do." Targeting this logic of trauma, which consigns subjects of Kwangju to hypostasized roles (hero, victim, perpetrator) reinforcing consensus and national identity, *A Boy Is Coming* insists that all speech about Kwangju is *not* possible; or better, that possible speech has not been exhausted in the accounting of the absolute community. *Boy* constructs its own logic of the event and what can be said of it,[178] exceeding or confusing the existing system of symbolization in its status as fiction. No explanation is forthcoming, answers are not available, there is no encounter with the risen dead among the gravestones.[179]

Displacing the Common Sense of Trauma   83

CHAPTER THREE

Fabricating the Real

Accounting for North Korea in Escapee Narratives and in Fiction

Each of us was given a pen and paper and
told to write down everything about ourselves.
—YEONMI PARK, *IN ORDER TO LIVE*

This chapter continues to think the difference between possible and impossible speech through examples of fictional and nonfictional representations of North Korea. Here too I assume that politics lies less in speech itself and more in the account that is *made* of speech. I begin with accounts that have been made of North Korean escapee testimony under a regime of human rights discourse that requires that the witness produce not only the facts but also the grounds upon which the veracity of those facts is judged, adhering to a logic of torture that guarantees the truth of language through the suffering of the body. I then turn to Adam Johnson's fiction dealing with North Korea which in my reading brings the identificatory discourse of human rights into an unexpected correlation with a dictatorial understanding of the relationship between speech and identity.

In chapter 2, Han Kang's novel raised the question of what it means to "write properly" the testimony of the survivor. *A Boy Is Coming* took as its theme the tension between the demand to document (to preserve, to remember, to make intelligible) and the aesthetic representation of historical disaster, and put forward situations that reject easy articulations in either register. The novel dislodged the name of Kwangju from its utility or political expediency as "fully known," freeing it to attach to other referents outside a historiographic logic and in response to the ethical imperative to return to and resist "that which was, but must not have been."

At the same time, the preceding chapters have shown that there is a persistent impulse toward the objective inclusion of the *real* as a condition of the political in art. Whether in the chronological form of the history of the nation, the detailed first-person depiction of the poverty and suffering of the migrant, or the narrative testimony of survivors of massacre, the real stands as both the guarantor and the product of what is understood as "political art." The mainstream reception of Han's novel as a work that delivers the truth of the May 1980 uprising and massacre through an expansion of veracious testimony and in the autobiographical voice of the author herself bears out this continuous demand.

The present chapter considers the way that documentary and literary uses of testimony intersect at the level of narrative form in the representation of North Korea. The drive to represent "the real North Korea" has drawn "little distinction . . . between claims to authenticity mounted through fictional cinematic images, on the one hand, and ostensibly disinterested documentary footage, on the other."[1] As we will see below, this "hunger" for the real[2] extends as well to the reception of literary fiction dealing with North Korea. But it is not simply that different aesthetic forms are pressed into service to deliver an accurate picture of North Korea. North Korea's relative isolation presents us with the dilemma of what one escapee calls an "unimaginable" real,[3] for which the facts of the matter are unknowable, whether withheld or inaccessible. The autobiography, memoir, or confession are then pressed into service as key sources of "information" about North Korea. These narratives are required to take on a documentary or probative function and, in so doing, level what Nichanian calls the "realist insult" at the witness.[4] This is one way in which the voice is silenced—in the demand that it provide proof of facts established by an external authority in accordance with the already known.

What manner of narration is sufficient to a situation in which the speaker must produce not only the story but also the backdrop of facts

Fabricating the Real 85

that provides the basis for judging the verisimilitude of the tale—in which "writing down everything about yourself" also forms the grounds for judging the veracity of that "everything"? As the first part of this chapter will show, within a human rights frame, speech is demanded of the defector or escapee—a demand that assumes that communication is not only inevitable but obligatory. Under this discursive regime, escapee narratives are subject to two forms of invalidation: they are inaccurate, or they are uninteresting, too conventional to be believed. They are thus subject both to Nichanian's "historiographic imperative," an injunction that "forbids any consideration of the event outside the coordinates of the fact,"[5] and at the same time to an aesthetic judgment that locates the failure of the testimony at the level of its verisimilitude within the confines of narrative form. The demand for speech leveled at North Korean escapees or defectors, which assumes that speech is all but involuntary, is met with reproof—a second mode of silencing—when the probative value of the narrative is shown to be lacking.

What is at stake is what Nichanian calls the "manifest impasse" between documentary and literary uses of testimony. "Testimony as document," he writes, "inherently excludes any recourse to art." From the perspective of history, the artistic representation of "the bestial, the inhuman, and the atrocious" may stand accused of embellishment or exaggeration in a way that "run[s] the risk of diminishing the reality effect that these descriptions must forcibly exercise." Thus "those who favor a literary treatment," he writes, "have nothing to oppose to the documentary conception of testimony and to the omnipotence of the archive."[6] Escapee narratives and fictional narratives alike are thus assigned the task of validating the facts "in the face of which no 'different opinion' can ever occur,"[7] producing a consensus in language.

In the second part of this chapter, I will argue that fiction presents a challenge to the archive—that which determines the meaning of statements, "normatively structured in advance"[8]—by putting forward its own world in which the *logic of naming* pushes directly against the logic of identification, and the *logic of story* resists the clear causality of the "progressive narrative of emancipation"[9] required of the escapee. Adam Johnson's fiction explodes the conventionality of veracious genres of biography and confession, drawing attention to the demand for identity and verisimilitude paradoxically shared by both human rights and

86 *Fabricating the Real*

totalitarian discourses, which employ a logic/practice of torture that aims to achieve the obligatory, involuntary correspondence of speech and truth, guaranteed by the suffering of the body.

TRANSCRIBING THE REAL:
THE (DIS)APPEARANCE OF THE SUBJECT

The demand for verisimilitude from texts related to North Korea is so habitual that when Adam Johnson published his Pulitzer Prize–winning *The Orphan Master's Son* in 2012, the critical response focused almost entirely on the uncanny accuracy of the novel in portraying the "real" of the North Korean experience—and this despite the fact that the novel continually foregrounds its own fictionality. Reviews described Johnson's work as "an epic journey into the heart of the world's most mysterious dictatorship"[10] and "an adventuresome journey into the depths of totalitarian North Korea and into the most intimate spaces of the human heart,"[11] providing "a rare glimpse into one of the world's least known countries"[12] and "open[ing] a frightening window on the mysterious kingdom of North Korea,"[13] taking "implausible fact and turn[ing] it into entirely believable fiction."[14] "Informed by extensive research and travel to perhaps the most secretive nation on earth,"[15] the novelist was said to have accomplished "the seeming impossible" in "masterfully render[ing] the mysterious world of North Korea with the soul and savvy of a native."[16] Barbara Demick goes so far as to write that she "assumed it had to be part of a memoir by a North Korean, so accurate were the details . . . he's managed to capture the atmosphere of this hermit kingdom better than any writer I've read."[17] Finally, the review in the *Washington Post* reads:

> Adam Johnson has taken the papier-mâché creation that is North Korea and turned it into a real and riveting place. . . . an instructive lesson in how to paint a fictional world against a background of fact. . . . It's this process of re-imagination that makes the fictional locale so real and gives the novel an impact you could never achieve with a thousand newspaper stories. Johnson has painted in indelible colors the nightmare of Kim's North Korea. When English readers want to understand what it was about—how people lived and died inside a cult of personality that committed unspeakable

Fabricating the Real 87

crimes against its citizens—I hope they will turn to this carefully documented story.[18]

In these accounts, the work of fiction is a well-researched and carefully documented travelogue, a window onto the unknown, a seeming memoir written with the "savvy of a native," turning "the papier-mâché creation" into a "real place." What is demanded of the fiction here is precisely what we will see demanded of escapee narratives—to make the unknowable known, to present the "background of fact" that will make of North Korea a "real place," and to adhere to the historiographic imperative and endure the "realist insult" in rendering witness testimony. When a "point by point" correspondence between the language of the text and "some extra-textual domain of occurrence or happening"[19] is required, the subject of the enunciation is strangely eliminated—whether in the case of the escapee, whose entire role within the human rights frame is reduced to the transcription of information or "primary data,"[20] or in the case of the author of fiction, who is naturalized into a "native" or a "North Korean."

But what makes escapee narratives or fiction political is not their representation of the facts of the matter, decided upon in advance and presented in a language adequate to veridical representation. Such a "politics" corresponds, as we have seen, to what Rancière calls the police, a "regime in which the parties are presupposed as already given, their community established and the count of their speech identical to their linguistic performance." This is a world of the fully visible, "a world in which everything is on show . . . and in which everything can be resolved by objectifying problems."[21] What we see in the reception of escapee narratives and in Johnson's fiction alike is the *disappearance* of politics in the full identification of the subject of North Korea. That is, if political activity is "whatever shifts a body from the place assigned to it" or "makes visible what had no business being seen, and makes heard a discourse where once there was only place for noise,"[22] then politics appears impossible in a situation where one's proper place has been fully identified and the limits of what can be said or seen have been established beyond doubt. Under the human rights frame within which escapee narratives are received and made known, and likewise under the totalitarian regime as represented in the novel, you must be what you say you are—any hint of

88 *Fabricating the Real*

performance is met with criticism. What is demanded of the subject is no less than a correlation of word and thing underwritten by the authenticity of being.[23]

In human rights discourse, the escapee or defector is understood to be fully identified, fully sayable. Identification makes visible, fixes in place, makes intelligible or legible, says everything there is to say. In keeping with the thrust of the book's argument—that the politics of art does not lie in its presentation of subject matter understood to be political— and against identification (the realist operation of texts claiming political status on such a basis), we will see the politics of the literary text emerge through a separate process of subjectivization. Where Han Kang raised the question of the boundaries of the realm of possible speech in representing historical disaster and atrocity, *The Orphan Master's Son* moves from within the confines of genre to a point where a fracture opens, pushing the logics of identification and verisimilitude to a breaking point and revealing in the process the various types of silencing carried out on the North Korean subject in the name of politics.

Political subjectivization, per Rancière, is a heterology, "never the simple assertion of an identity; it is always, at the same time, the denial of an identity given by an other, given by the ruling order of policy." Policy (or "police") is about "'right' names, names that pin people down to their place and work. Politics is about 'wrong' names,"[24] names that break with the police order, that "order of bodies that defines the allocation of ways of doing, ways of being, and ways of saying, and sees that those bodies are assigned by name to a particular place and task; it is an order of the visible and the sayable that sees that a particular activity is visible and another is not, that this speech is understood as discourse and another as noise."[25]

The North Korean subject is in this sense depoliticized in the context of a human rights discourse that understands itself to be apolitical and universal. The logic of identification—wherein the witness corresponds exactly with the text and disappears, silenced by the word—is challenged by the logic of naming in Johnson's fiction, a logic that allows the emergence of a subject "between nominations." As we will see, what is revealed in the process of pushing against the limits of referentiality is a strange correlation between human rights and totalitarian discourses in their demand for identification and the involuntary speech

Fabricating the Real   89

that accompanies it, speech that balances on the precarious edge between the factual and the factitious.

Against the determining classificatory logic of the archive, *The Orphan Master's Son* puts forward a heterologous subject, a body shifted from its designated place and role. Here the subject is a nameless being who does not accept the "right" name given to it, an outcast who is "denied an identity in a given order."[26] "Names come and go," the protagonist tells us. "Names change. I don't even have one."[27] This orphan who rejects his status as an orphan (his last words are "My mother was a singer," claiming his parentage to the end) runs the gamut of roles in the novel, from child laborer, kidnapper, military intelligence agent, diplomat, and inmate in a long-term labor camp to high-ranking government official, husband to the "national actress" of North Korea, and best friend of Kim Jong Il. The point is not simply that the main character occupies a series of roles and shows us some full spectrum of possibility, any more than the power of Han's novel was derived from its presentation of a range of fictional voices (the child, the woman, the laborer) that somehow automatically expands our knowledge and understanding of the event of Kwangju. Rather, the novel installs logics of naming and story that radically disturb the operation of identification—a deterritorialization of the logics of filiation and verisimilitude through the demonstration of a different rationale, a different world beyond the archival demand for the documentary real that corresponds with the already given.

Here too Rancière provides the useful term "literarity": the capacity of writing—"the orphan utterance, deprived of the voice that gives it meaning and legitimacy"—to produce an "imbalance in the legitimate order of discourse." This "disordering" confuses a communal harmony, the relationship between "ways of doing, ways of being, and ways of speaking."[28] Within the "manifest impasse" between literature and document and in contrast to the "legitimate order" of knowing North Korea, exemplified in the form of the escapee narrative, this chapter attempts to examine what happens when "testimony, in order to free itself from the realist option, tends toward that which is called art."[29] Working against the "right name" attached to the authentic, perfectly intelligible speaker by human rights discourse and dictator alike, we will see that "words that exceed the function of rigid designation" are put forward only to be "unceasingly contested by those who claim to 'speak correctly.'"[30]

90 *Fabricating the Real*

From the outset, then, writing carries a dual function. On the one hand, it is understood as an instrument utilized to underwrite the authority of the real or the original. On the other hand, writing is the "orphan word" that exceeds and supplements the limits of speech that define a dominant discursive order. This duality is captured in the figure of transcription that appears throughout *The Orphan Master's Son*. First, the act of transcribing presents a figure of knowledge without interpretation or understanding: in transcription, the aim is to bring the image or representation into exact correspondence with the referent, to the original, without deviation. The main character is sent to English school, where they have no interest in teaching him English— "he simply had to transcribe it"; as an intelligence agent, he is assigned to transcribe transmissions between the United States, Japan, and South Korea in the East Sea—"all night he clacked away on his typewriter, down there in the dark."[31] Later in the novel, an American rower kidnapped by the North Korean navy is assigned to write out by hand into notebooks the eleven-volume *Selected Works of Kim Jong Il*, "silently transcribing."[32] What is demanded is the conveyance of knowledge without interpretation, the delivery of "primary data" without any performance of meaning making.

At the same time, transcription represents a threat, an excess—in the rendering of thoughts or speech into written form, words are sundered from their origin, shifted into different contexts and made to mean otherwise. Under torture, the protagonist "types" in the air with his fingers, transcribing the words of his interrogators, disturbing the usual order of questioning; he "seemed to be typing" with his hands on his stomach, "as if he were transcribing the dream he was having," the narrator tells us.[33] The face of North Korea's national actress, Sun Moon, is "transcribed" as a tattoo onto the protagonist's chest; the names of martyrs are transcribed onto the identification papers of orphan children; the identity of the main character is repeatedly transcribed. Transcription can identify and, in so doing, eradicate the interpreting, thinking subject in the mechanical transmission of the unchanged word. At the same time, as Johnson's fiction reveals, transcription may become story: putting words and images into play, untethering language from its intended context, revealing the contingency of a symbolic order, and allowing other meanings and subjects to emerge.

Fabricating the Real 91

THE LOGIC OF HUMAN RIGHTS: "FORTUNE SMILES" AND NORTH KOREAN ESCAPEE NARRATIVES

Johnson's 2015 short story "Fortune Smiles" tracks the lives of two North Korean defectors after their escape and relocation to the South. "When they first arrived at Incheon airport and surrendered to authorities," the narrator tells us, "they didn't go free, as they'd expected." They instead spent eight weeks in the Hanawŏn "settlement support center," where they were "debriefed, interviewed, fingerprinted and subjected to a battery of physical and mental exams." Hanawŏn also functions as a kind of reeducation program, and the two main characters—DJ and Sun-ho—take classes there on finances, hygiene, "being pleasant," and avoiding crime.[34] Even when they are released from the center, they find that they are not free—they are required to go to meetings with case officers and support groups, and to attend English lessons.

One way to read the story, then, is as a meditation on individual freedom. South Korean behaviors are incomprehensible to the protagonist. "Passing a fitness center, DJ stared at rows of men running on treadmills. What force was driving them? What were they running from?"[35] "It was one thing to surrender to the rule of a murderous dictator," he thinks later, "but what unseen forces did these Southerners obey?"[36] The clearest and in its way most shocking example of this "all-powerful sense of order and compliance" that the story puts forward is the 2014 Sewŏl ferry disaster, which claimed over three hundred lives, most of them high school students.[37] DJ thinks of the disaster as he sits in a Lotteria restaurant with Sun-ho, eating fast food and looking at a nearby table of students in school uniforms: "As the ferry slowly sank, the students were told to wait in their cabins, and there they passed the time until the ferry rolled under the waves."[38]

Sun-ho also invokes the Sewŏl when he confronts a group of indolent high school students, telling them, "You are all passengers. And this whole fucked-up country is the ferry. You call us robots. You call us order-taking zombies. But we know what adversity is. We know what it is to survive, and I can tell you—not a single one of us would have drowned on that boat."[39] The same event appears again at the very end of the story. Just before he departs for a return journey to the North, Sun-ho speaks his last words to DJ, who is remaining in the South: "'Don't get on the

92 *Fabricating the Real*

ferry,' he said, his eyes large and intense. 'If you follow their rules, you'll become one of them.'"[40]

The perceived lack of freedom experienced in the North is balanced here with the seemingly bizarre and tragic subjection to norms of liberal individualism experienced in the South. This dilemma drives the thoughts and actions of the characters, who are caught between two unsustainable unfreedoms or subjections. The dilemma extends itself into their speech. We are attuned to the question of speech first by Sun-ho's silence, as he orders in a fast-food restaurant by pointing to images on the menu. The reason for the silence becomes clear when it is broken and his accent draws the unwelcome attention of others in the restaurant.[41] At work, DJ also maintains silence, listening to coworkers tell stories but unable to join in: "He'd never told a story in his life, at least not about himself."[42] Both Sun-ho and DJ mock "celebrity defectors," those "beautiful young women who wept as they told the most harrowing stories,"[43] with big eyes and a sad tale, "out to get famous by telling the world how victimized and pathetic we are."[44]

South Korea has offered the freedom to speak of events experienced in the North—"it was only here that [DJ] heard others speak, something impossible in the North."[45] Yet at the same time, speech is forced—both compelled and constrained. At the compulsory support group meetings for defectors, "you had to say three things that were great about life in the South. People listed the usual things: freedom, opportunity, the Internet, and so on."[46] When DJ's turn comes, he has trouble speaking until, pressured, he also responds with "I appreciate democracy, freedom and the variety of television programming."[47] He is not only forced to speak, but is forced, in what can only be called a performative contradiction, to speak the word "freedom."

Johnson's story dramatizes what I have called the impossibilization of impossible speech. When all possible speech is identified and demanded, what emerges is a kind of silencing. The story presents two linked forms of discourse that work to delimit the domain of the sayable: (celebrity) defector narratives and human rights. In the first case, a template is given: defector narratives must give "the most harrowing stories—of starvation, separation, suffering and torture. Always a baby died. Always there was the moment when the dark shadow of rape fell across the story, and the interviewer let the silence linger before shifting

Fabricating the Real   93

to the desperate escape."[48] Human rights discourse appears in a dispute Sun-ho has with a man at the DMZ, who is launching a basket of pamphlets attached to a balloon toward the North. "We must get the word out," he tells Sun-ho. "They know they're suffering," replies Sun-ho, who is launching a winter jacket with pockets stuffed with energy bars and lottery tickets. "They don't need you to tell them the regime is bad." "Kim Jong-un is a human rights violator," the man replies. "The UN made it official."[49]

Human rights, Christine Hong tells us, is the "dominant lingua franca for social justice projects" directed at North Korea today.[50] She analyzes the 2014 UN Human Rights Council's "Commission of Inquiry" report, which concludes—as Sun-ho's fictional argument at the DMZ does—with the decisive claim that the North Korean government has committed crimes against humanity. It is the rights framework that makes these crimes legible to the international community, sustains the "well-funded, transnational 'Korean human rights' industry,"[51] and aims to "rehabilitate" North Korean humans, who are then "precariously situated in the neoliberal economic order" and "poorly served in such a setting by abstract assurances of universal humanity."[52]

Wendy Brown, citing Michael Ignatieff, notes that it is rights language that "creates the basis for 'conflict, deliberation, argument and contention,'" a framework that provides a "'shared vocabulary from which our arguments can begin.'"[53] The subjects framed as victims in human rights discourse are cast as "yearning to be free of politics"[54] and seek empowerment through liberal individualism. Human rights discourse puts itself forward as apolitical or, as Brown has it, antipolitical, a "moral discourse centered on pain and suffering rather than [a] political discourse of comprehensive justice."[55] Liberal humanitarianism thus "relies on a violent gesture of depoliticization," Žižek agrees, "depriving the other of any political subjectivization."[56]

Human rights discourse—the simple reference to which stills the debate at the DMZ in "Fortune Smiles"—puts itself forward as apolitical yet at the same time as a shared language, the basis for argument and contention, bounding the debate about (in this case) North Korea within inviolable and supposedly universal limits of speech. It represents the subject of human rights violations as a victim, defined by suffering, and desiring freedom from politics and integration into liberal

94 *Fabricating the Real*

individualistic selfhood. "Human rights," as Rancière has it, "are no longer experienced as political capacities." The recipient of such rights "pure and simple is then none other than the wordless victim, the ultimate figure of the one excluded from the logos, armed only with a voice expressing a monotonous moan, the moan of naked suffering, which saturation has made inaudible." We are left only with the victim on the one hand and the executioner on the other: "the monstrous figure of a person who denies humanity."[57]

The humanitarian stage is characterized, Rancière writes, by "the impossibility of any mode of enunciation." The "heterological mode of political subjectification" that characterizes democratic politics is impossible in an order that has "decided to accept as legitimate only those claims made by real groups that take the floor in person and themselves state their own identity." No identity can be claimed if the speaker does "not possess native entitlement and the social experience" of the identity in question.[58] The role of "humanity" within such an order, the role of the "absolute victim that suspends . . . subjectification,"[59] is to be speechless. Here the impossibility of speech is encased within the fullness of human rights discourse, where the right to speak is claimed by consensus and the victim is rendered speechless as such.

"Fortune Smiles" dramatizes the depoliticization of the subject at the moment the defectors enter into "freedom" in part, as noted above, by representing difficulties of speech. Their entry into South Korea takes place only after their stories are *taken* at the Hanawŏn. The expected freedom is not forthcoming, an unfreedom extended to speech—DJ and Sun-ho are compelled to verbalize opinions not their own at the compulsory meetings, including the word "freedom" itself. The defectors are marked by the difference of their speech, their accents that *put them in their place*, make them identifiable to all others in their cultural difference. The defectors' speech is without platform, *silenced* through a dismissive lack of attention: "All the average defectors," DJ tells us, "they weren't news."[60] Speech goes unrecognized or misrecognized, as with the songs of the woman who defected with her accordion and now sings in the Seoul subways for money. Her songs are either not understood as North Korean by the passersby or are misunderstood, as when the onlookers perhaps mistake a song's praise of the Great Leader as a Christian hymn.[61] Finally, at the DMZ, speech is blocked through a simple

Fabricating the Real 95

reference to a human rights framework and to the crimes against humanity committed by the North Korean leader.

What we see unfolding is a struggle over the propriety of speech, the parameters of speech appropriate to the situation. When silence is broken, it is in the refugee intake facility, in the commercialized testimony of "celebrity defectors," or in the compulsory support groups. Speech here is in a way doubly impossible. At an individual level, it is not possible to speak *within* North Korea (a problem that is not solved once the defectors reach the South); at the same time, North Korea itself is enveloped by the impossibility of speaking *of* it—it is notoriously difficult to obtain information about what happens within North Korea from the outside. There are generally two ways of knowing anything about North Korea: satellite imagery, and defector or refugee testimony.[62] "Fortune Smiles" touches on both. Satellite imagery is a revelation to DJ, who uses it not to glean empirical knowledge but as an avenue to nostalgic memory as he looks at images of familiar places he can no longer get to. Defector testimony is limited to those "celebrities" whose descriptions of both absolute suffering and "progressive narratives of emancipation"[63] do not make sense to the protagonists. Such testimony is treated in human rights discourse, Hong points out, as "primary data," via a method that ascribes a "false positivism" to its sources.[64]

In migrant labor fiction, we saw that testimony is elided or *obscured* by the fantasy of frictionless speech, "impossible" speech outside of linguistic difference. The overwhelming presence of the witness in the narrative voice obscures the distance between the text and the events testified to. There, speaking for another is not only unproblematized but is the central narrative strategy of the stories analyzed in the first chapter. The proximity of the stories to the real is guaranteed through this apparent divorce of speech from context, achieving a human understanding across linguistic or cultural boundaries.

While witnessing and representing the traumatic event are recurring themes in Han Kang's *A Boy Is Coming*, we saw that the demand for testimony is openly *rejected* by the characters. The narrative voice balances between the two definitions of "witness" described by Agamben: the *testis*, the third person who testifies in a dispute between two conflicting parties, and the *superstes*, the one "who has lived through something, who has experienced an event from beginning to end and

96 *Fabricating the Real*

can therefore bear witness to it," the survivor who testifies to the event witnessed.[65] The narrators of Han's novel have experienced something— the massacre at Kwangju—that they bear witness to even as they reject the demands for their testimony. At the same time, the authorial voice, figured in the concluding chapter, stands as *testis*, and the novel as a whole works as a third-party adjudication testifying in the dispute of competing historical positions on the occurrence and responsibility for the events that occurred in Kwangju during May 1980.

"Fortune Smiles" opens the case of North Korean defector narratives, in which testimony is *obligatory*. Here the North Korean defector, escapee, or refugee encounters a kind of "compulsory discursivity" and is placed in the role of the witness who experienced something, while the role of third-party adjudication is assumed by an external voice, the voice of human rights discourse. The narratives of North Korean escapees are assumed to have a historiographic and documentary function, where proof of established facts is demanded in its accordance with the known. In such cases, Nichanian writes, "the survivor is . . . under the obligation to fabricate, all by himself, the scene, the gaze, and the event."[66] The result of such a process is shame, a shame experienced by the witness when testimony is "an appeal made to a third party, to the West, to the observer, to what Hagop Oshagan called 'civilized humanity.' . . . As survivors, we have never ceased . . . to appeal to the external gaze."[67]

Under a human rights regime, North Korean defectors address their stories to an international audience, a "civilized humanity" that listens and judges based on consensual criteria that insist on a coincidence between the verisimilar and the necessary, or the real and the possible.[68] It is before this "civilized humanity" that defectors must state their case, embodying the suffering that defines them and thus giving not only their words but also their being as proof. Testimony is demanded as document, and intersects with human rights discourse in the body or speech of the refugee, a *bodily speech* that guarantees the truth of the statements. This is exemplified in the logic of torture, which, as Theodore Hughes points out, attempts to "enforce the coincidence of words with truth" by "baring the body"[69]—an alignment between language and truth guaranteed by the suffering of the body.

What is demanded of defector narratives is precisely what is denigrated by DJ and Sun-ho in "Fortune Smiles"—that they in every case tell

Fabricating the Real 97

the story that is already expected or known by the listener, always corresponding to and representing the most horrifying violations in the most conventional and clinically accurate language possible. In this way the defector narrative functions both as "the verisimilar tale of social necessity"[70]—confirming what we believe we know about North Korea—and as a form of obscenity in Hal Foster's sense of being "too close to the scene" or "excessively close"[71]—a "world in which everything is on show.... The regime of the all-visible, of the endless presentation to each and every one of us of a real indissociable from its image."[72]

The real indissociable from its image evokes what Kellen Hoxworth has called "performative correctness." If "correctness" is signaled by an "ideal subject of politics as a subject of truth who is free from mystification," then one who "plays politics" is a "mere performer" who presents a "fake in contrast to putatively real politics."[73] Critique of North Korean escapee narratives has taken place along the lines of "unmasking the 'performative'" in conjunction with fact-checking of potential inaccuracies in testimony. As John Cussen puts it, defector narratives are

> too infrequently backed up by corroborative testimony. Too often controverted in their plot details by the memoirists' own spoken accounts of their childhoods in North Korea and of their lives in peril in China. Too transparently suborned by those several right-wing geopolitical leviathans whose "soft power" modus operandi include[s] the buying and shopping of human rights discourse. And, lastly, too fond of the spotlight themselves, these videogenic survivor-memoirists. In short, not to be relied upon in the all-important project of knowing what everyday life is like in North Korea, say the experts.[74]

In combination with factuality, what is demanded is the total absence of performance—as Hoxworth writes, "the only 'true' subjectivity is one impossibly devoid of performance."[75] A disjunction between subject, identity, and position[76] is intolerable. The escapee may not play a part; or rather, there is only one part to play, and that is the identity that guarantees the veracity of the narrative in a human rights discourse that treats testimony as "primary data."

98 *Fabricating the Real*

Among escapee narratives perhaps the most prominent example is Blaine Harden's biography of Shin Dong-hyuk, published as *Escape from Camp 14: One Man's Remarkable Odyssey from North Korea to Freedom in the West* in 2012. Following publication of the book, Shin admitted to having falsified various key aspects of his story. Harden then provided a new foreword to the book, included in subsequent editions, which details the necessary revisions based on new testimony. Admitting that it is difficult or impossible to verify defector accounts due to North Korea's insularity, Harden defends the veracity of the narrative in three ways even as he outlines the changes in Shin's story. First, he notes the traumatic nature of Shin's experiences growing up in the North Korean gulag—according to the logic of trauma, the story is *more true* or more accurately indicative of the traumatic experience if it arrives fragmented or disjointed.[77] Second, he points to the marks of torture on Shin's body as irrefutable evidence.[78] Finally, he claims that Shin had been unaware of the distinction between "fiction" and "nonfiction," a categorical difference that for Harden hinges on the relative importance of details.[79]

Harden rescues Shin's testimony by making its inaccuracies a sign of greater (traumatic) truth, reducing the importance of language by taking the body as the most irrefutable form of evidence, and pointing to the inherent mobility of truth under difference generic forms (what would be unacceptable as nonfiction might be acceptable as fiction, he implies). While this resuscitation of the veracity of Shin's account can explain individual elements of the revised testimony, the demand for realism is undisturbed. These formal elements (the logic of trauma, the signs of the body, the power of genre) are engaged not only to excuse but also to amplify the accuracy of the narrative. Whether language is whole or fragmented, whether the subject speaks of suffering with words or mutely with the body, whether in the form of fiction or nonfiction, the truth of North Korea within a human rights framework is inevitably arrived at through the "violent gesture of depoliticization."[80] Here again we have the impossibilization of impossible speech, as sense is made of the testimony of the defector, reducing the *possible* of language to consensual meaning under a "regime in which the parties are presupposed as already given, their community established and the count of their speech identical to their linguistic performance."[81]

Fabricating the Real 99

Under the "regime of the all-visible," a regime that presents a "real indissociable from its image,"[82] defector narratives are subject to a logic of proof, made to stand as documentary evidence with veracity located entirely in the realm of the factual. At the same time, as the case of Shin Dong-hyuk makes clear, because defectors must establish not only the veracity of their own narratives but also the ground of facticity itself, there is never any choice for escapees but to embody the truth in their testimony. Put differently, in the absence of information, the factual becomes factitious—something *made* in the process of the defector's testimony.

It is important to note that this "fabrication" does not imply agency. As one whose speech is received as information or data, the defector is entirely without political agency under the human rights framework. The North Korean defector is nothing but the North Korean defector. Appearance aligns seamlessly with the real as human rights discourse delimits the sense of defector narratives and deprives the speaker of subjectivity, which is "not simply a fight for the content of oppression it is ostensibly about but also a fight for the ownership—the propriety, the property—of speaking."[83] Defectors are subsumed within a police logic, their bodies fixed in place and corresponding to a fixed domain of possible speech.

Yeonmi Park's well-known escapee narrative and its critical reception reproduce this logic with even greater clarity. Park broke onto the international human rights scene in 2014 with a series of speeches and published the memoir *In Order to Live: A North Korean Girl's Journey to Freedom* in 2015. She faced almost immediate skepticism due to perceived inaccuracies in her tale and inconsistencies between different deliveries of her story—a response similar to that leveled against other escapee narratives.[84] The danger, Mary Ann Jolley wrote, was that if "someone with such a high profile twists their story to fit the narrative we have come to expect from North Korean defectors, our perspective of the country could become dangerously skewed. We need to have a full and truthful picture of life in North Korea if we are to help those living under its abysmally cruel regime and those who try to flee."[85]

Jolley's concern is remarkable for several reasons. First, here again the survivor is assigned the role of "fabricating the scene, the gaze, and the event." The situation is only known through the survivor's testimony; the event comes to light only through the witness of the one who was there.

100 *Fabricating the Real*

Park herself makes this claim explicit. In the prologue to *In Order to Live*, she writes that "only those of us who have escaped can describe what really goes on behind the sealed borders,"[86] the "unknowable" black box of North Korea. At the same time, the framing gaze of the defector is scrutinized for elements of subjective bias or error. Park has been criticized for misrepresenting her story, from contradictory aspects of her narrative (was it her mother and father who crossed over with her into China, or just her mother?), the question of whether she actually saw corpses floating down a river or witnessed her friend's mother being executed for watching illegally imported DVDs, to more general complaints that her suffering is exaggerated and that her family was better off in North Korea than she claims.[87]

The witness is thus charged with representing the scene to the human rights or "civilized" audience, but also—ostensibly because the story cannot be fact-checked—questioned as to the accuracy of her account. It is imperative that the account remain within the realm of the factual; it must fit with what the audience understands, in advance, to be veridical—it must correspond with the real, the known. This is the "shame and the ignominy of 'realism' "[88] that Nichanian writes of, the transformation of testimony into a "discourse of proofs"[89] that gives that testimony the very documentary function that Hong points out above. Again, the defector must produce not only facts but also the ground of facticity, the narrative guaranteeing the condition of factuality itself. The entire operation can be reframed in linguistic terms—the defector must bring the referent into immediate contact with the signifier while at the same time producing the factive, the linguistic context that signals the truth of the statement embedded within it.

The first demand places these witness accounts firmly in the category of modern realism, which Barthes defined as "any discourse which accepts 'speech-acts' justified by their referent alone."[90] This is almost too obvious in the case of defector narratives. The task of testimony is to reveal "what took place," what "actually happened" (in North Korea)—"'concrete reality' becomes the sufficient justification for speaking."[91] In Barthes's well-known examination of the role of the superfluous or useless detail in the literary text, under the regime of the "new" verisimilitude—while such details appear to denote the real directly—they in fact connote the category of the real itself. This in turn produces

Fabricating the Real   101

the well-known reality effect, "the basis of that unavowed verisimilitude which forms the aesthetic of all the standard works of modernity" and which aims "to make notation the *pure encounter of an object and its expression.*"[92] To produce the "referential illusion," the concrete detail—the having-been-there-ness of the narrative element—is thus "constituted by the *direct* collusion of a referent and a signifier; the signified is expelled from the sign."[93]

This is what Barthes means when he tells us that the "pure and simple 'representation' of the 'real,' the naked relation of 'what is' (or has been)" constitutes a "resistance to meaning." The brute "having been there" is "brandished as a weapon against meaning . . . as if, by some statutory exclusion, what is alive cannot not signify."[94] Both this *involuntary* signification, and the *elimination of the signified* (and with it, the necessarily interpretive or translational production of the conceptual content of the sign) point to the elimination of agency under a logic of torture that aims for the perfect correspondence of signifier and referent, of language and truth.

At the same time, the witness is required to produce not only the facts but also the factive—strictly speaking, a verb that presupposes that the sentence in which it is embedded is true, whose object is thus assigned the status of established fact.[95] Essentially, the factive signals a linguistic context that allows for the supposition that a statement is true. "She couldn't believe that in her own country a human's life had less value than an animal's," Yeonmi Park writes in her memoir,[96] or: "My mother couldn't believe the hospital just left the bodies out there in the open."[97] What is presupposed is that human life in North Korea in fact has less value than the life of an animal, or that there were in fact dead bodies left exposed in the hospital courtyard—the "belief" is factive, relying on the self-evidence of the truth of the sentence. The factuality of the text relies on the context in which it is situated, and which is also provided by the narrative. The verb assigns the status of fact to its object.[98]

The operation of the factive at the level of the sentence also characterizes the text as a whole, which is compelled to produce its own grounds of factuality at the same time that it presents the facts of the matter. Embedded in the discourse of human rights, the narrator is taken as an object ("having been there") and assigned the status of fact. No interpretation or translation is necessary—justified by the authenticity of experience,

102 *Fabricating the Real*

the escapee is deprived of agency and reduced to a voice speaking the truth of what could not be otherwise. The entire veracity of the text is subject to judgment based on the text containing an error or falsehood, not because an error calls into question a specific aspect of reality (the geographic location of a particular labor camp, or the type of handbag carried by the narrator's mother) but because it invalidates the *involuntary* nature of the testimony, that the signifier *cannot not* correlate with the referent.

There is some discomfort with this resistance to meaning in the "documentary" correspondence of referent and signifier. Establishing the truth is demanded of the defector—the "silence" that surrounds North Korea must be broken. Yet a kind of secondary silencing also underlies Jolley's call for "a full and truthful picture of life in North Korea" beyond that "narrative we have come to expect." Ironically, the danger is that defector stories will hew *too closely* to the established narrative, the consensus about what North Korea is and what happens there. If statements from escapees too closely "fit the narrative we have come to expect from North Korean defectors," she warns above, "our perspective of the country could become dangerously skewed." The speech of the escapee may be silenced in the face of skepticism regarding its facticity; and it is, paradoxically, potentially silenced as well when it hews too closely to the narrative that validates its facticity.

There are two insights to take from Jolley's journalistic commentary on Park's testimony. First, between the silence of the reclusive nation and the silencing of the untrustworthy witness emerges the silent victim of human rights discourse, whose enunciation is made impossible. The authentic "human" in human rights discourse is *speechless*, the "wordless victim" whose speech is inaudible in a context "saturated" by a human rights discourse that accepts only communications of the real in the "monotonous moans" of the escapees.[99] The reception of North Korean defector narratives bears this out. It is after all the degree of suffering that Park supposedly endured that becomes the flashpoint for debates regarding the veracity of her statements.[100]

Second, unexpectedly accompanying the demand for veridical speech and for testimony as document, there is a strange request for *something else*, something that does not "fit the narrative that we have come to expect," beyond the saturation of sense in human rights language, beyond

Fabricating the Real   103

the point at which the gap between expression (signifier) and the real (referent) is eliminated and "full visibility" is achieved. The anxiety of the commentator arises in the face of the reduction of narrative to the absolutely expected, to the consensual—here, the confluence of a pre-given "politics" with a representational mode most often described as "realist" and the subsumption of narrative to an external discourse that gives it its full sense while stripping the speech of political subjectivity. Something is lost or obscured in the identificatory overlap of speech and position that aims to plug "possible gaps between appearance and reality."[101]

Under the guise of achieving full visibility and sense, the escapee narrative and its reception perform a kind of silencing, an impossibilization of impossible speech resulting in a full identification of the "North Korean subject" and a definition of all speech utterable from that identified position. If human rights discourse provides the frame within which escapee speech is made fully intelligible, then the challenge to such powerful foreclosure will take the form of a literary de-identification, the inscription of "a subject name as being different from any identified part of the community"[102] that creates a dispute about the frame itself within which the given is given as such.[103] The question is how the voiceless can regain speech and hence intelligibility as subjects becoming political. In Hoxworth's terms, the case of defector narratives urges us to refuse the limited horizon of an "ideal subject of politics as a subject of truth who is free from mystification,"[104] a subject who is authentic only by virtue of being without performance, by virtue of being *identical to the identity assigned* in a given discursive context. "To rethink the subject of performance and politics," he writes, "requires a refusal of the promises of performative correctness and attentiveness to the performances of those who only appear as political subjects when subjected by the performative and its grammars of violence."[105]

REALIZING FICTION IN *THE ORPHAN MASTER'S SON*

In a recent article, Douglas Gabriel details how Russian director Vitaly Mansky's 2015 documentary film *Under the Sun* consists of both North Korea–sanctioned footage and of shots filmed without permission, intercut together in a way that seemingly "laid bare the artificial staging and choreography" behind the state's claims of happiness and prosperity. Captured in the moments when Mansky left his camera running between scenes is the direction given to the individuals appearing in the documentary. Voices remind those on screen "to act in certain ways,"[106] for instance, directing one of the main subjects of the documentary, eight-year-old Ri Jin-mi, "how to perform, instructing her . . . to act like she does at home rather than like she is performing in a movie."[107] This necessity of providing direction, in addition to subtle visual and aural cues expressed during the sanctioned portions of the documentary (facial expressions, tones of voice, and so on) led commentators to see "inklings of discontent" and a lack of "genuine belief" in the North Korean system.[108]

Mansky describes his method as "real cinema," requiring that the filmmaker "forego any script, and that the filming process be allowed to unfold without restraints," a mode of filmmaking with "no dramatization or reconstruction."[109] "I wanted to make a film about the real [North] Korea," Mansky claimed, "but there's no real life in the way that we consider. . . . There is just the creation of an image of the myth of a real life. So we made a film about fake reality."[110] At the same time, in a 2016 North Korean article reacting critically to the documentary, Jin-mi's mother is interviewed and asked about the unauthorized footage. "'In films that we . . . call documentaries,' she maintains, 'adults, of course, and even professional actors repeat scenes.' Put differently, Jin-mi's mother points out how there is always an element of acting in documentary films."[111]

What is most interesting here is Jin-mi's mother's commonsense rejection of the idea that a documentary film might present an undramatized reconstruction. Is not an unexamined division between "fake reality" and a somehow "realer real" at the heart of an ideological interpretation that seeks the "truth" of the North Korean between scenes or in readings of indicative gestures or facial expressions? This demand to eliminate performance is shared both by North Korean state officials (who instruct Jin-mi to avoid looking like she's acting in a movie) and by the documentary director who aims to make a film without dramatization or reconstruction and "made a film about [real] fake reality."

Gabriel's point is that critical reception of the film relies on a politics of truth that either reads North Koreans as they appear in North Korean media ("bask[ing] in the glory" of the military and ideological

Fabricating the Real   105

superiority of the regime) or as victims, the "suppressed citizenry." This is an either/or proposition that, he argues, explains North Korea in binary terms and ignores the complexity and ambiguity of individuals in relation to state and society.[112] What is more crucial in terms of my argument is that here too we see the "hunger" for the real that characterizes readings of North Korean escapee narratives, and the elimination of the subject—the gap between an actual and literal meaning—in the drive to align signified with referent where speech *cannot not* denote the real, *even when it is "fake."*

In his discussion of Krzysztof Kieślowski's turn from documentary to feature filmmaking, Slavoj Žižek points to the curious feeling that one gets while watching Kieślowski's documentaries, "as if (real-life) persons *play themselves*, generating an uncanny overlapping of documentary and fiction."[113] It was "to avoid *this* impasse that Kieślowski had to move to fiction: since, when we film 'real-life' scenes in a documentary way, we get people *playing* themselves (or, if not this, then obscenity, the pornographic trespass into intimacy), the only way to depict people *beneath* their protective mask of playing is, paradoxically, to make them *directly play a role*, i.e. to move into fiction."[114]

This neatly sums up the logic behind the turn to literature in the remainder of this chapter. I look to Adam Johnson's fiction to examine the capacity of art to overcome the stifling insistence that speech be treated as document, the drive to make all speech possible in "breaking silence," and the insistence that the subject only emerges in the absence of performance. Such insistence opens the individual to the shame of a kind of ontological fact-checking and puts into play the parallel logic of torture, for which the suffering of the individual body guarantees the correspondence of word and truth. The disturbing, too-perfect coincidence of testimony with a given narrative—the feeling that the story is *too* good to be true ("it's so real, it must be fiction")[115]—points to a tautogorical logic for which the real is "indissociable from its image" and hence immune to the appearance of the nonidentary subject.[116] As we will see below, Johnson exploits this logic, exposing the uncanny shift in sense that emerges when one is asked to play oneself in a scripted real.

From the title forward, *The Orphan Master's Son* focuses on the character and trope of the one without parents, without a family lineage that would provide a sense of order, place, and identity. The main character

106 *Fabricating the Real*

is apparently an orphan, yet believes that he is the son of the man who ran the orphanage where he grew up. The character has an indeterminate identity: his name throughout the first half of the novel, a "biography," is Pak Jun Do, though, like the other orphans, he is named after a famous North Korean martyr; "Jun Do" is explicitly related to "John Doe" in the text, not a missing person but "when you have the person, just not his identity."[117] The second half of the novel, dubbed a "confession," portrays a different character, Commander Ga, who nonetheless appears to be Jun Do through correspondences that emerge in the plot and in the dialogue and memory of the characters. The perpetual uncertainty around the identity of the main character undermines a logic of filiation, a "natural" situation that would give an original sense of identity or meaning to the character. The nominal splitting of the character also undermines the two genres into which the narrative is organized— biography, which tends to chronologically coordinate the character in historical time, and confession, which narrates the interiority of the subject. In the first case, the subject goes missing before the end of the biography is reached; in the second case, the interrogator—a self-professed biographer—seeks a confession from the wrong subject.

Chronologically reconstructed, *The Orphan Master's Son* is comprised of two main sections. Part 1, "The Biography of Jun Do," is the tale of a boy who grows up under harsh conditions in an orphanage in North Korea, becomes a zero-light DMZ tunnel fighter for the military, is recruited by the government to help kidnap Japanese citizens, and is eventually stationed aboard a fishing vessel with listening equipment and a typewriter, assigned to monitor international radio transmissions on the East Sea. Jun Do is recognized as a hero of the republic after a run-in with an American military vessel and is dispatched to Texas as part of a diplomatic mission. Upon the failure of the mission and his return to P'yŏngyang, Jun Do is sent to a long-term labor camp, Prison 33. Part 1 ends by telling the reader that "from this point forward nothing further is known of the citizen named Pak Jun Do."[118]

Part 2, "The Confessions of Commander Ga," picks up one year later and is narrated by a nameless Division 42 interrogator. One of his current prisoners is the former minister of prison mines, Commander Ga, who has been charged with killing his wife. The main character in this section is referred to exclusively as Commander Ga, but we learn that it is

Fabricating the Real   107

likely Jun Do, who in a twist of fate met Commander Ga at Prison 33, defeated him in hand-to-hand combat, and escaped the camp by assuming his identity. He returns to P'yŏngyang, takes up residence with Ga's wife, the actress Sun Moon, and aids the Dear Leader in staging a performance designed to humiliate an U.S. delegation visiting to undertake a trade of technology for an American hostage. At the same time, he puts into action a plan developed with Sun Moon, modeled after the film *Casablanca* and designed to get her and her children onto the American aircraft and safely abroad. The novel has three endings: Commander Ga's death in the chair of the "autopilot," a self-modulating torture device in Division 42; a retrospective narration of Sun Moon's defection and Commander Ga's arrest; and a North Korean state retelling of the event, which remolds Ga into a heroic martyr.

Read in this way, *The Orphan Master's Son* may be understood as a heroic tale of one man's resistance against totalitarianism, who, against all odds, aids a leading national actress and her family in defecting to the United States. Yet at the center of the novel's structure is an unmistakable torsion between two forms of the revelation of the self (the biography and the confession) and between two names, Jun Do and Commander Ga, which appear to refer to the same individual. Further, the novel is perforated by transcripts of broadcasts from North Korean state radio that tell or retell portions of the story in a different idiom. The reader is interpellated as a North Korean, hearing a state-sanctioned story from the first page (the opening line reads "Citizens, gather 'round your loudspeakers, for we bring important updates!"[119]). The address, by a North American author writing in English, is delivered from the position of the North Korean state; the addressee, an English-language reader who presumably understands that they are reading a work of fiction, is placed in the position of a North Korean listener. This opening move and the structure of the work overall eliminate any idea of identity at the base of a writer's authority to tell a story or any idea of cultural authenticity as the guarantor of the truth of the novel. Neither the author nor the reader preoccupy the position that they are required to assume in a model of performative correctness.

The opening section continues to address the reader with a rhetorical question: "Were you not assembled . . . to witness it firsthand? What are you going to believe, citizens? Rumors and lies, or your very own

108 *Fabricating the Real*

eyes?"[120] At first glance, this appears to intensify the situation of the addressee as a North Korean listener, who was, it is implied, actually there to see the events that are to be described. Yet, as the opening continues, it becomes clear that what has been witnessed firsthand are films, staged performances, awards presentations, broadcasts of news, speeches, public service announcements, and so on, including an opera performed by P'yŏngyang's "new opera singer," an invitation to which frames the first section of the novel as itself a long performance of "the story of the greatest nation in the world."[121] At the same moment that we are enjoined to believe our very own eyes, the objects of perception lined up to indicate the truth are without exception performances—on stage, on film, on the radio, and in Kim Il-Sung Square. The first pages of the novel thus open the question of the relationship between (empirical) truth and performance, couched in a language that itself enacts a relationship between state and individual.

There are two central logics that operate across both halves of *The Orphan Master's Son*: a logic of names and a logic of story. Conventionally, the autobiographical narrative is guaranteed through a kind of contract with the reader via the (real) name of the subject, appearing on the spine of the book and also in the narrative;[122] meanwhile, the confession, the disclosure or acknowledgment or avowal of the truth, is a story told in the intimate language of a self compelled to speak either out of guilt or belief. The problem set before the fiction is how to give voice to a subject without demanding such identification—how to tell a story that reveals truth outside the logic of the historiographic imperative or the humiliating demand for the real,[123] and how to "revisit the scene of subjection without replicating the grammar of violence."[124]

Logic of Names

Three compilations of names appear in the novel. First, there is rumored to be a master computer, controlled by the state—a master list of North Korean citizens, complete with location and dates of birth and death. Second, Jun Do encounters a phone book in a guest room during his visit to Texas, containing thousands of names. "He couldn't believe that you could look up anyone and seek them out. . . . It was unfathomable that a permanent link existed to mothers and fathers and lost mates, that they were forever fixed in type."[125] Finally, there is the box containing photographs that an inmate, Mongnan, takes of all individuals entering Prison 33, each holding a chalk slate with their name written on it. Clipped together with each is an "exit photo," taken upon their death.[126]

In the case of the master computer, to name is to identify for the purpose of punishment. "I'm ready to denounce," one of the prisoners under interrogation in Division 42 states. "There were many bad citizens who attempted to corrupt me, and I have a list, I'm ready to name them all."[127] The state interrogator who narrates the second half of the novel understands his work as that of a biographer—the desired result of torture is not a list of others' names, but a fixing of the identity of the one tortured. "Our team discovers an entire life, with all its subtleties and motivations, and then crafts it into a single, original volume that contains the person himself," he tells us. "When you have a subject's biography, there is nothing between the citizen and the state."[128]

This is how the biographer-narrator envisions the function of pain produced by the "autopilot," which "works in concert with the mind, measuring brain output, responding to alpha waves. Every consciousness has an electrical signature, and the autopilot's algorithm learns to read that script. Think of its probing as a conversation with the mind, imagine it in a dance with identity."[129] Here is the dream of scientific (or genetic) determination of the true self, the detectable "signature" that marks identity. It is this signature that the biographer seeks to capture at the moment of its elimination. The image given is one of a pencil and eraser moving in tandem, the writing that fills each page eliminated, leaving blankness. "They continue in lockstep this way, the self and the state, coming closer to one another until finally the pencil and the eraser are almost one, moving in sympathy, the line disappearing even as it's laid down, the words unwritten before the letters are formed."[130] Here the logic of torture is made perfectly clear: pain produces a complete overlap of language and truth, "a model of how to share everything,"[131] a light that blinds rather than illuminates,[132] the end result of which is *identification*. "Once we discover the inside of a subject, what makes him tick, we not only know everything he's done but everything he will do."[133] Everything that can be done or said is identified in advance. How does fiction resist this drive to determine all possible speech? Or as Hartman

110 *Fabricating the Real*

puts it: "Is it possible to construct a story from 'the locus of impossible speech' or resurrect lives from the ruins?"[134]

The difficulty with naming that began with the title of the book—the "son" of the "orphan master" has no filial identity, no proper surname assigned by position in a family—is carried forward with the edition notice, before the body of the text even begins. Beyond the "all characters appearing in this work are fictitious" and "all resemblance to persons living or dead is coincidental" disclaimer, the notice admits that, as a matter of fact, not all of the characters are fictional—some are "well-known real-life figures." The name of a character (Kim Jong Il, for instance) may signal the "real-life-ness" of the figure, referring to a "real" person in the world; yet, the notice tells us, the words spoken by or the situations in which the real-life character finds themselves are meant to be taken as entirely fictional. Here the real name is given but decontextualized and made to perform in unexpected ways.

The character of Jun Do/Commander Ga presents the obverse in that it is the real name that is sought, a name that would correspond to the identity of the fictional character before the reader. "I just wanted to find out his real name," the nameless interrogator and would-be biographer tells us;[135] "I could imagine the subject's true name, whatever that would turn out to be, embossed on the spine."[136] Yet the dynamic of torture, confession, and biography is broken in the case of the protagonist. "Names come and go," Commander Ga says. "I suppose I have a real one . . . but I don't know what it is."[137] Nameless, the character is open to definition. The identity of the protagonist has not been captured; interrogation under torture has not produced the proper name. "I've made very little progress on his biography," the interrogator tells us. "It doesn't even have an ending."[138] In apparent opposition to this decontextualization, the novel ends with an announcement of the name over the North Korean loudspeaker: "Forever, Commander Ga Chol Chun. In this way, you'll live forever,"[139] interred in the Revolutionary Martyrs' Cemetery as a hero of the nation.

Logic of Story

While obviously an anxious reaction to the loss of control over the story, this propagandistic ending contains a kernel of truth. The protagonist,

Fabricating the Real 111

(perhaps) an orphan named Pak Jun Do, named after a revolutionary martyr known for taking his own life as a test of loyalty to the regime,[140] has made his way in death to his proper home, the cemetery filled with bronze busts of national heroes. Here the rationale of the narrative weirdly prevails. Under the name "Commander Ga" and having aided in a defection and having been tortured to death by the state, the protagonist is nonetheless memorialized as "an inspiration to all,"[141] as a proper hero of the story. ("Believe it or not, the hero is me," Ga tells Sun Moon as he sends her off on the American plane.[142]) But a second, formal truth is also contained here, in that Jun Do is not able to escape this story told about him by the state. His identity is fixed in a narrative that is clearly unrealistic yet is understood to be true. We see this as soon as Ga undergoes the first round of torture. The interrogators send a message "deep into the bunker complex below us, where all the decisions were made," reading: "Is not Commander Ga." The reply returns immediately by vacuum tube. "When we opened it, the note inside read simply, 'Is Commander Ga.'"[143]

Here is an opening into the operative logic of story in *The Orphan Master's Son*, a logic that is repeatedly confirmed at both the diegetic and structural levels of the narrative and spans both major sections of the novel. Perhaps the most obvious example stems from Jun Do's time in the hold of a fishing boat as a spy, transcribing messages heard over the radio. The fishermen all have tattoos of their wives inked on their chests, and Jun Do is compelled to do the same in order to pass as a member of the crew. As he is unmarried, the Captain reproduces an image of North Korea's national actress Sun Moon from an available pinup calendar. What, Jun Do asks, is the point of tattooing your wife's face on your chest? "'There is only one reason,' the Captain said. 'It's because it places her in your heart forever.'" Yet Sun Moon has only been encountered on screen, while acting, or in the photos in the pinup calendar. "'When you see her movies,' the Captain tells him, 'that's not really her. Those are just characters she plays.'"[144] It is the not-real image of Sun Moon that is reproduced in ink on Jun Do's body.

Yet, as the novel progresses, Jun Do becomes known as "the man who loves Sun Moon,"[145] and eventually becomes (replaces) Commander Ga, minster of prison mines and Sun Moon's husband. A representation, the tattoo, drives the action of the narrative—the image prefigures the real.

112 *Fabricating the Real*

Despite the fact that love gradually develops between the protagonist and Sun Moon, the sense of acting or performance never diminishes. Their first kiss "started with the tilt of her head, her eyes flashing to his mouth, a hand slowly reaching to his collarbone, where it rested, and then she leaned in, the slowest lean in the world. He recognized the kiss. It was from *Hold the Banner High!*, the one she'd planted on the weak-minded South Korean border guard."[146] Their plan to escape the North is inspired by *Casablanca*, which they watch together. "'I must make it to the place where this movie was made,' she said. 'I have to get out of this land and make it to a place where real acting exists. I need a letter of transit and you must help me.'"[147]

What we see here is a doubling: performance becomes real in performance. Later in the novel, barely conscious after a severe beating, when asked by his interrogators how he first met Sun Moon, the protagonist replies: "So cold . . . She was on the side of the infirmary. The infirmary was white. The snow fell heavily, it blocked my view of her. The battleship burned. They used the infirmary because it was white. Inside, people moaned. The water was on fire."[148] In this abstracted, seemingly delusional account—which the interrogators fail at first to understand—Ga describes with *complete accuracy* his first encounter with Sun Moon, in Prison 33, during a projection of one of her films on the side of the camp infirmary. The verisimilitude of the recounting is lost because it cannot exist in the story of their relationship that prevails; it is not only the style of the prose that marks it as fantastical, but its departure from both the normal romantic plot and the biographical tale of Ga's marriage to Sun Moon.

This logic, by which the story takes precedence over the individual, runs throughout the novel. "Where we are from," one character tells Jun Do, "stories are factual. If a farmer is declared a music virtuoso by the state, everyone had better start calling him maestro. . . . For us, the story is more important than the person. If a man and his story are in conflict, it is the man who must change."[149] Jun Do reproduces this for an American interlocutor later in the first part: "You've got to understand—where he's from, if they say you're an orphan, then you're an orphan. If they tell you to go down a hole, well, you're suddenly a guy who goes down holes. . . . I mean if they tell him to go to Texas to tell a story, suddenly he's nobody but that."[150]

Fabricating the Real   113

Sun Moon's lament that she has never truly acted and her desire to reach a place where "real acting" exists makes sense in this context. As represented in Johnson's fiction, the North Korean citizen is always acting, is always playing a role in a story that originates elsewhere. *"I'll perform your story,"* she tells Kim Jong Il when she is first "discovered" as an actress on a train to a reeducation camp.[151] "You've never been one to shy away from authenticity," he tells her later; "you practically live your roles."[152] When there is no distinction between "real life" and performance—when everything has become performance—then there is no performance. What matters then is the *account* that is made of a word or act: the meaning that is assigned, for instance, to a tear rolling down the face of a professional actress.[153]

No matter how excessive the words, it is the dictator—the one who "says often" or "prescribes" (from the Latin *dictare*), whose words are obeyed and adopted as reality—who determines the sense of an utterance, the facts of the matter. "With the Dear Leader, citizens, remember," the loudspeaker tells us, "everything is possible."[154] Emerging from the mouth of the dictator, stories are factual. Attending a gala at the Grand People's Opera House, Sun Moon and Ga mimic this, attempting to convince one another that they are real, that they are the roles that they are playing. "'I am a talented actress and you are my husband,' she said. 'I am a talented actress and you are my husband.' Ga looked into her uncertain, unseeing eyes. 'You are a talented actress,' he said. 'And I am your husband.'"[155] The host, Kim Jong Il, sends a masked imposter out into the gathering, only to appear himself momentarily, pleased that he had fooled Ga into thinking the imposter was him. "'He thought it was me,' he announced to the delight of the room. 'But I am the real Kim Jong Il, I am the real me.'"[156] Per the edition notice, the entirely fictional nature of the work prohibits us from construing Kim Jong Il's declaration of realness as itself real. However, this does not detract from the force of the logic put forward—that the dictator tells the story, produces the consensus, "patching over the possible gaps between appearance and reality or law and fact."[157] "Tell me, Commander, what is your opinion of imposters?" Kim Jong Il later asks Ga as they contemplate the kidnapped and detained American rower. "'Do you think that, over time, a replacement could become the real thing?' 'The substitute becomes genuine,' Ga said, 'when you declare it so.'"[158]

The logic of having to correspond to the story in a context "where people had been trained to accept any reality presented to them"[159] is played out in the first part of the novel, when the second mate on Jun Do's fishing vessel steals a lifeboat and attempts to defect. The rest of the crew returns to shore to be questioned, but before making land, they determine the story that they will tell: that they were boarded by Americans, who threw the second mate overboard to the sharks, and that he could not be saved, even though Jun Do leapt into the water to try to rescue him. "All that's left is the proof," the Captain tells Jun Do, who, understanding the need to fabricate the real in accordance with the story, allows his arm and upper body to be badly mauled by a shark they had caught earlier. "Sharks and guns and revenge," he tells the Captain. "I know I thought it up, but this isn't a story that anyone could really believe." You're right, the Captain tells him, "but it's a story they can use."[160]

Facing the interrogators upon his arrival, Jun Do "understood that he was alone, and all he had was the story,"[161] which develops as he is tortured. "It was difficult to tell how long the old man had been working on him. All his sentences ran together to make one sentence that didn't make sense. . . . And suddenly the story was true, it had been beaten into him, and he began crying because the Second Mate had died and there was nothing he could do about it. He could suddenly see him in the dark water, the whole scene lit by the red glow of a single flare."[162]

Jun Do continues to tell the story of the last moments of the second mate's life to his torturer. "*It's dark, I don't know where I am*, he said. *I'm here*, I told him, *listen to the sound of my voice*. He asked, *Are you out there?* I put my hands on his face, which was cold and white. *I can't be where I think I am*, he said. *A ship is out there—I can't see its lights*. That was the last thing he said." His interrogator responds: "'*I can't see its lights?* Why would he say that?' When Jun Do said nothing, the old man asked, 'But you did try to rescue him, didn't you? Isn't that when you got bit? And the Americans, you said their guns were on you, right? . . . Earlier you said his last words were *All praise Kim Jong Il, Dear Leader of the Democratic People's Republic of Korea*? You admit that's a lie.'"[163]

Here the glow of the red light and the idea of a ship gone dark in the night are aspects transcribed and adopted from an earlier distress call made by two American women who were rowing around the world, a call picked up by Jun Do on his listening equipment aboard the fishing boat.

Fabricating the Real 115

"There's a ship out there, a ship without lights. We shot it with a flare. The red streak bounced off the hull. Is anyone out there, can anyone rescue us?"[164] Decontextualized ("I can't be where I think I am") and cited beyond the reason of the story-in-progress, the words fail to make sense to the interrogator. Yet at the same time it is this moment of indecipherability that compels the interrogator to certify Jun Don's story. " 'But the facts,' Jun Do said. 'They don't add up. Where are the answers?' " The old man responds: " 'There's no such thing as facts. In my world, all the answers you need to know come from here.' He pointed at himself."[165]

This scene points to how language can, inexplicably, circulate outside a dictatorial, identificatory logic. At the very moment when the veracity of speech should be guaranteed by terrible suffering, it is not fact but fiction that is *realized* and becomes true for both speaker and listener. It is here that the novel hijacks the power of story to determine. It is not "too good to be true," but rather "too fantastical to be a lie." It is also here that the reviewers of Johnson's fiction who find in it a "frightening window on the mysterious kingdom of North Korea" might discover themselves in a position structurally homologous to that of the interrogator, who realizes the truth precisely at the moment when the sense of the story "we have come to expect" fails. Against the realist demand for explanation, the novel destabilizes the normative link between language and truth; the suffering body produces a story that is not real, or better, that becomes real in its telling through the interpretive act of the interlocutor.

Thus it is neither Sun Moon's successful defection to the United States nor Jun Do/Ga's sacrificial death (paralleling the sense of *Casablanca*'s ending, Rick's failure to escape and his martyrdom[166]) that functions as the climax of the novel, but rather Ga's *refusal to explain what happened*, producing an event in excess of the determined real. The dictator is unable to understand the event of the defection as it happened—"he seemed not to recognize an event that occurred without his authorization";[167] to the one who must have "the last word,"[168] Ga's act is indecipherable and undermines identification. " 'I don't understand who you are,' the Dear Leader said to him."[169] When asked under torture to explain, Jun Do/Ga refuses. "I can't tell you," he tells the interrogator. " 'Why not?' 'Because this mystery is the only reminder to the Dear Leader

116 *Fabricating the Real*

that what happened to him is real, that something happened that was out of his control.' "[170]

In the end, *The Orphan Master's Son* both carries the logic of realism to a horrifying limit and puts in place a causal structure that takes advantage of the indeterminacy of the signifier and the determining power of the story to exceed the bounds of "possible speech," whether under a totalitarian regime or within a human rights framework that silences the victim. Under a police logic, "every word has a well-determined point of origin and point of destination, and is thus inscribed in an ordered arrangement of bodies in their place and in their function."[171] The dictator controls the master computer with the names of every North Korean citizen, has the "last word," can make the substitute genuine by declaring it so. Against this, we see words *adopted* by the orphan protagonist: the words of the rower through which he makes his confession; or the words of the minister of prisons, who, when sexually assaulting his victims, tells them that he is "giving them his scar," wounding them in a way that will give them something in common. "I've given you the scar that's on my heart," Jun Do/Ga tells Kim Jong Il as they watch the plane carrying the American delegation lift off from the P'yŏngyang airport. "I will never see Sun Moon again. And neither will you."[172] The words are not only borrowed (heard and reported by a victim of assault earlier in the novel, and also by Jun Do when he is attacked by Ga at Prison 33) and repurposed, but also figure the near future, in which the tattoo of Sun Moon is removed from the protagonist's chest with a box cutter—a literalization in which the scar is "given" for the dictator, who takes a "last image"[173] with which to remember Sun Moon by.

Such use of "words separated from their normal ambit" removes them from the "normal play of speech that designates, orders"; they become orphan words adopted and "spoken by someone we no longer know to anyone at all," reorganizing "the entire relationship between words and things, between the order of discourse and the order of conditions."[174] The narrative real of the novel is infiltrated by lines of dialogue, reproductions of scenes, and props (cars, wrenches, costumes, a tea set). The setting of the disastrous diplomatic meeting in Texas is simulated for the Americans at the Py'ŏngyang airport, but with rattlesnakes replaced by North Korean rock mamushi, a chuck wagon stolen

Fabricating the Real 117

from a Japanese theme park, a hand-painted Texas state flag, a custom-made Colt .46, and so on. Words and objects are cut loose from their proper contexts, and the performative aspect of language is brought disturbingly to the fore.

Not only words or props but stories too are "separated from their normal ambit" in the novel and function to disturb the narrative real. "Tell us your oldest memory," the interrogators ask Ga. Ga responds by recounting a fable in which a boy is lost by his parents and wanders the world, escaping the cold wind, a mine shaft, and fields of the dead and dying only to be captured by a bear, who speaks an unknown language and embraces the boy, warming him and feeding him honey. "Everybody recognized the story, one that's taught to all the orphans," the interrogator tells us, "with the bear representing the eternal love of Kim Jong Il. . . . And it gave us chills the way he told the story, as if it actually was about him and not a character he had learned about, as if he personally had nearly died of cold, hunger, fever, and mine mishaps, as if he himself had licked honey from the Dear Leader's claws. But such is the universal power of storytelling."[175]

Two things happen here: first, the story (a fable) is adopted as the speaker's own, structuring the diegetic reality of the main character. Second, the fable structures the shape of the fictional narrative itself, as the character undergoes a series of parallel trials over the course of the novel. It is no coincidence that Sun Moon's final performance before her defection is a musical rendition of the same fable but stripped of its moral ("finding the fatherly love of the Dear Leader"). Her performance, in a voice "edged with the things the song had left out," shifts the referent of the fable to Jun Do/Ga, rendering it a recounting of a real unauthorized by the state.[176]

At the same time, despite its reiterative shaping of the narrative real, such a recounting is not allowed to function as a document. Muddling the distinction between art and not-art, Johnson's prose functions as a decontextualization, a "denaturalization of discourse."[177] The novel compels us to understand language "not as a static and closed system whose utterances are functionally secured in advance by the 'social positions' to which they are mimetically related," but as having the capacity to introduce a break with "prior context," a break "crucial to the political operation of the performance."[178] This break is introduced in the process

118 *Fabricating the Real*

of a disidentification—a "removal from the naturalness of place," a fracture within an ethos and with the voice that is supposed to express its essence.[179] The politics of the text does not lie in the fact that it takes "North Korea" as its content—a "window" onto a totalitarian regime, making the fantastical appear as real, accomplishing the "seemingly impossible" by turning "implausible fact" into "entirely believable fiction." In Johnson's fiction, North Korea is not a mystery; "it's the most straightforward place on earth."[180] The novel is not the breaking of silence or a "speaking out," as if what is revealed to us is the true subject. Instead, by delinking words from prior contexts and putting in place a disorienting logic of cause and effect, the novel stands as a performance of a performance, with characters "playing themselves" to uncanny effect and in a way that disorders the logic of "performative correctness" that underlies human rights discourse and its realist demand.

DISPLACING "PERFORMATIVE CORRECTNESS"

In this chapter, we began again with possible speech, determined by "rules of speakability" that set limits on what may be said through a process of foreclosure or framing. That which is within the frame is recognized as sensible discourse, the speech of rational and intelligible beings. With the case of migrant labor fiction, those nationally, culturally, ethnically, and linguistically alien are brought into perfect comprehensibility through the fantasy of fluency that forecloses the speech of the migrant by encasing it within both the logic of monolingualism and within the politics of the *minjung*. The speech of the foreigner is brought seamlessly both into the Korean language and into a kind of eminently recognizable political discourse borrowed from the 1970s and 1980s labor movement. In Moon Jae-in's speeches on the anniversary of the Kwangju uprising and massacre, we saw that the unspeakable trauma of the past is remade into the foundation of national sentiment and a communal sense of belonging in the present. In both cases, the experience of the radically other is made intelligible and presented in terms that already exist as the common sense of the community.

With human rights discourse, we have another example of a mode of representation that relies on the verisimilar presentation of suffering, set in a narrative that dramatizes the emergence of truth via

Fabricating the Real 119

(autobiographical, confessional) acts of breaking a silence. Here too, we have a narrative mode that conceals both its status as representation, first in positing a perfect alignment of signifier and referent guaranteed by the suffering of the body, and second in its claim to an apoliticality that can then properly recognize and speak for the "human." Here too, the speech of others—speech assumed to be unintelligible, as linguistically, culturally, or experientially beyond the ken of a reader or listener—is presented as understandable, and this presentation itself is assumed to be a political act. Through a process of identification, the subject is put in their place and made intelligible; through biographical and confessional forms, that place—made tautologous with the subject—is explained to an audience eager to accept the story as fact.

Thus, on the one hand, the escapee from an "unimaginable" and unknowable space is made intelligible to the "civilized world" in the language of human rights discourse, with the testimony of survivors transcribed and underwritten by a correspondence of word and truth guaranteed by the authenticity of the suffering individual. On the other hand, and in excess of this possible speech, *The Orphan Master's Son* presents an actuality that exceeds the determined context of the "progressive narrative of emancipation." Establishing unfamiliar logics of name and story and setting its action in a multilayered, almost viscous medium of performance (as a theme, but also as the structure of rationality), the limits of what it is possible to say or do are put into question.[181] The truth content of the narrative is not determined by its verisimilitude—by the removal of any interval between signifier and referent—no matter how hard critics may have tried to put the novel forward as a "well-researched" documentary recounting of everyday life in North Korea. Scandalously undermining the truth claims of both (auto-)biography and confession and the "straightforward" discourse of totalitarian dictator and human rights regime alike, the orphan character embodies the "wandering excess" of the "orphan word"—not the identified and speechless martyr of human rights discourse consigned to reproducing their experience in conventional language for an audience that expects nothing else, but a subject "between nominations" who defers the moment of agreement between possible speech, visibility, and identity.

120 *Fabricating the Real*

The Orphan Master's Son takes advantage of the demand for documentary truth, making the direction from offscreen that instructs the subject to "act like you do in real life, not like you're performing in a movie" the organizing principle of the narrative.[182] Further, in Johnson's fiction, the characters are required to act *as if* it were real in a context that continually writes and rewrites the grounds of that real. What we get is a series of orthonymic returns, "the threatened displacement of one by an imposter who is oneself."[183] In so doing, the novel calls attention to the duplicity of a human rights discourse that denies the subject in demanding "performative correctness" (the authenticating force of no performance whatsoever) and at the same time requires both a narrative that conforms to the consensus of what is known—the parameters of possible speech—and *something more*, something that exceeds "the narrative we have come to expect from North Korean defectors." Against a human rights logic that demands the performance of a given identity and nothing more, Johnson presents characters who are perpetually disidentified, taken out of place. Jun Do/Ga, Sun Moon, and others are literally and figuratively orphaned, moving from position to position, role to role, untethered from filiation. In the end, it is impossible to fix the character by aligning *where* someone is with *who* someone is. The orphan and his "orphan words"—given to us in a system of shifting names, elusive senses, a strange causal domain—that is, given to us *in fiction*—are narrated outside claims of history or culture, verisimilitude or identity.

"Fortune Smiles" closes with an act that captures this sense of a transgression of positions and places. Having defected from the North, and having undergone a depersonalizing identification in the South, Sun-ho plans to undo his escape, to un-defect—both in the sense of repairing a wrong, a defect, but also to undo an undoing (*de-facere*). He attaches himself to six giant, helium-filled balloons tethered to a plastic desk chair with automotive fan belts and launches himself northward off the roof of a high-rise building in Kangnam, "snapped up into the sky, spinning wildly and swinging until he was no longer visible."[184] The short story ends with a transgression of identity but also of territory, one that leaves the main character hanging, swinging precariously in the airspace over the DMZ. In the following chapter, we will see this no-place of disidentification figured as a kind of utopia. In response to a police logic

Fabricating the Real   121

that *puts you in your place*—whether that place is a compulsory support group, Sun-ho's "home" in the maintenance closet of the Kangnam high-rise, or a cell in a psychiatric ward—we will see the transgression of the "ordered arrangement of bodies in their place and in their function"[185] in speech and writing that take leave of their proper context and emerge where none were thought possible.

CHAPTER FOUR

Disturbing Sensibility

Transgressing Generic Norms in Castaway on the Moon *and* I'm a Cyborg, but That's OK

> Through transgression, they find that they too, just like
> speaking beings, are endowed with speech that does not simply express
> want, suffering, or rage, but intelligence.
>
> —RANCIÈRE, *DISAGREEMENT*

As chapter 2 reread narratives of trauma as a piercing force emerging from the relationship established between past and present, in this final chapter, I read for the transgression of both space and bodies as mirrored in the transgression of generic norms. I examine examples from contemporary South Korean film that represent characters excluded from society: the suicidal castaway and the *hikikomori* in Yi Haejun's *Castaway on the Moon* (2009) and the occupants of a mental asylum in Pak Ch'anuk's *I'm a Cyborg, but That's OK* (2006). Both films appear to adopt the conventional form of the soteriological narrative, tracing arcs expected to result in the salvation of characters either in romantic love (rescue from loneliness and isolation) or medical cure (rescue from illness and death). We find that the logic that typically moves a character from a state of deprivation toward rescue or salvation via the transformative event fails, in the end, to give meaning to the apparently meaningless even as it harnesses the capacity of such a logic to foster hope and to work outside of the common sense of language. While the narrative arc in each film appears to be leading to a proper resolution, that resolution is in each case superseded by a moment of discomfort, a kind of inflection point where the curvature of the arc has vanished or is as yet undecided. What emerges is what Henri Lefebvre calls a "politics of the possible," which appears not at the level of the films' content but through their formal violation of genre norms—the explosion of conventions of the Robinsonade and the romantic comedy—and in the rejection of the logic of salvation. I argue that the films lay down the basis for moving beyond supposed universals of the national subject and the medicalized human body and toward a mapping of space beyond established sensibilities that bound what constitutes the human and its belonging with others.

In chapter 3, an analysis of Adam Johnson's fiction traced "words separated from their normal ambit,"[1] a fictional mode that intervened in the identificatory discourse of human rights and its constitution of subjects within the parameters of possible speech. There the wordless victim was paradoxically produced by a discursive framework that, in aiming to "give voice" to that victim, in fact gave all possible speech in advance, an overlap of speech and position that removes the capacity of the individual to exceed the common sense of the situation. A kind of transgression of identity was made possible through the appearance of impossible speech or a reordering of the sense of narrative language. In this chapter as well, we see subjects "out of place." These characters assume a capacity for speech intertwined with a mobility that exceeds the common-sense spatial logic that determines one's proper position in the social structure. Here it is not only the "orphan utterance" that wanders but also the characters themselves, an illegitimate or nonsensical mobility that "re-carve[s] . . . the space that is between bodies and that regulates their community," outlining, "on the topography of the community, another topography."[2]

The present chapter explores the possibility of reading contemporary South Korean cultural production outside of a framework of interpretation that identifies the subject tautologically, according to a spatio-cultural logic, and correspondingly delimits the possible meanings of that subject's speech. I provide a comparative reading of *Castaway on the Moon* (*Kimssi p'yoryugi*, dir. Yi Haejun, 2009) and *I'm a Cyborg, but That's OK* (*Ssaibogŭjiman kwaench'ana*, dir. Pak Ch'anuk, 2006), attempting to think through how these films represent a mode of relating that suggests

124   *Disturbing Sensibility*

a postnational or ecumenical sense of identity and belonging. This provides an opportunity to consider how film or art in general can formally convey a content that both reflects or stems from the reality of a situation—its historical linearity—and also exceeds the realist imperative to reproduce sameness. What is revealed is what Henri Lefebvre calls the "virtual" or the possible, a utopic dimension inherent in—but also impossible within—the place-specific situation of the present. What I find in tracing different levels of transgression in these films is a representation of otherness beyond the postcolonial ethical imperative to put oneself in the place of the other.

I look first at the establishment of distinct spaces in the two films—from an abandoned island in the middle of hyperurban Seoul to the cramped isolation of a high-rise apartment, from the fantastic space of the asylum in *Cyborg* to the isolation cells that separate the patients—and how the efforts made to cross the gaps between them critique the very discourses that establish categorizing space itself. The methods utilized by the characters to "step across" (*transgredi*) distance toward another—unconventional communication at a distance (telecommunication) in one case, the Freudian transference in the other—suggest discourses that exceed the particular cultural space of the films. These transgressions at the same time critique what David Palumbo-Liu calls "delivery systems," social discourses that establish purportedly universal norms "that convert otherness to sameness" and provide the boundaries and barriers to be transgressed. In this sense, it is important not to read these films, in their transgression of particular space, as advocates of the global. I argue instead that *Cyborg* and *Castaway* critique global delivery systems (national identity, urban space, psychiatry and health, and so on) in the process of pushing toward a new way of imagining being together.

I follow this with an analysis of transgression not as a simple "stepping across" but as a *violation* of space. First, the city space is infringed upon by the primitive island in *Castaway*, a violation that puts into motion a questioning of stable identities and the imagination of a postnational, postconsumer relationality between the two protagonists of the film. In *Cyborg*, it is the space of the human body that is transgressed, first in the fantasy of the patient who believes that she is nonhuman—or more precisely, a human supplemented by the nonhuman—and second

Disturbing Sensibility 125

in the (equally fantastic) surgery performed on her body to ensure that she can both retain her identity as a cyborg and survive (be healthy) as a human. If *Castaway* critiques urban-capitalized and nationalized identities, *Cyborg* exceeds the limits of the medicalized patient and calls into question psychiatry's somatic and normalizing understanding of health.

While these transgressions establish a basis for moving beyond supposed universals of the national and the medicalized human body, we also see a violation of genre norms, as conventions of the Robinsonade and romantic comedy are uncomfortably exceeded. Both *Cyborg* and *Castaway* refuse the narrative closure of redemption, evading a cure in the case of the former and love in the case of the latter, allowing a remnant of transgression to remain in each case that leaves the characters in crisis—"rescued" but still outside the norm, unsaved yet no longer in need of salvation. If the characters remain different, then the films themselves also reject generic sameness at the narrative level, formally mirroring their content and enabling an interpretive method to develop that attempts to map a space beyond established sensibilities of what constitutes the human and its belonging with others. Against the "voyage that finds back the places exactly as they were written about,"[3] that literally puts speech in its place, we see something like Schweinitz's "hybrid-genre cinema" with films that "conspicuously emphasize the lack of coherence" between different generic elements, seeking not "to immerse the viewer in a homogeneous 'possible world' of the imagination but present an exposed . . . construct of heterogeneous signs." One could say, he writes, that such films "create an intentionally *impossible* world."[4] Both *Cyborg* and *Castaway* reject the mode of silencing through total visibility we saw in the migrant labor fiction in chapter 1, transgressing form to allow for the generation of speech out of place and the appearance of subject positions not usually visible.

The relationship between the normal and the pathological is mapped onto topographical space in both films, and linked to the question of (national) community. If nationality is "constituted through representations of community conveyed through a regime of fantasies and conceptual forces . . . the sentimental feeling of the 'we' enabled by these regimes within modern national communities,"[5] then how do the characters transgress space, physical boundaries, taboos, and so on in an

126 *Disturbing Sensibility*

effort to establish a "feeling of the 'we'" beyond identification with the nation? If culturalism links ethnic, national, and linguistic identities and "postulates cultural difference only between the interior and exterior of a certain national or ethnic community,"[6] then how do these films question the capacity of language to communicate experiences that exceed both available concepts and existing norms?[7] If contemporary medical discourse objectifies and identifies the patient and paternalistically reduces the human being to the disease diagnosed, how do these films represent the invisible or unvoiced through the transgression of established boundaries or imaginations of subjectivity and community?[8]

We will examine the way that these films put forward their fictions—not as works of imagination or flights of fancy, but as *operative* in the sense that they actively construct situations, convoke populations, institute relations of inclusion and exclusion, and establish relations between situations and their meanings.[9] Both *Cyborg* and *Castaway* dramatize, topographically and topologically, the situation of subjects rendered or judged incapable of occupying "the space-time of political things"—rejecting the prohibition against considering "certain categories of people as political beings" and allowing them voice.[10] Rather than understanding these "light" films as apolitical, approaching from this angle allows us to see art as political not in its message but rather in how it configures space-time—how it brings about "a reframing of material and symbolic space." If politics is "the configuration of a specific space, the framing of a particular sphere of experience, of objects posited as common and . . . of subjects recognized as capable of designating those objects and putting forward arguments about them,"[11] then these films are political in their transgression and reframing of known space.

I assume a context of globality—that we are "all living in the same global 'situation.'"[12] At the same time, globalization, with its familiar universalization of particular discourses, is not treated as a free or progressive context. Rather, globalization interacts with national identities to enable a movement beyond identification with either, a way of "being together as social beings"[13] that emerges from what Palumbo-Liu calls the "vital resistance of otherness."[14] It is not only the resistance but also the prolongation of difference in these two films that points to Lefebvre's "worldwide" (*mondial*), which tends to "break obstacles, explode boundaries, and drag along that which opposes it." Though clearly not

Disturbing Sensibility   127

national, the reframed space of *Cyborg* and *Castaway* is also not precisely the real space of the global (deterritorialized space managed by national states). Instead, planetary space "gives itself to the human species as theater and scenario, field of the possible, and sudden appearance of the unforeseen."[15] The films consider certain possibilities that are "founded on [this global, empirical, historical] reality" but that also give us a "perspective on the real,"[16] a *virtual* and future-oriented take on postnational space and identity—an "enacted utopia"[17] that presents us with the possible object, a "constellation of [the] existing and nonexisting."[18] This then puts into motion "a process of alteration, a . . . process that alters the very distribution of resemblance and de-semblance, reality and appearance, and the intelligible and the sensible . . . which alters, at the same time, our very sense of the real."[19]

The characters in *Cyborg* and *Castaway* are characters who transgress, stepping across space, violating norms, exceeding the limits of the acceptable or probable. They are not only criminalized (penalized, incarcerated, isolated by the state and the medical establishment) but are also often invisible to those around them. They assume a capacity for mobility and act with a strange freedom through an unseeing social space (the city, the online community, the asylum and network of doctors), a system that does not register their presence or registers their presence only as that which must be isolated or expunged from the social body. The characters are thus not only alienated or incarcerated but finally exceed what Rancière calls the sensible itself, the "law that divides the community into groups, social positions, and functions. The law implicitly separates those who take part from those who are excluded, and it therefore presupposes a prior aesthetic division between the visible and the invisible, the audible and the inaudible, the sayable and the unsayable."[20]

As the characters make visible the invisible (with the telephoto lens in *Castaway*, or the transference in *Cyborg*), the films also visualize fantasy as inseparable from the filmic real and thus in and of themselves realize the unseen. In both form (visual and narrative style) and content, the films bring to light the discomfiting possibility of *something else.* If the sensible (or Palumbo-Liu's "delivery systems") consists of "the rational administration and control of social processes . . . the clear categorization of every individual, of every 'visible' social unit," then "disturbing

128 *Disturbing Sensibility*

such orders of the visible [audible, sayable] and proposing different lateral links of the visible, unexpected short-circuits, etc., is the elementary form of resistance."[21] Or as Rockhill puts it, the "essence of politics consists in interrupting the distribution of the sensible by supplementing it with those who have no part in the perceptual coordinates of the community, thereby modifying the very aesthetico-political field of possibility."[22]

The characters in *Cyborg* and *Castaway* transgress binaries of identification—sane/insane, human/nonhuman, city/country, healthy/sick, alone/together, social/asocial—and as a consequence these films are able to critically stage the development of an ecumenical community, outside the comprehension of existing categories of "same" and the "different" that make knowledge of the other possible. Ecumenopolitical space is therefore inherently transgressive, bridging real and virtual, praxis and theory—"at one and the same time product and work: an ensemble of places, and [the] result of a creative and thus artistic activity, both conscious and unconscious."[23] Discourse is mapped improperly or inaccurately onto space in these two films, beyond available concepts. In the resulting gap, we see that both present not only utopic space—nonspace—but also *eutopic* space, putting into motion those for whom mobility is not intelligible or permissible in the current configuration of the sayable.[24]

TRAVERSING SPACE IN *CASTAWAY* AND *CYBORG*

These two films may not at first glance appear to provide an opportunity for serious reflection of any sort. Presenting themselves as slightly offbeat romantic comedies, they are easily interpretable as lighthearted forays into the oddities of contemporary life through the perspectives of characters who are either figuratively or literally cast away from society. *Castaway* features Mr. Kim, a bankrupt and suicidal businessman (played by Chŏng Chaeyŏng) paired with a pathologically agoraphobic recluse, Ms. Kim (Chŏng Ryŏwŏn). *Cyborg* takes place in a mental asylum and focuses on the lives of inmates, notably Yŏnggun (Im Sujŏng)—who has been placed in the hospital after a suicide attempt following the institutionalization of her grandmother—and her fellow inmate Ilsun (Chŏng Chihun).

Disturbing Sensibility 129

The first step in thinking through the role of transgression in these films—and how that transgression might point to a possible understanding appropriate to a postnational global community—is to examine the apparently simple motion of "stepping across" that is emphasized in each film.

Castaway is grounded in the clever duality of its title. *Kimssi p'yoryugi*, more literally "a record of Kim adrift," can refer to either or both of the protagonists. Mr. Kim, whose credit card debt and failed romance (among other reasons) prompt him to attempt suicide by leaping from a bridge, regains consciousness only to find himself washed up on a deserted island in the middle of the Han River. Unable to swim and powerfully afraid of the water, he is trapped on the uninhabited island set literally in the middle of the teeming megalopolis of Seoul. At the same time, Ms. Kim resides on an island of her own making, a *hikikomori* isolated in the bedroom of her small apartment in a high-rise building overlooking the river. Her only contact with the outside world comes via social media, though she uses the text function on her mobile phone to communicate with her mother, who also resides in the apartment. The isolation of the characters is established early in the film—through the title, which suggests the story of the shipwrecked castaway, through the introduction of the unexpected island and the unlikely survivor Mr. Kim, and through the later introduction of the unmistakable *hikikomori*. The remainder of the story is the working out of a mutual exodus.

Castaway is set in motion by an initial egress. Mr. Kim's attempted departure from life results in his unexpected "going out" from the city (the establishing shot shows us the familiar skyline) and into the uninhabited space of the deserted island. Visually, we see the character transform from a modern, rational urban dweller—complete with suit, glasses, mobile phone, credit card debt, manners, and so on—to a barely clothed "savage," eating wild mushrooms for food until he gradually learns to forage and to catch and cook fish and birds to sustain himself. He takes up residence in an abandoned "duck boat" and—in pursuit of his dream of making a bowl of noodles (*jjajangmyŏn*) for himself—begins the process of sowing corn and other vegetables, of becoming self-sustaining. The tone of the opening scenes is humorous, stemming partly from the unexpected reversal—from suicide attempt to desperate attempt to hang on to life—and partly from the film's tongue-in-cheek

130 *Disturbing Sensibility*

take on the tale of survival. At the same time, a soteriological element of potential redemption is introduced early on, as Mr. Kim discovers a particular kind of edible plant—the salvia—and is moved to choose life over death by the sweet taste of the flower, the name of which derives from the Latin *salvere* (to feel healthy, to heal) or the noun *salus*, one possible meaning of which is "salvation."

After setting in motion the process of redemption for Mr. Kim, *Castaway* progresses by moving both central characters toward culminating moments of egress—departures from their situations of isolation. Following the opening sequences, we are introduced to Ms. Kim, also isolated but within an urban residential unit. Her communication with the outside world takes place online via an array of avatars, facades that hide her true identity and allow her to take on desired urbane or public characteristics that her isolation, asociality, and her scarred face will not allow in actuality. Both characters in a sense face self-imposed exile, and it is "going out" from this condition of isolation or invisibility that brings them together.

The transgression of the space between Mr. Kim and Ms. Kim takes place optically, in the voyeuristic relationship that Ms. Kim develops with Mr. Kim as she watches him through the telephoto lens of a camera that she uses primarily to photograph the moon. Two times a year—in the spring and in the fall, during the national civil defense drill, when the city streets are emptied of pedestrians and automobiles, Ms. Kim opens her curtains to daylight and photographs the deserted spaces of the city. The national defense ritual renders the earth alien and depopulated, a moonscape. The castaway, however, has slipped the bonds of nationality and remains active on his deserted island during the drill, and Ms. Kim's lens is drawn to him and the message he has written in English on the beach in large capital letters: "HELP." She grows increasingly fascinated by this alien life-form (*woegye saengmyŏngch'e*), and begins to interact virtually with him by interposing her finger between the lens and its target.

When the message carved into the beach changes from "HELP" to "HELLO," she is given the opportunity to make contact. Ms. Kim literally comes down to earth from the heights of her apartment building to deliver a message, inserted into a bottle and thrown onto the island (shown spinning across the backdrop of the city skyline). Her outfit as

Disturbing Sensibility   131

she leaves her apartment for the first time in years—a motorcycle helmet with reflective face shield, an umbrella to shield her from headlights and the gaze of passersby—marks her own status as an explorer on an alien world. While the distance between the two characters can initially be crossed only with the help of the telephoto lens, here communication begins the process of bringing the characters out of their respective isolation and into proximity.

It is in the process of their long-distance and faceless dialogue—exchanging messages such as "HOW ARE YOU?" or "FINE THANK YOU, AND YOU?"—that a crisis of identity develops. When queried "WHO ARE YOU?," Ms. Kim is unable to answer, unwilling to reveal her identity but also unwilling to present one of her avatars in response. The crisis of identity is embodied in the film by a storm that destroys Mr. Kim's carefully cultivated farm and dwelling. Agents of the government arrive for a cleanup operation on the public land and ask the same question of Mr. Kim: "Who are you? What are you doing here?" He is named "homeless" by the agents, despite his protests that this is his land—crucial not only because he feels that it is his home but also because his analog communication with Ms. Kim is predicated on his remaining rooted in this particular place.

After Mr. Kim has been rousted from his island by agents of the government and reenters the now-unfamiliar space of the city dirty, in the tattered remains of his suit and with a formidable beard, Ms. Kim gives chase, realizing that his departure from the island will make it difficult if not impossible to locate him again. Once again the national civil defense drill intervenes, causing Mr. Kim's bus to pull off the road and allowing Ms. Kim to cross a bridge—the moon visible in broad daylight and now returned to its proper location in relation to the earth—and catch the bus. Her appearance is disheveled, and the passengers on the bus greet her with stares and shocked silence. She introduces herself in English, giving him her proper name and asking again, "Who are you?" They exchange a smile, and as the bus lurches forward, grasp hands—the first face-to-face dialogue and physical contact between them coming in the last few seconds of the film.

In this way, *Castaway* brings together the two "aliens"—who continue to distinguish themselves from other city dwellers in their appearance, behavior, and even language—after a lengthy process of egress, of

132 *Disturbing Sensibility*

"going out." *Cyborg* works in much the same way, presenting two characters who must cross a gap and move toward relationality. In the case of the latter film, however, this stepping across is not a movement of egress but of *regress*, and the gap between the characters is crossed not through a voyeuristic optics and faceless communication but through the shared space of fantasy and the violation of the human body.

If "tele-" is a figure for the long-distance communication that crosses the space (along with the ironically tossed message in a bottle, a perfect medium for the island bound) between Mr. Kim and Ms. Kim in *Castaway*, then transference is the action that allows for intersubjective communication and relationality among the patients isolated in the space of the asylum in *Cyborg*. If *Castaway* begins with an initial egress, with *Cyborg* we have an opening regress as the film begins with the female protagonist Yŏnggun's admission to the psychiatric hospital following what appears to be a failed suicide attempt. Here she is introduced to a variety of patients suffering ailments ranging from mythomania and antisocial personality disorder to psychosis. Yŏnggun herself is being treated as delusional but also as anorexic, and much of the tension in the film revolves around the doctors' attempts to force her to eat. Yŏnggun believes that she does not require food because she is a cyborg, and goes about the asylum hallways at night talking to her fellow mechanical expatriates—the fluorescent lights, drink dispensers, and so on; she also carries a case of batteries that she periodically uses to "recharge" her energy.

The other patients understand Yŏnggun's fantasy as real and defend her right not to eat; in visual terms, the film also treats the delusions of the patients as real, presenting brilliantly conceived fantasy scenes woven together with more realistic or mundane moments in a way that brings them seamlessly into the narrative flow. It is this impulse to take seriously the fantasies of the characters, exhibited both in the community of patients and, formally, by the film, that is taken up by the male protagonist Ilsun.

Ilsun arguably occupies more the role of therapist than patient, and is sharply distinguished from the hospital's psychiatrists, who routinely adopt a medicalized mode of treatment in contrast with Ilsun's more psychoanalytic approach. Ilsun establishes a ritual with other patients wherein he adopts their symptoms—in one instance, he takes on a

Disturbing Sensibility 133

traumatized patient's tendency to take the blame for even the smallest transgression, adopting his behaviors (walking backward, thanking others profusely, being overly polite, constantly apologizing, etc.)—leaving that patient free of debilitating symptoms and, in a sense, cured. The transfer is symbolized through the painting of the patient's face and the exchange of a mask, and by a single word uttered by Ilsun at the moment of exchange: *chŏndal*, or "transfer."

Freud defines transference as the transfer of conflicts and related emotions onto the relationship between the analyst and analysand, an integral part of the psychoanalytic treatment and something that the analyst might point out to the patient, bringing to consciousness what had been repressed or unconscious.[25] Transference mediates between fantasy and reality, desire and obstacle: "The transference . . . creates an intermediate region between illness and real life through which the transition from the one to the other is made. . . . a *playground* in which it is allowed to expand in almost complete freedom and in which it is expected to display to us everything in the way of pathogenic instincts that is hidden in the patient's mind."[26] In *Cyborg*, the space of the asylum—brightly colored, populated by gardens and large, retrofuturistic metal structures—functions as such an intermediate region, a visual "playground" within which patients' fantasies are allowed some level of free expression. It is this environment that Ilsun utilizes in taking on the position of the analyst, actively transferring the patients' symptoms onto himself.

This is precisely the relationship that Ilsun strikes up with Yŏnggun, who is desperate to rid herself of empathy (*tongsimjŏng*) so that she can revenge her grandmother by killing the "whitecoats" who took the elderly woman (sans her dentures) from her home and institutionalized her. Ilsun agrees to "steal" Yŏnggun's empathy, and they enact the ritual of transfer in the subterranean steam tunnels beneath the well-ordered space of the asylum. Yŏnggun's subsequent attempts to carry out a massacre are vividly depicted in the sort of stylized violence that we are familiar with from director Pak Ch'anuk's work, but they all come to naught—she doesn't have the requisite strength to bring her fantasy to full realization.

Unlike the psychiatrists, who patronize Yŏnggun each time they speak with her, Ilsun enters further and further into her fantasy. The film makes clear, for instance, that he can actually *see* and *hear* the fantasy

134   *Disturbing Sensibility*

violence that ensues once she is freed of her empathy. Ilsun also insti-gates the asylum-wide hunger strike in protest of the plan to force-feed Yŏnggun. Finally, it is Ilsun who strikes upon a method for solving the contradiction of Yŏnggun's anorexia—you can be a cyborg and eat too, he tells her, and performs a "surgery" to install a "rice megatron" directly into her body, a tiny machine that will allow Yŏnggun the cyborg to pro-cess human food and use it for energy. Ilsun thus not only enters into Yŏnggun's fantasy but also trespasses upon her body, unclothing her and drawing a "door" on her back through which he pretends to insert the megatron.

The extension of his empathy across the boundaries that separate the inmates of the hospital ultimately yields a catharsis, a regression into Yŏnggun's past and an explanation for her psychosis. The playground of transference leads to the healing regression of catharsis. The film visu-alizes this at several points, including one fantasy where Ilsun holds Yŏnggun's grandmother in place (against the tension of an elastic band—signifying her mortality—pulling her into the distance) on a Swiss mountaintop so that Yŏnggun can have the final conversation with her that she's been denied throughout her incarceration; and the penultimate scene, which I will deal with below, where Ilsun and Yŏnggun return to the past and "translate" the grandmother's last words. Thus an initial regression—from rational human being to medicalized subject—is resolved through the transgression or "stepping across" of Yŏnggun's fan-tasy and her body, yielding a countering regression that mirrors the psy-choanalytic denouement of catharsis.

AGAINST THE NATURALNESS OF PLACE

If transgression in its simplest form—a stepping across—is central to the action and characterization of the films as demonstrated above, the films also announce the relevance of this *transgredi* to the relationships between human subjects as they become a medium exploring connec-tions between self and other. Here I turn to the ways in which space is utilized as a figure for relationality, before turning to a narrative analy-sis of the two films.

The work of art, David Palumbo-Liu holds in *The Deliverance of Oth-ers*, can help us to "meditate on the ways we are connected to, and act in

Disturbing Sensibility 135

relation to, others."[27] Though writing specifically on literary aesthetics, Palumbo-Liu's insight—that literature allows both the development of sameness, an overcoming of distance, and the elaboration and consideration of difference, in its presentation of those radically other from an "us"—can also be brought to bear on these two films and their dramatization of relationality. Literature "engenders a space for imagining our relation to others and thinking through why and how that relation exists, historically, politically, ideologically" and in turn "creates new forms of narration and representation."[28] At the same time, literature questions the consensual universality of categories, what Palumbo-Liu calls "delivery systems"—social discourses that "set conventions for both communication and behavior" and that create and maintain "norms that convert otherness to sameness," "tamping down" extreme behavior and readjusting the radical other to the "system of behaviors and emotional expression proper to society."[29] For Palumbo-Liu, these systems that bring us others include categories such as the rational, the family, the body, and the affective.

These films establish the relationship between self and other as a problem of identity formation that exceeds the national. In the following section, I show how *Cyborg* and *Castaway*, in violating our narrative and generic expectations, also move past a postcolonial ethics of "putting oneself in the place of the other" and suggest a radically other model of relationship. In the final section and following Lefebvre, I discuss how this model is based in the reality of the situations depicted but also signals possibility, a (virtual) postnational aesthetics beyond the empirical yet identifiable along the refractive surface of these films.

The question of identity is raised most overtly in the case of *Castaway*'s Ms. Kim, who has isolated herself in her bedroom and who interacts with the outside world via her computer through what she describes as her profession. This work consists of maintaining several identities and broadcasting (invented) activities for each. Here the medium, social networking software, does not allow an imagining of relationality for Ms. Kim, but rather gives her the opportunity to manipulate others' imaginings of her—a unilateral flow of information that dictates how others see her but behind which she cannot be seen.

For Mr. Kim, this situation is in a sense reversed—he is utterly unable to present any aspect of himself to "them," represented visually in the

136 *Disturbing Sensibility*

film by the cityscape that faces him mutely across the wide river separating his island from the mainland. He is shown shouting at the distant city, dropping his pants ("Can you see me now?"), attempting to flag down a tourist cruise boat, and so on, in each case unable to make any impression of himself on others. When the elements that provided him with a sense of identity in his life as an urbanite are stripped away—credit cards, national ID card, job, girlfriend—Mr. Kim becomes first invisible and then *something else*, what Ms. Kim sees through her telephoto lens, transformed from indebted, suicidal, "civilized" city dweller into a "perverse," "lonely"—incomprehensible, unintelligible—alien.

While distance is established between each character and others, this transformation of Mr. Kim into a survivalist—a free, agriculturally self-sustaining "primitive" island dweller—allows him to replace the "HELP" written on the beach with "HELLO," a new visibility that promotes, rather than discourages, relationality. The transformation also draws in Ms. Kim, a change visually indicated by the replacement of photographs of the moon obsessively pasted to her wall with photographs of the island and Mr. Kim. She begins to follow his attempt to survive on the island with a clinical interest that turns to imagined participation (her "physical" interactions with Mr. Kim through the interposition of her finger between the lens of her camera and the distant island) and eventually becomes communication and an egress from the small apartment bedroom into the wider city space. Put differently, the film dramatizes the overcoming of the exigencies of contemporary (urban) life—which produce alienation and distance—through an encounter with radical otherness, and the overcoming of distance and difference through imagined and then (in the final moment of the film) realized relationship.

In this way, an initial transgression of acceptable social behaviors—taking up life as a squatter on a deserted island in the Han River, or the radical isolation of the *hikikomori*—becomes the very basis for establishing what the film suggests is the possibility of relationality. Each character maintains "false" relationships with others until they pass beyond the limits of the acceptable, violate social norms, and find themselves "out of place." Social relationships are presented via spatial metaphor. The characters are visually separated from others in space (the locked room, the deserted island) and it is the overcoming of this distance, through

Disturbing Sensibility 137

the telephoto lens and then through the missions that the astronaut Ms. Kim makes onto the surface of an alien world (or, as she sometimes sees it, the moon) and the establishment of indirect communication that yields a sense of hope and belonging for both.

Norms of legal and evidentiary truth—we could say norms of realism—are not violated without consequence, however. Ms. Kim is eventually discovered behind her false fronts, and her multiple identities are cruelly dismantled amidst the revelation of her "lies." Mr. Kim is also discovered after a powerful storm destroys his home and crops, when a city cleanup crew arrives on the island. Netizens punish Ms. Kim in a scene that can be described as traumatizing, an unwanted revelation of her identity; while, as we saw above, Mr. Kim is punished by the invading city authorities, dressed in uniforms and military-style camouflage outfits, representatives of the state who chase him around the island and eventually corner him. His protestation against their identification of him as a homeless man or squatter, and their responses, are revealing. "Who are you?" they ask him. "What are you doing here?" "This is my land," he tells them. "I have to stay here." "You're not allowed to be here," they maintain. "This is a migratory bird sanctuary, off limits to the general public."

This is a remarkable moment. As a trespasser on the island, Mr. Kim is accused of being an outsider who does not belong; this very charge of not belonging in a particular place brings him into the "public" that is by definition excluded from the land. He is excluded from his dwelling place by virtue of this inclusion, compelled to adopt an identity that would eliminate the relevance of the island for him as home while awarding him a place in the national public.

The militarized cleanup crew eventually removes his tattered suit from the scarecrow where it had been repurposed, and dresses Mr. Kim in it. The significance is unmistakable: Mr. Kim is being forced back into the trappings of a scarecrow or hollow man, compelled to abandon his newfound identity as an island dweller and return to ordered space. In order to make him excludable from his island home, he is counted as part of the "general public" but is almost immediately excluded from that public when, without a home, he finds no place in it. He is only briefly intelligible as a subject—in Rancière's terms, he is brought into "the police figure of the population exactly identical to the counting of its parts" only long

138 *Disturbing Sensibility*

enough for that dominant order to exclude him as a "part of those who have no part."[30] Thus he finds himself deposited on a sort of bench in a street-side park, shoeless, filthy, dressed in a ragged overlarge suit—now appearing precisely as a "homeless man" in his proper nonplace amidst the well-ordered space of the city. His thoughts turn to suicide, and he boards a bus headed for the 63 Building, the emblematic skyscraper on the south side of the Han River from which he presumably intends to throw himself.

If the question of identity and overcoming distance between self (something) and other (something else) is taken up at the level of the plot in *Castaway*, in *Cyborg* the theme is introduced formally from the opening credits. A sequence of translucent gears and cogs reveals the names of those who have worked on and acted in the film—the inner workings of film production or the mechanics or technology "behind the scenes." The computer-generated machinery transposes into a scene of identically clad factory workers, assembling radios along a production line, while the nondiegetic music continues, linking the two scenes, and mingles with the instructions spoken through the factory loudspeaker. A third aural level breaks in, with the question "Were there any sudden changes in Yŏnggun's behavior prior to this?" We continue to watch the assembly of radios, while what we eventually learn is a conversation between Yŏnggun's psychiatrist and her mother continues as a sort of voiceover.

The functional, visual, and aural overlap continues throughout the opening scene, and a sense of confusion begins to emerge as voices overlap with spaces to which they do not obviously correspond or within which they are not strictly possible. The first contradictory claim is by Yŏnggun's mother, who holds that "Yŏnggun raised her grandmother" before correcting herself with, "No, I mean, my mother raised Yŏnggun," explaining Yŏnggun's tendency to talk like an elderly person. When the scene shifts to the psychiatrist's office, we continue to hear the instructions over the loudspeaker in the factory, linking together not only disparate spaces but also times. When the psychiatrist asks if she might meet the grandmother, it is revealed that the elderly woman has been institutionalized for dementia, after eating nothing but *mu* for six months. The psychiatrist's hesitation gives us reason to suspect ambiguity here, as *mu* commonly refers to "radish" but could also mean

Disturbing Sensibility 139

"nothing" (無), significant in that we later learn that Yŏnggun is diagnosed with anorexia.

Linguistic overlap continues as Yŏnggun's mother, a butcher, takes a call on her mobile phone—carrying on two conversations at once, she orders meat and continues to discuss her childhood headaches with the doctor, then mistakenly orders head meat (rather than tongue). Turning back to the story, we see the present-day mother speaking in the voice of her childhood, a young girl's voice emerging uncannily from the older woman's mouth. The sound from the factory continues into the flashback, as we see the younger mother discover her own mother feeding radish to a group of mice. Aural overlap continues as the character of the mother as a child speaks in the voice of the adult mother of the narrative present.

We return to the factory, hearing both the dialogue from the psychiatrist's office and the instructions over the loudspeaker, which begin to seem strange. The mother reveals that Yŏnggun's grandmother believed the mice to be her own offspring, and herself to be the "mother mouse" (at which point the camera focuses on the computer mouse that the psychiatrist is manipulating, adding to the sense of multiple, overlapping meanings). In the factory, Step 9 of the instructions is to "cut left wrist with knife," insert the stripped ends of wire, bind with duct tape, and plug into wall socket. The view shifts to the exterior of the factory (as lightning strikes and the lights flicker inside, suggesting Yŏnggun's electrocution but also the bringing-to-life of Frankenstein's monster), and we hear the psychiatrist ask: "Did Yŏnggun ever say she had a different sort of existence [that she was something else] as well?" "Never," responds her mother. "Yŏnggun is a human being." As the credits come to an end, a light bulb containing the title of the film, *I'm a Cyborg, but That's OK* spins into view on Yŏnggun's big toe just as her mother says, "She'll be OK, won't she?," providing the final aural overlap of the opening scene.[31]

This opening formally indicates the central theme of becoming something else, introducing the logic of the film and at the same time training the viewer to be attentive to overlap between generations, past and present, words (the same word spoken in another's voice, the same word taking on different significance depending on context), humans and animals, the mechanical and the human, and ultimately fantasy and reality (both the fantasy of the film itself and the fantasies of individual

140 *Disturbing Sensibility*

characters in the film). Form prefigures content—it is acceptance of the fantasy form that leads us into Yŏnggun's reality, and acceptance of her fantasy (via the transference) through which Ilsun is able to connect with and in a sense heal his patient.

Linguistic malleability persists throughout the film ("I'm not a *ssaik'o* [psycho], I'm a *ssaibogŭ* [cyborg]!" insists Yŏnggun, while her mother persistently mispronounces the term as *"ssaiborŭ"* [cybor]). Stylistically as well we see a tendency to blur the distinction between fantasy and reality. There is simply no clear boundary between scenes of the filmic "real" and scenes of fantasy. To take only one example, a patient is shown singing on a bench, apparently in the Swiss Alps, until our perspective narrows on her face, then pulls back to show that she's looking at herself in a mirror, and pulls back again to show the mural of the Alps painted on the wall behind her. We have no indication that our initial impression— that she is on a mountainside—is incorrect, until the film reveals its game. This *blind spot* that the viewer faces is similar to the blind spot that the psychiatrists encounter when they look at the patients. It is the mirror that is necessary to reflect what resides in the blind field, held in a position that allows a visual angle on or refraction of the object(s) otherwise unattainable. Both the failure of language as a communicative medium and the tendency to present "blindingly" positive representations of fantasy scenes mark such areas of occlusion.[32] The doctors also fail to communicate with their patients (or even with each other about their patients), narrating their ailments in medicalized terms, and they treat the patients paternalistically, blind to their fantasies.

The transgression of the body thus takes place at two levels that are overtly compared in the film: one based in the adoption of another's fantasy (Ilsun becomes the "doctor" who "operates" on Yŏnggun), and one a paternalistic interference on the part of the psychiatrists, who medicalize Yŏnggun and treat her as "the anorexic."[33] Anorexia is significant here partly because it bridges the psychic/somatic divide— treatment of the patient requires not only a medical act but also an engagement with the psyche.[34] This is not, however, how Yŏnggun's case is handled by the professional staff at the hospital. She is treated as a passive subject and made to endure electroshock therapy (EST), solitary confinement, and force-feeding through a nose tube. Ilsun's position— particularly during the absurd hunger strike that he organizes to protest

Disturbing Sensibility 141

the force-feeding—works against the operation of rational discourse (medicine, psychiatry) on the body of the patient, holding that it is unethical to intervene against the patient's wishes no matter the medical benefits. "All paternalistic interventions involve a restriction of freedom of action or of choice," and Ilsun defends Yŏnggun from this restriction of autonomy.[35] He works against the medicalized fixing of her identity by entering into (by *transgredi*, by violation) her fantasy, enabling her belief that she is a cyborg (body-as-fantasy), while ethically (nonpaternalistically, without medicalizing her body as an object of discourse) attending to her physical needs as a human being, supporting the "alternative meanings" through which she can therapeutically "reconstruct or reauthor" her life.[36]

With *Cyborg* as well as with *Castaway*, we see an imagination of relationality that exceeds the topological frameworks within which the subject is typically interpreted: one national, and one medical.[37] In the process of transgressing (national) space and (physical) boundaries, new forms of narration and representation are created that draw attention to the themes of self and other, of becoming another, and that are formally critical of the easy boundaries and identities established by dominant discourses of nation and medicine. The films processes of formal "transgression" that "outline, on the topography of the community, another topography,"[38] are paralleled in their narrative development, and below I demonstrate how the films veer from the expected track and themselves violate genre expectations. Violations of form paired with violations of narrative expectations combine to produce discomfort and to mitigate the reduction of the potential of the films to imagine the relation of self to (radical) other in an unfamiliar context, beyond both the particularity of the nation and the "sameness" of the global.

GENERIC TRANSGRESSIONS

The penultimate scene of *Cyborg* shows us Ilsun and Yŏnggun immediately following her resumption of eating and a cathartic session with Yŏnggun's still-uncomprehending psychiatrist. The two sit on a couch in a common room, Ilsun writing furiously on a piece of poster board. We learn that he is transcribing Yŏnggun's memory of the shape of her grandmother's lips silently mouthing words on the other side of a thick

142 *Disturbing Sensibility*

piece of glass, an event that furthermore took place in a fantasy that occurred while Yŏnggun was undergoing EST (a fantasy that in turn visually refers to a previous fantasy of being able to see her grandmother's lips moving silently through the glass rear window of the ambulance in which the "whitecoats" took her away).

On the one hand, this points to a major theme in the film, the separation of characters from one another at the level of verbal communication—the impossibility of speech. Whether in fantasy or in "real life," characters are separated from one another's spoken language on a consistent basis: cell walls, the thick glass of an incubator, the window at the back of an ambulance, distance, silence, mouth-covering masks, and so on appear with great frequency and literally prevent communication. At the same time, communication between doctors and patients is often completely impossible or consists of a series of miscommunications, owing to insurmountable differences in the discourses out of which each speaks—that is, a refusal on the part of the doctors "to hear the words exiting their mouths as discourse."[39]

On the other hand, Yŏnggun has been attempting to reach her grandmother and hear her final words regarding the meaning of existence throughout much of the film. Here, we can interpret the final scene as a culmination of this search, as the two main characters—now "healthy"—carry to fruition Yŏnggun's wish. Ilsun and Yŏnggun understand the transcription as a message from the grandmother regarding the meaning and purpose of Yŏnggun's life, and carry out those instructions *to the letter*. "You're a nuke bomb," the disjointed message reads. "Your purpose zov existence zis world zend. Knee da billion bolts." The final scene shows them on a mountaintop in a thunder-and-lightning storm, raising a metal antenna to the sky in order to gather the energy necessary—"a billion volts"—to, as the transcription commands, end the world. They fail, and the film ends with sunrise on the mountaintop and a startling rainbow arcing across the sky.

The closing moment of the film is discomfiting for a number of reasons. First of all, it defeats our expectations of a "happy ending," expectations raised by reference to the romantic comedy genre that the film generally holds to, "a film which has as its central narrative motor a quest for love, and which portrays this quest in a light-hearted way and almost always to a successful conclusion."[40] While the main characters seem to

Disturbing Sensibility   143

be together in the final scene, it is more in cooperation with one another than in a romantic unity. Second and also against the "happy ending" convention, the two fail in their bid to carry out the grandmother's instructions. Third, the instructions are themselves ominous in a way that reduces our pleasure in the union of the two characters around a common task.

Finally, and tying each of the above together, is Ilsun's continued devotion to Yŏnggun's fantasy. While consistent with his "treatment" of Yŏnggun throughout, his willingness to remain in the fantasy gives the ending a sense of irrationality, disrupting the salvific story of the cure that runs through the film. Her anorexia has been resolved, and her cathartic revelation to her psychiatrist that she is a cyborg seems to have her on the path to recovery as well. Yet here the fantasy persists—the goal is not a cure, but the "world's end." While this is consistent with Pak Ch'anuk's statement that "this movie is not interested [in] the concept of a cure,"[41] it raises the uncomfortable question of how the film's "couple of the year" (per the marketing for the movie upon its release) will continue on in their relationship from this point forward. Will it not be an exhausting life, to persistently maintain Yŏnggun's fantasy? This defeats our expectations, which were engendered by the parallel narrative arcs of cure and romance, neither of which are brought to a satisfactory conclusion.

If *Cyborg* pairs the development of romance with a curative process, *Castaway* focuses on a romance developed over time in the context of a survival story—a story of mutual rescue. As we have seen, Mr. Kim and Ms. Kim can each be seen as castaways. At the same time, the film plays with the conventions of the tale of survival, commenting on its form even as the development of the story depends on the tension around the rescue of each character from their respective but increasingly linked predicaments. In this sense, we can think of *Castaway* as a Robinsonade, "often also referred to as 'desert-island romance,' 'survival story,' or 'castaway story,'"[42] and which might be defined as "a story or an episode within a story where an individual or group of individuals with limited resources try to survive on a desert island."[43] Broadly speaking, the Robinsonade "repeats the themes of *Robinson Crusoe*; usually it incorporates or adapts specific physical aspects of Crusoe's experience and is an obvious rewriting of the Crusoe story."[44]

144 *Disturbing Sensibility*

The story of a "civilized man" marooned on a desert island, encountering the "primitive," and wrestling with solitude and survival has been written in faithful adherence to Defoe's original text or rewritten with an ironic and often postcolonial distance, as with J. M. Coetzee's *Foe*, Derek Walcott's *Pantomime*, or Marianne Wiggins's *John Dollar*.[45] This "rewriting" has been a key concept in postcolonial literary criticism, and generally constitutes a revision or restaging of the imperialist work in ways that both call attention to the original's complicity (with empire, with colonial epistemologies, and so on) and exploit or expose those aspects of the original text in ways critical of that complicity—a shift "from *original inscription* to parallel script."[46]

Castaway appears to fall into the latter category in its lighthearted approach to Mr. Kim's island survival story, made clear, for instance, in his frequently comedic voiceover. However, the film exceeds a specifically postcolonial critique. Tension persists not between Mr. Kim and island-dwelling natives or other representatives of the primitive, but between the castaway and the city, a constant and ironic backdrop to his efforts. Further, as seen above, Mr. Kim struggles with representatives of the nation, evicted from the island precisely because it is in the possession of the state, an emblem—as public land set aside for the citizenry—of civilization.

This double reversal calls into question who is civilized and who is primitive, and certainly the film plays with this problem—for instance, in Mr. Kim's efforts to establish a self-sustaining agriculture on the island and Ms. Kim's mimicry of this in her bedroom, where she grows corn seeds in empty canned-corn tins. At the same time, the romance that develops between Mr. Kim and Ms. Kim depends in large part on their status as outsiders, and it is in the closing scenes that Ms. Kim is able to trace Mr. Kim through his difference—made visible in the process of his double displacement—from other occupants of the space of the city. Having watched his eviction from the island through her telephoto lens and realizing that she will lose all contact with him now that he is no longer immobilized, she runs from her building and, nearly struck by a passing car, gives chase. Losing her way at one point, she hears a well-dressed couple remarking, "He's like Tarzan, practically a savage," and is able to follow the "uncivilized" trail that he leaves as a twice-homeless outsider in the city.[47]

Disturbing Sensibility   145

Ms. Kim is aided for the second time by the civil defense drill, which causes Mr. Kim's bus to pull to the side of the road and allows her to catch up. Here again, an easy distinction between national and postnational is difficult—it is the seasonal ritual of the civil defense drill that brings the couple together in the first place and here brings them together at last—their outsider status exceeds, but is also enabled by, the context of both the city and the nation-state. She boards the bus, and introduces herself to Mr. Kim, in English, giving her birth name and asking, "Who are you?" The conversation is viewed by the busload of passengers, properly immobilized by the state ritual and stunned into silence by the events unfolding before them, an unintelligible scene of the illegitimate seizing of mobility paired with an incomprehensible speech situation. The contrast between the two "castaways" and the city dwellers is made even more conspicuous by their choice of English.

But this confluence of two soteriological narrative arcs—the mutual rescue of the civilized from the uncivilized (from isolation and into community) and the development of a romantic relationship between the two main characters—is disrupted in the final moment of the film, when the bus jerks unexpectedly back into motion, and the two Kims, gazing into each other's eyes, are compelled to grasp hands in order for Ms. Kim to keep her balance. Their grimaces of happiness and tears of cathartic relief are replaced by a shocked, wide-eyed silence as they make physical contact for the first time, and it is at this point that the film closes. It is an uncomfortable moment that raises the same quotidian questions as *Cyborg*'s conclusion: What now? How will this new community of two survive? Will their radical otherness be absorbed into the sameness of the city and the national community? Will they remain together in isolation? We are left with one of *Cyborg*'s refrains: "Give up hope," Yŏnggun is told, "but give it all you've got!"[48]

The happy ending here remains elusive at nearly all levels: we are uncertain as to the proper definitions of the civilized and the primitive; we are uncertain about the resolution of the romantic subplot; and we are skeptical of the capacity of the rescue to perpetuate the continued survival of the characters in the hostile environment of the megalopolis. As in *Cyborg*, this film refuses narrative closure and the satisfaction of redemption. The characters do not "put themselves in the place of the other" but rather enable each other's radical and discomfiting otherness.

146   *Disturbing Sensibility*

They struggle toward community and belonging, but the stories end with continued (if shared) isolation, while genre conventions are rejected in place of indeterminacy. If, as Palumbo-Liu argues, "delivery systems" such as those referenced in the films—medicine, love/affect, the urban, national community, literary convention—are designed to convert otherness to sameness, then against this we find instead portrayals of an interaction with the other that is "radically altered," one that raises a dispute, makes a problem, puts "ethical choices . . . into crisis."[49] Their stories are not woven into familiar narratives and thus made familiar in their difference—the operation of the realist text—but rather insist on sustained difference within the apparently familiar, and in the process raise questions of how one comes into community with another in a setting that is at once specific and general, the shared situation of globality.

THE POLITICS OF THE POSSIBLE

In *Cyborg* and *Castaway*, minor transgressions (from errors in pronunciation to unpaid credit card debt) are paired with major encroachments—the appearance of an uninhabited island at the center of the city in *Castaway* and the mechanical at the very heart of the human in *Cyborg*. Through this pairing, the minor transgressions become major—the main character of *Cyborg* insists that she is not "psycho" but "cyborg" and is incarcerated in the asylum, while the male lead in *Castaway* is marooned on the inexplicable island, adopting the identity of a castaway. Both plots thus involve the radical separation of the individual from the social.

The films suggest that the redemptive return to sociality is achieved not through the retraction of transgression but rather through its validation. Transgressions of the body (by the mechanical) and the cityscape (by the primitive) are naturalized, as the overcoming of preestablished boundaries becomes a figure for relationality in a global era. Yet, transgression in each film is not treated as an event the solution to which brings a comfortable retention of preexisting boundaries or categories; rather, it takes place within a globalized context that has already eroded these boundaries. "Aren't we all living in the same global 'situation?'" Palumbo-Liu asks, and the films echo this in content and form— normative discourses (psychiatry, urban space, literary tropes and

Disturbing Sensibility   147

conventions) are not limited to any particular place. At the same time, the universality of the sensible and its "delivery systems" come under critique, and we can see the films—in their treatment of the theme central to both, the ethics of the relationship between self and other— moving toward something beyond the global, some other way of relating to another, some other way of conceiving community.

Both *Cyborg* and *Castaway* make transgression the basis for transformation into something else without celebrating it as an iconoclastic principle of political action. While the characters transgress physical and psychical boundaries, the films themselves trespass on our genre expectations, playing on formal innovations that call attention to slippages and gaps in language not only to emphasize themes of identity and difference but also to undermine our confidence in representational veracity and interpretive certitude. Here speech emerges without a place, from the mouths of those "just like speaking beings" who are themselves no-place, or out of place—a *literariness* that "undoes the relationships between the order of words and the order of bodies that determine the place of each." In *Cyborg* and *Castaway*, not only are "words separate from their normal ambit"[50] but space too is delinked from the usual logic of origin and destination, "another topography" mapped out on the existing lay of the land that calls into question the naturalness of place and the relationship between the order of words and the order of bodies.[51]

Narrative arcs of love and cure—arcs of redemption—are disrupted at the very moment of the characters' coming together. If these films resist the "delivery systems" of nationalist and medical discourse through the transgression of space and bodies and of expectations regarding the separation of fantasy and reality through their form, we also then see resistance against the "delivery system" of narrative itself, its norms of communication and action that might "convert others to sameness." While the narrative arc in each film appears to be leading to a proper resolution, in each case that potential resolution is superseded by a moment of discomfort, a kind of inflection point where curvature has vanished or is as yet undecided.

I have drawn on Palumbo-Liu's work on self and other in a global era and particularly on his reading of cultural texts as both as registers of this new situation and as a means of imagining ways of "being together" appropriate to the postnational. At the same time, these films arguably

148 *Disturbing Sensibility*

move beyond a question that limits his analysis, that of "how . . . we regulate the influx of otherness so as not to destabilize the system."[52] At levels of both content and form, these films provide a systematic disruption that pushes against the boundaries of intelligibility, leaving us in a sense with "too much otherness." In Palumbo-Liu's model, literature is transgressive because its perspective is exterior to the system, and is consequently able to show "another way of conceiving . . . relations between people."[53]

Certainly one key aspect of these two films is that "there is no outside"[54]—the island emerges unexpectedly at the heart of the city, the *hikikomori* experiences alienation in the midst of tens of millions, and the patients are released from the asylum only in shared fantasies of escape and freedom. Even as we are confronted with the insistent voices of those who have no grounds to speak and the mobility of those who have no right to move, the political subjects of these films emerge at the very heart of things, not ex nihilo but created "by transforming identities defined in the natural order of the allocation of functions and places into instances of experience of a dispute."[55]

Thus, while the virtual *possible* emerges from within the real as a transgressive fantasy, it is important to point out that these transgressions span a distance not from inside and outside but an imaginative distance between self and other, the result of attempts to communicate with—to join the fantasy of—those who are radically other. It is in this sense that I read the films as utopian, as presenting a "no place" that "seeks a place of its own." The island, the isolated apartment, the asylum with its subterranean steam tunnels, the mountaintop on which *Cyborg* comes to a close—these are utopic spaces *at the heart of the real*, revealed in the filmic process of transcending "the closed and the open, the immediate and the mediate, near and far orders within a differential reality."[56]

In his analysis of the worldwide, Lefebvre advocates a "politics of the possible," a movement toward "unrealized possibilities embedded within extant social and political institutions."[57] From within the worldly and the representable emerges that which was previously unsayable, the possible that is exposed in transgression. It is this *"possible* considered at one and the same time as founded on reality, and as perspective on the real"[58] that emerges in *Cyborg* and *Castaway* to point to the imagination

Disturbing Sensibility 149

of future identities but also to shed light on the present and the past.[59] These films draw us into fantasy in a way that produces discomfiting anxiety around the potential fulfillment of that desired future.

If the essence of politics is this interruption of sensibility, the troubling of those who count and those who do not, and the formal disruption of the normative gap between the visible and the invisible through the inclusion of "those who have no part in the perceptual coordinates of the community"[60]—the castaway, the antisocial asylum inmate, the psychotic, the *hikikomori*—then these films work toward a virtual or possible mode of human relations that, following Doxiadis, we might provisionally call "ecumenopolitical." For Doxiadis, the ecumenopolis—the world or universal city of the future—is a fine-grained space, a continuation of "man's desire to overlap as many . . . personal kinetic fields as possible,"[61] yet a space that signals a moment of crisis and dissociates humans from one another, requiring intervention "so that man who, at present, sees his values disintegrating around him, may be able to find them again."[62]

Within a city made of the world—the world made city, the world-made city—the two films resist the idea of globalization-as-homogenization through the representation of a disorganization of spaces of sameness. At the same time, they exceed a compartmentalization of space that would mesh seamlessly with accepted discourses of national or bodily normality, in the cohabitation of cyborgs and humans, the violation and manipulation of bodily cavities and organs, or the reduction of distance between the castaway (the "local") and the ("cosmopolitan") isolate.[63] If settlements are a "biological extension" of humans or "macrobiological systems,"[64] then we can read the disruption of both urban space (through the intrusion of the island) and bodily space (through the insertion of the machine) as parallel indicators of an unsettling shift beyond the familiar.

The films thus challenge not only sensibility but also the methodology through which we approach national cultures and the relationship between art and politics. If *Castaway* and *Cyborg* insist on a sustained difference within postnational space, then clinging to what Jusdanis sees as the false ecumenicity of comparison[65] produces a blind spot that prevents us from seeing the *possible object*, outside of empirical fact yet not fictional in the sense of being imaginary.[66] At the same time, such a

150 *Disturbing Sensibility*

blind spot itself indicates the need for a refractor, a parallax view that calls attention to a shift not only in the object viewed but also in the subjective position of the viewer.[67] National as well as postcolonial analyses, with their insistence on cultural authenticity,[68] are reductive of an emerging reality based not in the local (with its logic of distinction) but the worldwide.

Conclusion

> The iridescence that emanates from artworks . . . is the appearance of the affirmative *ineffabile*, the emergence of the nonexisting as if it did exist. Its claim to existence flickers out in aesthetic semblance; yet what does not exist, by appearing, is promised. The constellation of the existing and nonexisting is the utopic figure of art.
>
> —THEODOR ADORNO, *AESTHETIC THEORY*

Impossible Speech has introduced works of literature and film that present figures understood in advance as political: the foreign migrant laborer, the traumatized victim of state violence, the North Korean defector or escapee, and those "cast away" from the social, including the urban precariat and the mentally ill. Assigning speech to such characters is often understood as a political act. The artwork is then received as evidently political on the basis of its surface presentation of such figures, revelatory of a politics conventionally defined as "the set of procedures whereby the aggregation and consent of collectivities is achieved, the organization of powers, the distribution of places and roles, and the systems for legitimating this distribution."[1] Against such a politics of art, which in its pervasive realism and drive to make visible relies on the identification of characters within a pre-given situation who must perform correctly and in accordance with a "verisimilar tale of social necessity,"[2] I have followed Rancière in understanding politics as a speech situation—as the very decision on what may be said, seen, or heard in a given situation, an adjustment in the configuration of sensibility linked to a configuration of subjects.

This has led me to focus for the most part on texts that resist the archive, that "system that governs the appearance of statements and generates social meaning,"[3] a set of norms that "precede the possibility of description" and structure the sense of statements in advance.[4] Such a structuring force exhibits a greater polarity in response to language that threatens established boundaries of the sayable. We have seen this force emerge, sometimes unexpectedly, in any number of ways: in the quiet avowal of the link between the "tie of language" and the "tie of blood" in migrant labor fiction that ostensibly aims at eradicating cultural-linguistic difference; in the confidence that there is "nothing left to be said" about the Kwangju uprising and massacre, that the event is fully visible in speech that is fully legislated; in the compulsory discursivity of human rights discourse and the common plot of the defector narrative that must give a "full and truthful picture of life in North Korea" and in the drive to read fiction about North Korea as witness testimony; and in the salvific, normative logic of the well-ordered society in which the good of "keeping one's place" is reflected both in the organized space of the city/asylum and in the narrative arcs of cure and romance.

Where such a force gives meaning, we have seen that it often does so by capturing the contingent or the apparently inexplicable in a familiar form. Trauma, autobiography, confession, the Robinsonade, and the romantic comedy work to place characters into roles corresponding to a generic norm and to achieve a kind of consensus, a term also borrowed from Rancière and signaling an identity between the verisimilar and the necessary or the real and the possible.[5] Examples of such "possibilized" speech woven into the preceding chapters demand that the literary or film work take on the status of document, subjected to a logic of proof and read on the basis of evidentiary standards. This in turn yields what Nichanian, writing of the Armenian genocide, calls "realist shame"—the "shame of testimony" compelled to express the inexpressible in order to satisfy the archival drive and to reach consensus where consensus should never be reached. This persistent demand for the real in language yields the "primary transformation of testimony into a discourse of proof and its engulfing into the archive, through which the survivor is literally deprived of his own memory"[6] in the name of the transparent communication of full and factual knowledge.

Even as they dispute the limits of the sayable, these examples from literature and film have in no way denied the actuality of the subject

Conclusion   153

matter they deal with. It is not a matter of denying the existence of any truth, or submitting subjects to some free play of meaning. Rather, in each case, by bringing those not expected to speak or act onto the stage, they introduce a certain constitutive ambiguity in the formal representation of that subject matter, a gap between the signifier and the referent that destabilizes consensual meaning. Mark Anderson points out that the epigraph to the first story in W. G. Sebald's *The Emigrants* can be translated in at least two different ways, due to a grammatical ambiguity in the German.[7] "Zerstöret das Letzte / die Erinnerung nicht" can be rendered as "Doesn't memory / destroy the last remnants?" or as "Destroy every last thing / [but] not memory."[8] This ambiguity captures the dilemma that each chapter raises. Memory is that which must not be destroyed—the fictional texts analyzed above are drawn again and again to the event of atrocity, whether in the past or threatening the present. At the same time, as Sebald also points out, forcing speech—saying something that cannot be described, bringing into speech "experiences exceeding what is tolerable,"[9] actually *erases* memory,[10] occluding the event, whether in the form of stereotypical memories,[11] "characteristic turns of phrase,"[12] or "routine accounts of human suffering."[13] Memory, or memorization, destroys "the last remnants." At work is a kind of pre-censorship,[14] a determination in advance of the limits of meaning, an establishing of the boundaries of the sayable that exclude, obnubilate, produce a "scandalous deficiency"[15] in its memorization of the past.[16] We are left with a kind of voyeurism, pictures of massacres treated as "pornography."[17]

Thus, in each chapter, we have seen both a drive to approach and to *make* the event or the subject *appear*, and at the same time a resistance against a communicative model of language that takes the content of the material to be everything and its form to be nothing.[18] In this resistance, a gap opens between making visible and making invisibility impossible; and between an incapacity of speech—"the silences, throat clearings and coughs, hesitations, stitched loosely together"[19]—and a compulsory discursivity that makes not-speaking impossible, determining the parameters within which speech will be intelligible and forcing speech to occur within those parameters. What is also resisted is an easy *understanding* of the subject, whether the foreign migrant laborer, the victim of the historical disaster of Kwangju, the prisoner of a North Korean long-term

154   *Conclusion*

labor camp, the homeless man in the well-ordered space of the city, the shut-in confined to her room and dreaming of a depopulated and razed urban landscape, or the patient deemed antisocial and psychotic who is incarcerated and subject to an electroshock therapy that resembles, in its own way, a device meant to restore the patient to a sense of shared reality signaled by the correspondence of language with the already known.[20]

The issue has not been to read these texts for what they make visible, but rather to read for points of resistance against attempts to make invisibility impossible, against the obscuring consensus that forecloses the possible senses of language. Chapter 1 illustrated the "pre-censorship" that Sebald describes—the "apparently unimpaired ability . . . of everyday language to go on functioning as usual" in the face of "experiences beyond our ability to comprehend," the inability of eyewitness accounts to exceed the "bounds of verbal convention," and the capacity of such conventional language to "banish memory."[21] Through the conceit of fantastical translingual fluency, unbounded by ethnic or national qualification and presented in the seamless language of the narrator, the migrant laborer protagonists are paradoxically reduced to mute bodies. Here the anxious effort to "break the silence" of the migrant laborer runs aground on the continued identification of speech with ethnic-national community and the monolingualism that operates on the very surface of the text. Despite efforts to make the foreign laborer visible, she literally disappears by the end of the text, dissolved into the straightforward telling of a "verisimilar tale of social necessity" in perfectly conventional language.

The idea that speech may be "possibilized" in a way that silences the subject continued into chapter 2, which opened with Moon Jae-in's addresses on the state's annual observance of the Kwangju uprising and massacre. Here the historical entered into the dynamic of visibility and invisibility. The question was not only to define all possible speech related to the disaster, including the definition of the impermissible speech of the Kwangju deniers, but also to make the event fully visible through the historiographic presentation of facts in the most realistic language possible. In this way, the state may declare the event to be fully known, over and done with, even as it repeatedly returns to Kwangju as a founding trauma, the "spirit of May" that legitimates a present-day organization of the national community. Such discourse legislates the

Conclusion 155

boundaries of the sayable with its memorization of the past, a reiteration that in its production of a numbing loss of memory paradoxically defies Moon's injunction that we "never forget."[22] Against this common sense, *A Boy Is Coming* insists that the traumatic past remain unrepresentable while accepting the ethical task of approaching the event again and again in order to "write it properly." Here the image of the past pierces— rather than standing as a stable, fully-known origin of—the present moment, enacting a refusal to "destroy memory" while at the same time expanding the potential politics of Kwangju outside of the narrow boundaries of nationalist history. What we see in Han's novel is the representation of erasure or silencing that does not deny the historicity of the event but rejects the translation (or foreclosure) of speech into something that would *make sense* of atrocity.

If chapter 1 addresses the disappearance of the political subject in the possibilization of all speech and chapter 2 interrupts the total visibility of Kwangju by focusing on a literary narrative that pushes back against the easy achievement of consensus and meaning around historical disaster, chapter 3 looks to representations of North Korea to identify the particular horror that emerges when the realist dream of the complete overlap of speech and reality is achieved. Against a human rights discourse that aims to make the subject visible through an absolute accountability to their speech—speech seized and deemed true or false in a situation totally saturated by the account of the defector or escapee—fiction disturbs an identificatory logic by allowing the political subject to emerge in a "denial of an identity given by an other."[23] Adam Johnson's North Korea fiction challenges both the link between ways of saying and ways of being assigned to the bodies of North Koreans, and the expectation that facticity itself be produced in the testimony of the escapee.

As Johnson's fiction undermines the expected veracity of the genres of biography and confession, chapter 4 exploits the generic expectations of the Robinsonade and the romantic comedy. Against the normative logic of consensus or identification that "puts everyone in their place" in a well-ordered society, *Castaway on the Moon* and *I'm a Cyborg, but That's OK* operate via a logic of spatial and linguistic transgression that ultimately rejects the telos of salvific narratives of rescue, cure, or love. Such transgressions (both spatial and generic) work to make place unintelligible, tracking those who are "out of place"

156 *Conclusion*

and enacting a critical failure in the overlap of symbolic and material space. The protagonists of these films have disappeared or have been segregated from social space and have experienced a concomitant condition of unintelligibility. Yet far from "giving voice" to these marginalized subjects, the films refuse in the end to bring the characters into the communicational language of common sense. Instead, a blind spot remains that prevents us from seeing the possible object outside of the grid of empirical fact yet also gives us something approaching the "constellation of the existing and nonexisting" that is Adorno's utopic figure of art.[24] What is revealed is the relationship between the rules of speakability and the assignment of one's position or place. In a sense, one must keep one's place and speak from that place in order for one's words to be heard and understood, and in order to retain the rights assigned to the one occupying that place or position. Following from *The Orphan Master's Son*, the films of chapter 4 reveal again that identity rooted in culture or place is another aspect of sensibility, linked to speech in the establishment of sense and non-sense.

The goal has been to undertake the difficult task of approaching the moment where the fictional text produces an "imbalance in the legitimate order of discourse"[25] over and against a consensus that would frame the boundaries of intelligible language and reaffirm identities conforming to the common sense of the community. At the same time, none of the works examined have in fact exceeded familiar speech. None are written in a strange, alien language. Where a "storming of language"[26] has occurred, it has emerged from *within* logics of monolingualism (the tie of blood and language), historiographic truth, witness testimony, and social normativity. Each of these logics seeks to fix, to define, to identify—to link, as Rancière has it, a way of speaking with a way of doing and a way of being. Each of these logics *silences* the subject in its own way: overwhelming the speech of the other through the representational authority of the author or narrator; determining the limits of permissible speech under the historiographic imperative; subjecting witness testimony to judgment based, in the end, on the demand for absolute correspondence between word and thing, the probative value of the language derived from its representation of a real that cannot not be; and through the appearance of heterologous political subjects from the tight grid of the asylum or the administered space of the city.

Conclusion 157

Consequently, my readings have not been suspicious or "ideological"—I have not sought some truth of the text as (intentionally or unconsciously) concealed beneath the obscuring form of the artwork. Instead, I have looked for the sense of the text on its surface, so to speak—in the operations by which the text establishes the logic of a situation, and positions its characters to speak (or not) or act (or not) within the rationality of that situation. We have seen many examples: Kim Ŭnsuk, who works with the words of others, transcribing silent speech onto the page of Han's fiction; Pak Jun Do/John Doe, who exists between names and who transcribes the words of others, even those of his captor at the moment of torture; those abandoned on unpopulated islands in the Han River, in the cells of the asylum, in the locked rooms of high-rise apartment buildings who develop their own language and, as a result, their own sense of community. It is not a linguistic determinism that is at work here, but the establishing of logics of speech within which new subjects may emerge who stretch or fracture the existing and well-ordered logics of genre and society. The experiences these characters undergo are linguistic in the sense that they do not happen outside of "established meanings," but neither are they fully "confined to a fixed order of meaning."[27]

Each text calls out to be read as politically engaged not in terms of its content, but in that each puts forward a situation in which language—no matter in how familiar a way it appears or is used—is in dispute. As noted above, I have leaned throughout on Rancière's definition of politics as a speech situation, a dispute over the bounds of what constitutes intelligible speech and the subjects who are allowed to, or charged with, speaking intelligibly. This does not take place outside of known language, but occurs within the fixed order that nonetheless does not fully confine it. As we saw so clearly in *Castaway on the Moon*, the appearance of the subject is not the descent of the alien new into an existing reality, but emerges from within it, from the very center of things.[28]

Such an approach may be charged with making the problem overly complex. After all, doesn't "impossible speech," no matter how destabilizing initially, become frankly "possible" at the moment of its utterance? Yet the works of fiction and film that I've tried to address here aim precisely at that boundary, to make complex the moment when language enters into consensus. It is the habit of dominant discourse to

158   *Conclusion*

achieve hegemony "precisely by its capacity to convert, recode, make transparent, and thus represent even those experiences that resist it with a stubborn opacity."[29] Impossible speech becomes possible in its utterance—it may be captured, archived, or authorized as soon as it appears. But each chapter has attempted to grasp the performance of the moment in which the utterance calls into question its grounds of legitimacy and, in doing so, adjusts the terms of that legitimacy as an effect of its own performance.[30] Unauthorized speech assumes authorization in the act of its performance and, in doing so, challenges the boundaries that determine what counts as discourse.

Throughout the book, I have tried to provide examples that take advantage of the inherent capacity of fiction to challenge "possible" speech normatively structured in advance and to oppose the lines drawn by foreclosure by redrawing those lines.[31] This redrawing is the occasion of "impossible speech," where those not asked, expected, or authorized to produce discourse do so nonetheless, challenging the grounds upon which what is deemed sayable, hearable, or visible are decided. Whether the refusal of testimony and expansion of "Kwangju" in *A Boy Is Coming*, the logic of naming and the determining power of story in *The Orphan Master's Son*, or the displacement and transgression by which the narratives progress in *Castaway on the Moon* and *I'm a Cyborg, but That's OK*, these works are understood to be putting forward formal arguments that alter both how the content is to be received and the boundaries of the genres that typically determine the possible range of meaning. Part of the task of the book, then, has been to recognize the complexity of literary and filmic representation and to come to some idea of fiction that allows for a politics beyond the commonsense definition of the term. *Impossible Speech* is oriented against a naïve realist reading of literature that draws a one-to-one correlation between the text and some extratextual reality and assumes that political art is that which deals with subject matter already considered political. Instead, I understand politics as a fight for the propriety of speaking itself,[32] a struggle that perhaps best takes place in the work of imaginative art not absolutely reducible to a given reality.

The preceding chapters review works that delink the question of representation from the question of referentiality[33]—or better, insert the requirement of interpretation between the word and the thing,

Conclusion 159

wrenching open a gap between the real and the possible. Each of the core chapters marks a moment in which the text resists the archival demand or the realist imperative, the insistence that the artwork participate in bringing the event or object into full visibility. Each chapter breaks with the "naturalness of a place" or identity and the speech that links them: with regimes of victimhood and trauma, regimes of compulsory discursivity and the demand for testimony, and with regimes of social normativity. Interpretation becomes necessary when comfortable generic forms, which tend to guarantee the truth of the narrative, are undermined by "illegal" texts that rove within their boundaries and challenge the project of understanding itself. "What counts, when one attempts to elaborate an experience, is less what one understands than what one doesn't understand," Lacan writes. "Interpreting is an altogether different thing from having the fancy of understanding. One is the opposite of the other."[34] The point is not to deny the historical world of facts, but to recognize what Claude Lanzmann called the "obscenity of understanding," the obscenity of any attempt to bridge the gap between atrocity and its *engendering* out of prior causes—the attempt to give a context that allows explanation of that which brooks no explanation. Such an attempt constitutes "obscenity as such"—it establishes the intelligibility of atrocity in its very communication, a logic of cause and effect that *makes sense* of that which sense must not be made of.[35] In the difference between interpretation and explanation, where the former recognizes the gap between what one sees or hears and the meaning that is attributed to it, we find an imperative to avoid reducing the event or the subject to the surely known, placed comfortably into a situation or context by which cause and effect can be clearly described— the transformation, as Nichanian puts it, of "the 'mneumogenic' narrative into a discourse of proofs."[36]

I have noted that "impossible speech" is not speech that is strictly "not possible," nor is it the successful representation of fantastic or impossible content.[37] Impossible speech does not signal a kind of unrepresentability, something that is rendered unspeakable as a property of the event or that exceeds the capacities of human representation in language. It is rather the introduction of a break in the perfect agreement between the real and the possible. Rancière calls this introduction of a break *dissensus*, a dispute about what is given, a disagreement over the boundaries of

160 *Conclusion*

what is allowed into discourse and what is excluded from the frame. Such a dispute emerges when the speech of those who cannot be understood within a given social configuration—those who are deemed unfit for political life—is represented as speech rather than as mere noise.[38]

When impossible speech appears, it indicates not a pre-given subjectivity but the process of subjectivization, the coming into being of a speaking subject who is momentarily "between nominations."[39] Such a subject comes into being between pre-given identities, where the experience of the other is made intelligible and presented in terms that already exist as common sense. In texts ordinarily labeled "political," the speech of others—speech assumed to be somehow unintelligible, as linguistically, culturally, or experientially beyond the grasp of a reader or listener—is presented as understandable. This making intelligible itself is *assumed to be a political act.* This book has not only challenged this assumption, holding that *explaining something away* produces a flattening (from the Latin *ex-planus*), a reduction of significance; it has gone so far as to suggest that such an idea of the "politics of art," participating in the archival drive to classify and to explain, actually drains the artwork of its radical potential to intervene in the coordinates of the perceived real.

Perhaps nowhere is the logic of *the only possible speech* on clearer display than in debates surrounding the so-called comfort women—those women pressed into sexual slavery under the authority of the Japanese Imperial Army in the 1930s and 1940s. Here the demand for identity in suffering, the bounding of possible speech, and the compulsory discursivity required of witnesses whose testimony provides not only the facts of personal experience but also the grounds for deciding on facticity itself all come together on the stage of international human rights politics, resulting in a strange silence born of the perfect coincidence of the subject and the location/identity from which that subject speaks.[40]

Agamben famously points out that there are two words for "witness" in Latin: *testis*, the third party who bears witness in a trial or dispute between two other parties; and *superstes*, a "person who has lived through something, who has experienced an event from beginning to end and can therefore bear witness to it."[41] The first has to do with the acquisition of facts under the law; the second, with the ethical authority born of experience.[42] In the case of the comfort women, confusion arises because

Conclusion   161

they are asked to stand as witnesses in both senses—as those who underwent the experience and can speak of it, and as those who are charged with bearing witness in the quasi-legal setting of international human rights law.

But there is a third way in which the comfort women are asked to stand as witness, best accessed through the Greek term *martis*, for "martyr"—which, as Agamben also notes, is derived from the verb meaning "to remember."[43] They are asked to engender *belief* in others through their sacrificial *suffering*, which grounds both the legality and factuality of their testimony (*testis*) and the authenticity and ethical force of their experience (*superstes*).

The 2017 film *I Can Speak* (*Ai k'aen sŭp'ik'ŭ*, directed by Kim Hyŏnsŏk) is a comedy/drama understood to be "based on the true story of comfort women." Here all three senses of testimony come together in a way that produces, paradoxically, the silencing of the witness. On the face of it, the film seems to accomplish quite the opposite. The main character, an elderly woman named Na Okpun (played by Na Munhŭi), initially appears as a cantankerous and rule-bound nuisance who is widely despised by her neighbors for her habit of continually reporting their minor violations to the local government office (dropping a cigarette butt on the street, improper signage, etc.). As she shouts at one pedestrian early in the film: "It is our civic duty to follow [the letter of] the law!" For reasons at first unknown to the audience, Na wishes to learn English; through a series of coincidences, she ends up being tutored by one of the civil servants she'd been submitting complaints to, Pak Minjae (played by Yi Chehun). Eventually we learn that she is estranged from a brother—the two were separated when they were children—who now lives in Los Angeles and can speak only English. Pak assumes that it is to reunite with her brother that Na is learning English.

The sense of loss that pervades a film that otherwise largely opens as a comedy is intensified when we meet Na's friend, Chŏngsim, who suffers from dementia signaled not only by her forgetfulness but also by her rapid decline into speechlessness. It is in fact her friend's loss of speech that compels Na to learn English. We learn late in the film that Na and Chŏngsim were abducted into sexual slavery, placed in one of the "comfort stations" in Manchuria at the age of thirteen, and that Chŏngsim saved Na's life when she tried to kill herself to escape the horrifying and violent extremes of the camp. Chŏngsim had planned to testify at a hearing in the United States in support of the passage of U.S. House of Representatives Resolution 121;[44] she has written the script, but it needs to be read aloud. Na is pressed into this role by two activist figures, at the bedside of her silent friend.

It is thus well over halfway through the film that we learn that Na was enslaved, after which the "comfort women" drama must unfold at a rapid clip. The tension centers on the fact that she has not been legally verified as having been a comfort woman. Petitions are circulated and the verification process is expedited. Even so, Pak himself must rush to the House Chambers with a photograph of Na as a young girl in the camp—documentary evidence of the truth of her story that will make her speech permissible. As he pushes his way past the guards and into the room, Na takes matters into her own hands, ascending to the podium in front of the room of almost entirely white legislators (there are also several Japanese lobbyists present), saying three words in English—"I can speak," the film's title words—then stepping away from the microphone and unexpectedly lifting her shirt to expose her bare abdomen, marked by cuts, burns, and tattoos (including the Japanese imperial flag) inflicted during her time in Manchuria. "No evidence, you say?" she shouts. "I am the evidence. All the survivors are the evidence."[45]

The focus on compulsory discursivity and the location of truth in the factuality of narrative places the comfort woman in the role of the witness who experienced something, and whose experience then forms the basis for adjudicating a dispute. Her narrative is required to take on a documentary function and as such falls under what Nichanian has called the "historiographic stranglehold," a directive that "forbids any consideration of the event outside of the fact."[46] When probative function is attached to testimony as its primary or sole value, a "realist insult" is leveled at the witness, demanding verisimilitude—providing proof of established facts in accordance with the known.[47] In such cases, "the survivor is . . . under the obligation to fabricate, all by himself, the scene, the gaze, and the event."[48] As we saw in chapters 2 and 3, the result of such a process is shame, a shame experienced by the witness when testimony is "an appeal made to a third party, to the West, to the observer, to . . . 'civilized humanity.'" As survivors, Nichanian writes, "we have never ceased . . . to appeal to the external gaze."[49]

Conclusion 163

It is before this "civilized humanity" that comfort women must state their case, embodying the suffering that defines them and thus giving not only their words but also their being as proof. Testimony is demanded as document and intersects with human rights discourse in the body or speech of the refugee, or a *bodily speech* that guarantees the truth of the statements. The comfort woman must speak "as herself" and only as herself, when "herself" overlaps perfectly and tautogorically with "comfort woman." The colonized (for here "comfort women" appear as those who remain colonized *into the present*, as fully identified in an imperial/national discourse of power that assigns their speech meaning) do not have the option of *not speaking*. This demand for total visibility is exemplified in the logic of torture, which attempts to "enforce the coincidence of words with truth" by "baring the body"[50]—an alignment between language and truth guaranteed by the suffering of the body.

What we see as Na exposes the marks of torture upon her body is a different kind of "torture," the demand that language and truth align in a testimony guaranteed by attestations to the suffering of the body. In terms of the film's plot, this becomes most obvious in the attitudes of Na's neighbors, who welcome her into their community with open arms only once she has correctly and publicly confessed her identity. Her suffering qualifies her for entry into the community. To put it differently, her testimony as *superstes*, one who underwent, and her role as *testis*, to testify in the adjudication in the U.S. Congress of a dispute between two parties (Japan and Korea)—is underwritten by the third term *martis*, the demand that she expose her suffering as a guarantee of the truth of her statement and as a form of remembrance. It could be argued that such testimony is both obscene (in Lanzmann's sense) and pornographic (per Sebald), available to voyeuristic enjoyment.

Identification ("keep your place"), the logic of the only possible speech, and total visibility align in Na's appearance before the "civilized humanity" of the U.S. Congress. Such representations shore up a consensual ideal of community that continues to exclude and silence those represented by aligning the political act with the breaking of silence. These representations do not shift the parameters of what counts as legitimate speech or expand the roster of those authorized to speak.

164 *Conclusion*

Instead, they reinforce the mandated agreement between the real and the possible and harden the correlation between the place that one occupies (comfort woman, migrant laborer, Kwangju survivor, North Korean escapee, incarcerated patient, homeless person, etc.) and the speech that is permissible and expected as emerging from that identity of place and subject.

One of the subplots of *I Can Speak* is the coming together of a "family" outside of a logic of genetic heredity. Neither Pak nor Na have families of their own (Pak's parents died when he was younger, and he has raised his younger brother). The crucial moment occurs when Pak is in an interview for a prestigious government position. The interviewers ask him to confirm that he has only one family member, his younger brother. He replies affirmatively, then hesitates, and says "Hanmyŏng tŏ issŭmnida"—there is one more. Beyond being a touching affirmation of Na's growing importance in his life, the line may also be understood as referencing the well-known novel published by Kim Sum the year before (2016), titled *Hanmyŏng*.[51] The title taps into a central anxiety in the comfort women movement, namely, that due to their advanced ages, one day soon, there will be only "one left" (and eventually none) to testify to the historical atrocity.

Kim's novel notoriously includes over three hundred footnotes referencing testimony recorded by comfort women—witness testimony that is woven together into a fictional plot and spoken by fictional characters. In this technique, we find the first point that distinguishes the novel, which is not itself totally unproblematic, from *I Can Speak*—this self-conscious citation of actual testimony that at the same time achieves distance from a reproduction of that testimony as fact.[52] The novel also stages speech in an entirely different way. In *I Can Speak*, the main character must learn English in order for her speech to be intelligible to the American (or human rights) audience; she must testify before "civilized humanity" for her claims to be valid; and she must put forward her own body as proof, verifying the truth of her discourse. Na can speak but she can speak *only* as a comfort woman. The entire thrust of the movie is in the community's effort (English lessons, the legal verification process, and so on) to enable her to speak who she truly is, who she cannot not be.

Conclusion   165

Against this foreclosure—the total identification of the subject with a prearranged position—*Hanmyŏng* stages speech in three ways: the aforementioned technique of citation, for which the characters enunciate speech not properly their own along a logic of iteration or replacement; the contrast between noise (where the comfort women are treated as animals, "reduced to voices signaling pain" [Rancière]) and intelligible sound/speech, which may or may not be possible ("No speech whatsoever can explain my suffering," the narrator tells us in the words of Kim Poktong, taken from a 2015 interview);[53] and finally, through the denial of a clear correlation between identity and speech. This is possible in part because the figure of the comfort woman is split into two characters in the novel: one (largely silent) woman who watches the "last one" in televised interviews and who mediates the reader's view through her own experiences and memories; and the "one left," who speaks publicly of her ordeal. An ambiguity appears in the contradiction that arises in the statements of the two main characters: the effort of the silent narrator to claim her victimhood, which she does, realizing that "I too am a victim" ("Nado p'ihaejayo");[54] and the effort of the "one left" to distance herself from victimhood—"I am not a comfort woman" ("Nanŭn wianbu aniya")—while at the same time claiming the status of witness ("yŏksa ŭi sanjŭngin," the "living witness of history").[55] The paired statements (I am not a victim, I am a living witness) disturb the easy identification of the figure of the comfort woman, especially when those attentive to the footnotes realize that both are cited from the testimony of a single individual, Yi Yongsu.

Hanmyŏng resists the "realist shame" that Nichanian writes of, which "seizes testimony at the very moment it is uttered and instantly puts it at the service of historiographic refutation."[56] The novel admits the possibility of unrepresentability and makes a problem of testimony, privileging interpretation over proof. There is "living proof," but it is not the obscene documentary proof or verification of the facts of *I Can Speak*. It is rather a kind of *monumental* proof that in its very appearance in the public realm, the "space of general visibility," can *create* a problem[57] instead of contributing to a supposed solution or *dispersal* (from the Latin *solver*, "to loosen") of a problem.

Hanmyŏng concludes with the insolubility of the experience of the narrator, the collective narrator constructed out of hundreds of direct quotations. The final lines of the novel, delivered in the narrative present, read:

여전히 무섭다는 걸.
열세 살의 자신이 아직도 만주 막사에 있다는 걸.[58]
(That she is still scared.
That she is her thirteen-year-old self, still in those barracks in Manchuria.)

Antithetical to *I Can Speak*, a solution or a happy ending is not arrived at through the exposure of the witness's body before the "civilized" audience. The historical moment is made to pierce the narrative, with trauma emerging out of the relationship between past and present and remaining enigmatic—unsolved—in a way that, as we saw in chapter 2, demands interpretation or translation but does not invite the hereditary transmission of a melancholic "victimhood nationalism."[59] Furthermore, these closing lines are once again direct quotations, from testimony of Chinese and Indonesian victims of the Japanese military comfort women system, respectively.[60] In the end, Kim removes the question from a strictly national(ist) purview, a conflict between two states (Japan and Korea) that structures public discourse and affect around the comfort women issue and demands proof of the witness in both historical and legal terms. This is precisely the opposite of *I Can Speak*, in which the specifically national subject emerges through trauma—a trauma that entirely defines the identity of the protagonist and at the same time guarantees her membership in the national community, a trauma dissolved only in the obscene confession of the body demanded by the human rights logic of the "civilized" audience and in a situation in which all possible speech has been memorized and decided upon in advance.

The texts that I have reviewed in this book reject at every turn the euphemism that silences both by signaling something that "cannot be uttered for reasons of modesty or civility" and by proposing that one "observe religious silence"[61] before that which is *understood by all* and hence requires no place in speech. Euphemisms produce a kind of double silencing: the silence demanded by propriety, which insists that the thing itself not be spoken, or be spoken otherwise; and the silence of the adherent before the sacred, the impermissibility of additional speech

Conclusion   167

beyond the scripture that constitutes both the facts of the matter and the grounds of facticity within which those statements find their meaning. The comfort women thus bear the triple burden of witnessing in the experiential, judicial, and theological senses of the word. In place of euphemisms, the stories, novels, and films above perform a kind of catachrestic attack on correct speech and push back against the silencing that takes place when speech is understood as full of a meaning available to all. Such texts meet the realist demand—that speech obviate the necessity of interpretation in embodying the real itself (whether as the *truth* of trauma, the *fact* of experience, or the *diagnosis* and *location* of one's condition)—by opening again, even if only momentarily, a gap between the *really possible* and the *fully realized*, an interval prior to the absorption of the real into the actual[62] and to the retrospective act that gives that potentiality of the real its anachronistic status as given.

Euphemism and realism appear to present opposing logics: one that can speak only obliquely, one that aims at the appearance in language of the thing itself. After all, isn't the solution to euphemisms to name the real thing, to say the true word? Yet both produce a kind of awed silence before language, the power of which is either assumed and deflected (in the case of euphemisms) or on apparent display (in the seeming capture of the referent). In both cases, speech is already full of understood meaning—a consensus has been reached on what may be said of the matter. Yet it is here, where the sense of speech is most fully established or fully possibilized—where the archival force has its way, where impossible speech is made impossible—that the work of art may exceed its documentary function and, appearing in "the space of general visibility . . . creates a problem."[63] The works above observe moments where what had been solved precipitates—both in the sense of occurring unexpectedly, and in the sense of falling out of solution, a crystallization that is not one thing or the other and which disturbs the uniformity of the homogeneous mixture. Such works breach the limit of solubility.

This iridescent emanation is, Adorno tells us in the epigraph above, "the appearance of the affirmative *ineffabile*, the emergence of the nonexisting as if it did exist." It is the ineffable—the unutterable, that which may not be spoken—that appears and disrupts the logic of a representational politics that would limit meaning to that which is understood to be sayable. In revealing the pervasive realism that characterizes

168   *Conclusion*

approaches to the politics of literature, and in challenging the deadweight of correspondence that makes of every work of art a historical document, the texts above strive to reveal and to adjust the border between the intelligible and the unintelligible, between speech that is given as possible and that which is understood in advance to be impossible. In putting forward an impossible speech, each text marks a limit, the "dark margin encircling and limiting every concrete act of speech,"[64] and, in so doing, brings the adjustment of that limit into the realm of the imaginable possible.

Notes

INTRODUCTION

1. The thin veneer of fictionality separating this from a biographical narrative is made even more apparent in the fact that the name of the attorney, Song Usŏk, is clearly a placeholder—a combination of the director's given name and the family name of the actor (Song Kangho).

2. See Mun Kwangyu, "Yŏksa wa sŏnbi chŏngsin ŭi sohwan kŭrigo chinsil ŭi him—Yang Usŏk ŭi *Pyŏnhoin*" [Summoning history and the spirit of the classical scholar, and the power of truth: Yang Usŏk's *The Attorney*], *Hyŏndae yŏnghwa yŏngu* [Contemporary film research] 10, no. 1 (2014): 69–93; or Yuk Chŏnghak, "Ch'ŏnman kwangaek tolp'a yŏnghwa *Pyŏnhoin* ŭi munhwasahoejŏk ŭimi" [Surpassing the ten million viewer mark: The sociocultural significance of *The Attorney*], *Kanguk ent'ŏt'einmŏnt'ŭ sanŏp hakhoe nonmunji* [Journal of the Association of the Korean Entertainment Industry] 9, no. 1 (2015): 23–33. The film was released in late 2013, following the election of Park Geun-hye and the initiation of the more authoritarian mode of governance that she brought to her troubled presidency (2013–2017), before her eventual impeachment and conviction on charges of bribery, extortion, and abuse of power.

3. Chŏng Pyŏnggi, "Yŏnghwa *Pyŏnhoin* ŭi sŏnt'aek kwa nurak kŭrigo konggam ŭi chŏngch'ihak—konggam ŭi posusŏng kwa minjujuŭi ŭi posusŏng" [Conservative empathy and conservative democracy: Selection and omission in *The Attorney* and the politics of empathy], *Kyŏngje wa sahoe* [Economy and Society] 106 (2015): 271–295.

4. Chŏng, "Yŏnghwa *Pyŏnhoin* ŭi sŏnt'aek kwa nurak kŭrigo konggam ŭi chŏngch'ihak," 287–288.

5. Marc Nichanian, *The Historiographic Perversion*, trans. Gil Anidjar (New York: Columbia University Press, 2009), 8.

6. "이제 진실이 그 모습으로 들어냈습니다.... 명백한 상황이 있고, 증인이 있고, 증언이 있습니다."

7. Gavin Miller, "Literary Narrative as Soteriology in the Work of Kurt Vonnegut and Alasdair Gray," *Journal of Narrative Theory* 31, no. 1 (Fall 2001): 304.

8. Michael Root, "The Narrative Structure of Soteriology," *Modern Theology* 2, no. 2 (January 1986): 145.

9. Root, "The Narrative Structure of Soteriology," 147.

10. Root, "The Narrative Structure of Soteriology," 154, 146.

11. Jacques Rancière, *The Lost Thread: The Democracy of Modern Fiction*, trans. Steven Corcoran (London: Bloomsbury Academic, 2017), 66.

12. Judith Butler, *Excitable Speech: The Politics of the Performative* (New York: Routledge, 1997), 134.

13. Slavoj Žižek, "Against Human Rights," *New Left Review* 34 (July/August 2005): 125.

14. Slavoj Žižek, "Against Human Rights," 130.

15. Butler, *Excitable Speech*, 155.

16. Jacques Rancière, *Disagreement: Politics and Philosophy*, trans. Julie Rose (Minneapolis: University of Minnesota Press, 1999), 28.

17. Rancière, *Disagreement*, 29–30.

18. Jacques Rancière, *Aesthetics and Its Discontents*, trans. Steven Corcoran (Cambridge: Polity Press, 2009), 24.

19. Rancière, *Disagreement*, 30.

20. Rancière, *Aesthetics and Its Discontents*, 24.

21. Rey Chow, *Writing Diaspora: Tactics of Intervention in Contemporary Cultural Studies* (Bloomington: Indiana University Press, 1993), 111.

22. See Nancy Fraser, "The Politics of Framing: An Interview with Nancy Fraser," interviewed by Kate Nash and Vikki Bell, *Theory, Culture and Society* 24, no. 4 (2007): 73–86.

23. Butler, *Excitable Speech*, 140–141.

24. Jacques Rancière, *The Names of History: On the Poetics of Knowledge*, trans. Hassan Melehy (Minneapolis: University of Minnesota Press, 1994), 98.

25. Gilles Deleuze and Félix Guattari, *Kafka: Toward a Minor Literature*, trans. Dana Polan (Minneapolis: University of Minnesota Press, 1986), 48.

26. Jacques Rancière, *The Edges of Fiction*, trans. Steve Corcoran (Cambridge: Polity Press, 2020), 135–136.

27. Chin Ŭnyŏng, "Kamgakjŏgin kŏt ŭi punbae: 2000 nyŏndae ŭi si e taehayŏ" [The distribution of the sensible: On the poetry of the 2000s], *Ch'angjak kwa pip'yŏng* [Creation and criticism] 36, no. 4 (2008): 79.

28. The focus here is instead on disidentification as the mark of subjectivization, a disidentification that "inscribes a subject name as being different from any identified part of the community" (Rancière, *Disagreement*, 37).

29. Butler, *Excitable Speech*, 133.

30. As Chin writes in her essay on the "disappearance" of politics from the poetry of the 2000s in South Korea, "the mere fact that someone puts forward some assertion, that one speaks of the laborer or the common person and not the aristocrat or the bourgeois, is not sufficient" to render the text "political" ("Kamgakjŏgin kŏt ŭi punbae," 79). "Political" art is not a matter, as Adorno puts it, of the open treatment of social matters, "the claim that the sculpture of a coal miner a priori says more, socially, than a sculpture without a proletarian hero" (Theodor Adorno, *Aesthetic Theory*, trans. and ed. Robert Hullot-Kentor [Minneapolis: University of Minnesota Press, 1997], 229–230). Rather, it is an introduction of a break in the "sensible matrix of society" (Chin, "Kamgakjŏgin kŏt ŭi punbae," 81) through a work of art that disrupts "the relationship between the visible, the sayable, and the thinkable without having to use the terms of a message as its vehicle" (Jacques Rancière, *The Politics of Aesthetics: The Distribution of the Sensible*, trans. Gabriel Rockhill [London: Continuum, 2004], 63, cited in Chin, "Kamgakchŏgin kŏt ŭi punbae," 81).

31. Butler, *Excitable Speech*, 133.

32. Saidiya V. Hartman, *Scenes of Subjection: Terror, Slavery, and Self-Making in Nineteenth-Century America* (New York: Oxford University Press, 1997), 11. Hartman is paraphrasing Michel Foucault, *The Archaeology of Knowledge*, trans. A. M. Sheridan Smith (New York: Vintage, 1972), 130–131. The archive is not the sum of all of the texts of a given culture, a set of documents attesting to a cultural past (or a continuing cultural identity), or the institution that preserves such texts for future generations. "The archive is the first law of what can be said, the system that governs the appearance of statements as unique events," Foucault writes. It is "the general system of the formation and transformation of statements," a "system of discursivity" and "the enunciative possibilities and impossibilities that it lays down" (Foucault, *The Archaeology of Knowledge*, 129–130).

33. Butler, *Excitable Speech*, 140–141.

34. Here we see, precisely, the identity of the verisimilar and the necessary, a reality compelled to conform to what is already known—a reality that cannot not

be (Rancière, *The Lost Thread*, 66–67) and a representation that must mimetically reflect it.

35. See Jean-Jacques Lecercle, "Storming Language," *Crisis and Critique* 5, no. 2 (November 2018): 205–216.

36. See David Perkins, *Is Literary History Possible?* (Baltimore, MD: Johns Hopkins University Pres, 1992), 1–3.

37. Rancière, *The Edges of Fiction*, 135–136.

38. Dominick LaCapra, *Writing History, Writing Trauma* (Baltimore, MD: Johns Hopkins University Press, 2014), xiv. See also Dominick LaCapra, *History and Its Limits: Human, Animal, Violence* (Ithaca, NY: Cornell University Press, 2009), especially chap. 3: "'Traumatropisms': From Trauma via Witnessing to the Sublime?"

39. See Han Kang, *Human Acts*, trans. Deborah Smith (London: Portobello Books, 2016).

40. See Philippe Lejeune, *On Autobiography*, ed. Paul Eakin, trans. Katherine Leary (Minneapolis: University of Minnesota Press, 1989), especially pp. 3–30.

41. See Edward Said, *Orientalism* (New York: Vintage, 1979), 72. For all of the figures of speech used to describe the Orient, Said writes, "it is frequently enough to use the simple copula *is*." Here is the "quasi-invisibility of the 'there is,' which is effaced in the very thing of which one can say: 'there is this or that thing'" (Foucault, *The Archaeology of Knowledge*, 111).

42. Michiko Kakutani, "A North Korean Soldier Finds His 'Casablanca,'" review of *The Orphan Master's Son*, by Adam Johnson, *New York Times*, January 12, 2012, https://www.nytimes.com/2012/01/13/books/the-orphan-masters-son-by-adam-johnson-review.html.

43. David Ignatius, review of *The Orphan Master's Son*, by Adam Johnson, *Washington Post*, January 9, 2012, https://www.washingtonpost.com/entertainment/books/book-review-the-orphan-masters-son-by-david-ignatius/2012/01/02/gIQAIZWZmP_story.html.

44. Barbara Demick, "A Spot-On Depiction of North Korea," review of *The Orphan Master's Son*, by Adam Johnson, *Guardian*, February 17, 2012, https://www.theguardian.com/books/2012/feb/17/orphan-masters-son-adam-johnson-review.

45. See Hal Foster, "Obscene, Abject, Traumatic," *October* 78 (Autumn 1996): 106–124.

46. Rancière, *Disagreement*, 29–30.

47. Rancière, *The Politics of Aesthetics*, 3.

48. Rancière, *Aesthetics and Its Discontents*, 24–25.

49. Rancière, *Aesthetics and Its Discontents*, 24.

50. See Cho Yŏnjŏng, "'Kwangju' rŭl hyŏnjaehwa hanŭn il: Kwŏn Yŏsŏn ŭi *Legat'o* (2012) wa Han Kang ŭi *Sonyŏni onda* (2014) rŭl chungsim ŭro" [The task of the making present of "Kwangju": With a focus on Kwŏn Yŏsŏn's *Legato* (2012) and Han Kang's *A Boy Is Coming* (2014)], *Taejung sŏsa yŏngu* [Journal of popular narrative] 20, no. 3 (December 2014): 101–138.

51. John Frow, *Genre* (London: Routledge, 2015 [2006]), 12.

52. Frow, *Genre*, 15–16.

53. Yury Tynyanov, "On Literary Evolution," in *Readings in Russian Poetics: Formalist and Structuralist Views*, ed. Ladislav Matejka and Krystyna Pomorska (Champaign, IL: Dalkey Archive Press, 2002 [1927]), 32, cited in Jörg Schweinitz, *Film and Stereotype: A Challenge for Cinema and Theory*, trans. Laura Schleussner (New York: Columbia University Press, 2011 [2006]), 78.

54. See Frow, *Genre*, 7–10.

55. Tzvetan Todorov, *Genres in Discourse* (Cambridge: Cambridge University Press, 1990 [1978]), 19–20.

56. Janet Giltrow, "Meta-Genre," in *The Rhetoric and Ideology of Genre: Strategies for Stability and Change*, eds. Richard Coe, Lorelei Lingard, and Tatiana Teslenko (Creskill, NJ: Hampton Press, 2002), 203, cited in Frow, *Genre*, 12.

57. Todorov, *Genres in Discourse*, 19–20.

58. Frow, *Genre*, 11.

59. Butler, *Excitable Speech*, 136.

60. Rancière, *Disagreement*, 30.

61. Wendy Brown, "Freedom's Silences," in *Censorship and Silencing: Practices of Cultural Regulation*, ed. Robert Post (Los Angeles: Getty Research Institute, 1998), 313–314.

62. Brown, "Freedom's Silences," 314.

63. "Politics is primarily conflict over the existence of a common stage and over the existence and status of those present on it. . . . It concerns the speech situation itself and its performers." The speech situation: bringing to light a "wrong," a confrontation, "the contradiction of two worlds in a single world: the world where they are and the world where they are not, the world where there is something 'between' them and those who do not acknowledge them as speaking beings who count and the world where there is nothing" (Rancière, *Disagreement*, 27).

64. Brown, "Freedom's Silences," 315.

65. See Lecercle, "Storming Language," 205–216.

66. See Rancière, *The Lost Thread*, 67; and Rancière, *Disagreement*, 112.

67. Butler, *Excitable Speech*, 140.

Introduction 175

1. THE RETURN OF THE REAL IN SOUTH KOREAN FICTION

1. Winner of the Yi Sang Literary Prize in 2003, Kim Insuk's "Sea and Butterfly" was originally published as "Pada wa nabi" in *Silch'ŏn munhak* [Praxis literature] (Winter 2002): 257–290. The story was also published in English translation in 2008.
2. Kim I., "Pada wa nabi," 260.
3. Kim I., "Pada wa nabi," 286; Kim Insuk, "Sea and Butterfly," in *New Writing from Korea* (Seoul: Korean Literature Translation Institute), 1:178.
4. Kim I., "Pada wa nabi," 287; Kim I., "Sea and Butterfly," 179.
5. On the idea of a system of immobility/mobility, see for instance "migrant containment" in Hae Yeon Choo, *Decentering Citizenship: Gender, Labor, and Migrant Rights in South Korea* (Stanford, CA: Stanford University Press), 2016.
6. Naoki Sakai, *Translation and Subjectivity: On Japan and Cultural Nationalism* (Minneapolis: University of Minnesota Press, 1997), 8.
7. Kang Chingu, "Hanguk sosŏl e nat'anan ijunodongja ŭi chaehyŏn yangsang" [Aspects of the representation of migrant laborers in Korean fiction], *Ŏmun nonjip* [Journal of language and literature] 41 (2009): 262–263. On the exclusion of the "outside" as a condition of the imagination of the ethnic nation in migrant labor fiction, see Yŏn Namgyŏng, "2000 nyŏndae Hanguk sosŏl ŭi ijumin chaehyŏn yŏngu—chŏnjiguhwa, minjok kukka, ijumin ŭi kwangye rŭl chungsim ŭro" [Representing the migrant in Korean fiction of the 2000s—with a focus on the relationship between globalization, the ethnic-national state, and the migrant], *Kugŏ kungmunhak* [National literature and language] 165 (2013): 63–85.
8. Hwang Hodŏk, "Nŏmŭn kŏsi anida—kukkyŏng kwa munhak" [Not crossed—state borders and literature], *Munhak tongne* [Literary community] 13, no. 4 (2006): 426; cited in Yŏn Namgyŏng, "Hanguk hyŏndae sosŏl e nat'ansan chŏpgyŏng chidae wa kusŏngdoen chŏngch'esŏng" [The borderland and the construction of identity in recent Korean fiction], *Hyŏndae sosŏl yŏngu* [Modern fiction] 52 (2013): 264.
9. Yŏn, "Hanguk hyŏndae sosŏl e nat'ansan chŏpgyŏng chidae wa kusŏngdoen chŏngch'esŏng," 276–277; see also Yŏn Namgyŏng, *T'algyŏnggye sayu wa sŏsa ŭi yulli: Hanguk munhak kwa iju* [Post-border reason and the ethics of narrative: Korean literature and migration] (Seoul: Ihwa yŏja taehakkyo ch'ulp'an munhwawŏn, 2017).
10. Yi Kyŏngjae, "2000 nyŏndae tamunhwa sosŏl yŏngu: Hangugin kwa ijumin ŭi kwangye yangsang ŭl chungsim ŭro" [A study of multicultural fiction of the

2000s: On aspects of the relationship between Koreans and migrants], *Hanguk hyŏndae munhak yŏngu* [Modern Korean literature] 40 (2013): 249–250.

11. Yi K., "2000 nyŏndae tamunhwa sosŏl yŏngu," 251.

12. Hayden White, "The Fictions of Factual Representation," in *The Literature of Fact*, ed. Angus Fletcher (New York: Columbia University Press, 1976), 22.

13. Jacques Rancière, *The Future of the Image*, trans. Gregory Elliott (London: Verso, 2007), 13.

14. Rancière, *The Future of the Image*, 13–15.

15. Alexander Weheliye, *Habeas Viscus: Racializing Assemblages, Biopolitics, and Black Feminist Theories of the Human* (Durham, NC: Duke University Press, 2014), 51.

16. Rancière, *The Future of the Image*, 25.

17. Paul Gilroy, *The Black Atlantic: Modernity and Double Consciousness* (Cambridge, MA: Harvard University Press, 1993), 2.

18. Naoki Sakai, "Introduction: Nationality and the Politics of the Mother Tongue," in *Deconstructing Nationality*, ed. Naoki Sakai, Brett de Bary, and Iyotani Toshio (Ithaca, NY: East Asia Program, Cornell University, 2005), 6. See also Christopher Hutton, *Linguistics and the Third Reich: Mother-Tongue Fascism, Race and the Science of Language* (London: Routledge, 1999), 286.

19. William Whitney, *Language and the Study of Language: Twelve Lectures on the Principles of Linguistic Science* (London: Trübner, 1867), cited in Hutton, *Linguistics and the Third Reich*, 271.

20. Sigmund Freud, "Screen Memories," in *Early Psycho-Analytic Publications (1893–1899)*, vol. 3 of *The Standard Edition of the Complete Psychological Works of Sigmund Freud*, ed. James Strachey (London: Hogarth, 1962), 301–322.

21. The story has also been published in English translation: Kim Chaeyŏng, "Elephant," in *New Writing from Korea*, 1:182–208.

22. Kim Chaeyŏng, "K'okkiri," in *K'okkiri* (Seoul: Silch'ŏn munhaksa, 2008), 11; Kim C., "Elephant," 184.

23. Kim C., "K'okkiri," 14; Kim C., "Elephant," 186.

24. Kim C., "K'okkiri," 25; Kim C., "Elephant," 196.

25. Young-A Park, Do-hoon Lee, and Keith B. Wagner, "Changing Representations of the Urban Poor in Korean Independent Cinema: *Minjung* Heroes, Atomized Paupers, and New Possibilities," *Quarterly Review of Film and Video* 34, no. 4 (2017): 362.

26. Park, Lee, and Wagner, "Changing Representations of the Urban Poor," 372.

27. See Timothy Lim, "Rethinking Belongingness in Korea: Transnational Migration, 'Migrant Marriages' and the Politics of Multiculturalism," *Pacific Affairs* 83, no. 1 (March 2010): 51–71.

1. The Return of the Real in South Korean Fiction

28. Sakai, "Introduction," 24. Or as Hutton puts it, "the logic of the mother-tongue idea is that a particular individual should be the speaker of a particular language" (*Linguistics and the Third Reich*, 286).

29. Jin-kyung Lee, "Immigrant Subempire, Migrant Labor Activism, and Multiculturalism in Contemporary South Korea," in *The Routledge Handbook of Korean Culture and Society*, ed. Youna Kim (London: Routledge, 2017), 152.

30. Rey Chow, *Not Like a Native Speaker: On Languaging as a Postcolonial Experience* (New York: Columbia University Press, 2014), 57.

31. Kang C., "Hanguk sosŏl e nat'anan ijunodongja ŭi chaehyŏn yangsang," 253.

32. Yŏn, "Hanguk hyŏndae sosŏl e nat'ansan chŏpgyŏng chidae wa kusŏngdoen chŏngch'esŏng," 258.

33. Kim C., "K'okkiri," 25–26; Kim C., "Elephant," 197.

34. Dipesh Chakrabarty, *Provincializing Europe: Postcolonial Thought and Historical Difference* (Princeton, NJ: Princeton University Press, 2000), 7.

35. The falseness of this delinking is represented in Akkas's painful attempts to bleach his skin white, an act that adheres to a gruesome logic in a situation where "language possession is translated into and receives its value as skin color" (Chow, *Not Like a Native Speaker*, 3).

36. I refer to the version of the story published as "Kalsaek nunmul pangul" in Kang Yŏngsuk, *Ppalgang sok ŭi kŏmjŏng e taehayŏ* [On the black in the red] (Seoul: Munhak tongne, 2009), 191–216. The story has also been published in English translation as "Brown Tears" in *New Writing from Korea*, 1:132–151.

37. Kang Y., "Kalsaek nunmul pangul," 202; Kang Y., "Brown Tears," 139.

38. Kang Y., "Kalsaek nunmul pangul," 194; Kang Y., "Brown Tears," 132.

39. Kang Y., "Kalsaek nunmul pangul," 199; Kang Y., "Brown Tears," 136–137.

40. Kang Y., "Kalsaek nunmul pangul," 199–200; Kang Y., "Brown Tears," 137–138.

41. Kang Y., "Kalsaek nunmul pangul," 202.

42. Kang Y., "Kalsaek nunmul pangul," 205.

43. Kang Y., "Kalsaek nunmul pangul," 213.

44. Kang Y., "Kalsaek nunmul pangul," 210.

45. Kang Y., "Kalsaek nunmul pangul," 213.

46. Kang C., "Hanguk sosŏl e nat'anan ijunodongja ŭi chaehyŏn yangsang," 261.

47. Kang Y., "Kalsaek nunmul pangul," 214; Kang Y., "Brown Tears," 150.

48. Kang Y., "Kalsaek nunmul pangul," 214.

49. Kang Y., "Kalsaek nunmul pangul," 216; Kang Y., "Brown Tears," 151.

50. Yi K., "2000 nyŏndae tamunhwa sosŏl yŏngu," 278.

51. Su Kyŏng, "Hwansang sosŏl losŏŭi Hanguk ijumunhak" [Korean immigrant literature as fantasy fiction], presented at the Seminar on Memory and Migration, Kyumun Research Institute, Seoul, Korea, May 19, 2017.

52. Rancière, *The Future of the Image*, 14–15.

53. Jacques Rancière, *Aesthetics and Its Discontents*, trans. Steven Corcoran (Cambridge: Polity Press, 2009), 24.

54. Rancière, *Aesthetics and Its Discontents*, 24–25.

55. Hwang Chongyŏn, "A Postmodern Turn in Korean Literature," *Korea Journal* 47, no. 1 (2007): 5–6.

56. Rancière, *Disagreement*, 102.

57. Rancière, *The Lost Thread*, 66.

58. Jacques Rancière, *Disagreement: Politics and Philosophy*, trans. Julie Rose (Minneapolis: University of Minnesota Press, 1999), 112.

59. Judith Butler, *Excitable Speech: The Politics of the Performative* (New York: Routledge, 1997), 140–141.

2. DISPLACING THE COMMON SENSE OF TRAUMA

1. "5.18 kinyŏmsik: Mun Chaein Taet'ongryŏng kinyŏmsa chŏnmun (2019)" [Full text of President Moon Jae-in's commemorative speech on the anniversary of May 18 (2019)], https://www1.president.go.kr/articles/6318.

2. "5.18 kinyŏmsik: Mun Chaein Taet'ongryŏng kinyŏmsa chŏnmun (2020)" [Full text of President Moon Jae-in's commemorative speech on the anniversary of May 18 (2020)], https://www1.president.go.kr/articles/8639.

3. Cho Yŏnjŏng, "'Kwangju' rŭl hyŏnjaehwa hanŭn il: Kwŏn Yŏsŏn ŭi *Legat'o* (2012) wa Han Kang ŭi *Sonyŏni onda* (2014) rŭl chungsim ŭro" [The task of the making present of "Kwangju": With a focus on Kwŏn Yŏsŏn's *Legato* (2012) and Han Kang's *A Boy Is Coming* (2014)], *Taejung sŏsa yŏngu* [Journal of popular narrative] 20, no. 3 (December 2014): 111.

4. The commission (5.18 Chinsang kyumyŏng chosa wiwŏnhoe) was established by law in 2018 and commenced its activities in May 2020.

5. Cathy Caruth, *Unclaimed Experience: Trauma, Narrative, and History* (Baltimore, MD: Johns Hopkins University Press, 1996), 2.

6. Caruth, *Unclaimed Experience*, 3–4.

7. Dominick LaCapra, *Writing History, Writing Trauma* (Baltimore, MD: Johns Hopkins University Press, 2014), xii.

8. LaCapra, *Writing History, Writing Trauma*, 22–23.

9. LaCapra, *Writing History, Writing Trauma*, xv.

10. Part of the ceremonies in 2019 and 2020, for instance, included those assembled singing "Im ŭl wihan haengjingok" (March for the beloved), the song performed in 1981 at the posthumous wedding ceremony of Yun Sangwŏn, killed defending the Provincial Office during the uprising, and Pak Kisun, a night-school teacher who died after inhaling poison gas.

11. As Rey Chow reminds us, "defilement and sanctification belong to the same symbolic order" (Rey Chow, *Writing Diaspora: Tactics of Intervention in Contemporary Cultural Studies* [Bloomington: Indiana University Press, 1993], 54).

12. See Cho Sŏnghŭi, "Han Kang ŭi *Sonyŏni onda* wa Hollok'osŭt'ŭ munhak: Kot'ong wa ch'iyok ŭi chŭngŏn kwa wŏnhan ŭi yulli rŭl chungsim ŭro" [Han Kang's *A Boy Is Coming* and Holocaust literature: With a focus on the testimony of suffering and shame and the ethics of resentment], *Segye munhak pigyo yŏngu* [Comparative world literature studies] 62 (Spring 2018): 7.

13. Yi Suk, "Yesulga ŭi sahoejŏk ch'aengmu: P'ongnyŏk ŭi kiŏk kwa ingan ŭi ponjil—Han Kang ŭi *Sonyŏni onda* rŭl chungsim ŭro (2014)" [The social responsibility of the artist: The memory of violence and the essence of the human—with a focus on Han Kang's *A Boy Is Coming* (2014)], *Hyŏndae munhak iron* [Journal of modern literary theory] 60 (2015): 444.

14. This reading of the novel runs against the author's own repeated statements on the matter. When the novel won the Italian Malaparte Prize in 2017, for instance, the Italian press quoted Han as saying at the awards ceremony that "this book is not something that was written for me. I only wanted to lend my senses, my being, my body, to the people who suffered death (in the Kwangju People's Uprising), to those who remain, and to their families" ("Sosŏlga Han Kang, *Sonyŏni onda* ro It'alia Mallap'arŭt'e munhaksang susang" [Author Han Kang awarded the Malaparte Prize for *A Boy Is Coming*], *Hangyŏre* [Hankyoreh], October 2, 2017, http://www.hani.co.kr/arti/culture/culture_general /813384.html).

15. "침묵과 헛기침과 망설임, 헐겁거나 뻑뻑한 단어들을 덧붙이고 꿰매 어떤 내용을 완성할 수 있었을까" (Han Kang, *Sonyŏni onda* [A boy is coming] [Seoul: Ch'angbi, 2018 (2014)], 152). All translations from the novel are my own.

16. "Sosŏlga Han Kang, *Sonyŏni onda* ro It'alia Mallap'arŭt'e munhaksang susang."

17. Cho Y., "'Kwangju' rŭl hyŏnjaehwa hanŭn il," 132.

18. Han, *Sonyŏni onda*, 24.

19. Han, *Sonyŏni onda*, 25.

20. Han, *Sonyŏni onda*, 174. The term translated as "fuckers" here, *yŏnnom*, combines derogatory gendered terms for both women and men. A literal translation would be something like "bitch bastards." Though not entirely accurate, in my view "fuckers" is an adequate term in that they are being addressed precisely through a threat to their reproductive capacities, a "drying up" that is a threat of extermination. Sŏnju has in fact been rendered permanently unable to bear children (she is raped with a ruler during her torture), and unable to bear the touch or the gaze of men. My argument in this chapter does not center on the precise definition of "massacre," but it is worth pointing out that the targeting of reproductive capacity, a threat to the future of an entire group, is

180   *2. Displacing the Common Sense of Trauma*

one of the possible points where "genocide differs qualitatively from mass murder" (Michael Rothberg, *Traumatic Realism: The Demands of Holocaust Representation* [Minneapolis: University of Minnesota Press, 2000], 161).

21. See Yi S., "Yesulga ŭi sahoejŏk ch'aengmu," 447, 452–453. Kim Yŏngch'an points out that Han Kang was clearly aware of the strategy, citing a 2015 interview with the author in which Han notes that although Tongho has died, use of the second person gives the perpetual ability to "call" the "you" of the narrative into the present from multiple perspectives. See Kim Yŏngch'an, "Kot'ong kwa munhak, kot'ong ŭi munhak: Han Kang ŭi *Sonyŏni onda* wa *Nun han songi ka nongnŭn tongan* ŭl chungsim ŭro" [Suffering and literature, literature of suffering: With a focus on Han Kang's *A Boy Is Coming* and *While a Snowflake Melts*], *Urimalgŭl* [Our speech and writing] 72 (March 2017): 307; and Kim Yŏnsu, "Sarang i anin tarŭn mallonŭn sŏlmyŏng hal su opnŭn" [It cannot be explained in words other than love], *Ch'angjak kwa pip'yŏng* [Creation and criticism] 165 (Autumn 2014): 312–332.

22. Han, *Sonyŏni onda*, 17.

23. Han, *Sonyŏni onda*, 22.

24. Han, *Sonyŏni onda*, 10. Here we have introduced, in the voice of a boy thinking over his school lessons, a question that runs through the novel: Is the text aiming at empirical description, or is what we encounter on the page avowedly figural?

25. Han, *Sonyŏni onda*, 114; my emphasis.

26. Han, *Sonyŏni onda*, 115–116.

27. Han, *Sonyŏni onda*, 58–59.

28. Han, *Sonyŏni onda*, 17.

29. Han, *Sonyŏni onda*, 17–18.

30. Judith Butler, *Excitable Speech: The Politics of the Performative* (New York: Routledge, 1997), 160.

31. Jacques Rancière, "Who Is the Subject of the Rights of Man?," *South Atlantic Quarterly* 103, no. 2/3 (Spring/Summer 2004): 304.

32. Jean-Jacques Lecercle, "Storming Language," *Crisis and Critique* 5, no. 2 (November 2018): 205.

33. Michel de Certeau, *La prise de parole* [The capture of language] (Paris: Seuil, 1994).

34. Cho Y., "'Kwangju' rŭl hyŏnjaehwa hanŭn il," 102.

35. Lecercle, "Storming Language," 207–208.

36. Lecercle, "Storming Language," 209.

37. Lecercle, "Storming Language," 209, paraphrasing de Certeau.

38. LaCapra, *Writing History, Writing Trauma*, 23.

39. LaCapra, *Writing History, Writing Trauma*, 44.

2. Displacing the Common Sense of Trauma 181

40. Jung-woon Choi, "The Formation of an 'Absolute Community,'" in *Contentious Kwangju: The May 18 Uprising in Korea's Past and Present*, ed. Gi-Wook Shin and Kyung Moon Hwang (Lanham, MD: Rowman and Littlefield, 2003), 6. See also Jung-woon Choi, "The Kwangju People's Uprising: The Formation of Absolute Community," *Korea Journal* 39, no. 4 (Summer 1999): 238–282.

41. LaCapra, *Writing History, Writing Trauma*, 70.

42. Cho Y., "'Kwangju' rŭl hyŏnjaehwa hanŭn il," 104–105.

43. Cho Y., "'Kwangju' rŭl hyŏnjaehwa hanŭn il," 105–106.

44. Jean-Luc Nancy, *The Inoperative Community*, ed. Peter Connor, trans. Peter Connor, Lisa Garbus, Michael Holland, and Simona Sawhney (Minneapolis: University of Minnesota Press, 1991), 10.

45. Judith Butler, *Precarious Life: The Powers of Mourning and Violence* (London: Verso, 2004), 21–22.

46. Han, *Sonyŏni onda*, 202.

47. Han, *Sonyŏni onda*, 175.

48. Han, *Sonyŏni onda*, 212–213.

49. Sigmund Freud, *Beyond the Pleasure Principle*, trans. and ed. James Strachey (New York: Norton, 1961), 12.

50. Theodor Adorno, *Aesthetic Theory*, trans. and ed. Robert Hullot-Kentor (Minneapolis: University of Minnesota Press, 1997), 260.

51. LaCapra, *Writing History, Writing Trauma*, 46.

52. Han, *Sonyŏni onda*, 162.

53. Han, *Sonyŏni onda*, 207.

54. Han, *Sonyŏni onda*, 135.

55. Han, *Sonyŏni onda*, 207. The reference here is to a January 20, 2009, rooftop protest at an abandoned building in central Seoul, with participants calling attention to and resisting the eviction and forced relocation of residents by urban developers. The government mobilized a SWAT team; in the clash, a fire was ignited and five residents and one police officer were killed.

56. Cho Y., "'Kwangju' rŭl hyŏnjaehwa hanŭn il," 128.

57. Ji-Eun Lee, "(Dis)embodiment of Memory: Gender, Memory, and Ethics in *Human Acts* by Han Kang," in *Routledge Companion to Korean Literature*, ed. Heekyoung Cho (New York: Routledge, 2022), 362.

58. Cho Y., "'Kwangju' rŭl hyŏnjaehwa hanŭn il," 133.

59. Yi S., "Yesulga ŭi sahoejŏk ch'aengmu," 444.

60. Sŏ Yŏngch'ae, "Kwangju ŭi poksu rŭl kkumkkunŭn il: Kim Kyŏnguk kwa Yi Haegyŏng ŭi changp'yŏn ŭl chungsim ŭro" [The work of dreaming the dream of Kwangju's vengeance: With a focus on the long fiction of Kim Kyŏnguk and Yi Haegyŏng], *Munhak tongne* [Literary community] 78 (2014): 2.

182 *2. Displacing the Common Sense of Trauma*

61. Cho Y., "'Kwangju' rŭl hyŏnjaehwa hanŭn il," 133–134.

62. Cho Y., "'Kwangju' rŭl hyŏnjaehwa hanŭn il," 128.

63. Cho Y., "'Kwangju' rŭl hyŏnjaehwa hanŭn il," 128. Cho takes this phrase from Kim Sangbong. See Kim Sangbong, "Ŭngdap ŭrosŏŭi yŏksa: 5.18 ŭl saenggakham" [History as response: Thoughts on May 18], *Minjujuŭi wa ingwŏn* [Democracy and human rights] 6, no. 2 (2006): 139–156; my emphasis.

64. Butler, *Excitable Speech*, 137. Butler is paraphrasing Wendy Brown, "Freedom's Silences," in *Censorship and Silencing: Practices of Cultural Regulation*, ed. Robert Post (Los Angeles: Getty Research Institute, 1998), 313–327.

65. Jacques Rancière, *The Future of the Image*, trans. Gregory Elliott (London: Verso, 2007), 13–15.

66. Shoshana Felman and Dori Laub, *Testimony: Crises of Witnessing in Literature, Psychoanalysis, and History* (New York: Routledge, 1992), 225.

67. Han, *Sonyŏni onda*, 13.

68. Han, *Sonyŏni onda*, 176.

69. Cited in Cho Sŏnghŭi, "Han Kang ŭi *Sonyŏni onda* wa Hollok'osŭt'ŭ munhak," 11; see Kim Yosŏp, "Yŏksa ŭi nun kwa mal haejiji anŭn sonyŏn: Cho Kapsang ŭi *Pam ŭi nun* kwa Han Kang ŭi *Sonyŏni onda* e taehayŏ" [The eye of history and the unspoken boy: On Cho Kapsang's *The Eye of Night* and Han Kang's *A Boy Is Coming*], *Ch'angjak kwa pipy'ŏng* [Creation and criticism] 43, no. 3 (2015): 478.

70. See Hwang Chŏnga, "'Kyŏl ŭl kŏsŭllŏ yŏksa rŭl solchil' hanŭn munhak: *Pam ŭi nun* kwa *Sonyŏni onda*" [Literature that "brushes history against the grain": *The Eye of Night* and *A Boy Is Coming*], *An kwa pak* [Inside/outside] 38 (May 2015): 58–81.

71. Cho Sŏnghŭi, "Han Kang ŭi *Sonyŏni onda* wa Hollok'osŭt'ŭ munhak," 10.

72. Cho Sŏnghŭi, "Han Kang ŭi *Sonyŏni onda* wa Hollok'osŭt'ŭ munhak," 12; Giorgio Agamben, *Remnants of Auschwitz: The Witness and the Archive*, trans. Daniel Heller-Roazen (New York: Zone Books, 1999), 33. To testify is thus "to place oneself in one's own language in the position of those who have lost it" (Agamben, *Remnants of Auschwitz*, 161); the value of such testimony "lies essentially in what it lacks; at its center it contains something that cannot be borne witness to.... The survivors . . . bear witness to a missing testimony" (Agamben, *Remnants of Auschwitz*, 34).

73. Cho Y., "'Kwangju' rŭl hyŏnjaehwa hanŭn il, 133.

74. "증언의 공백을 메우고 있는 작품" (Cho Sŏnghŭi, "Han Kang ŭi *Sonyŏni onda* wa Hollok'osŭt'ŭ munhak," 12).

75. Kim Yŏngch'an, "Kot'ong kwa munhak, kot'ong ŭi munhak," 298.

76. Kim Yŏngch'an, "Kot'ong kwa munhak, kot'ong ŭi munhak," 302.

77. Han, *Sonyŏni onda*, 211; my emphasis.

78. Jean-Luc Nancy, *The Ground of the Image*, trans. Jeff Fort (New York: Fordham University Press, 2005), 37. See also Rancière, *The Future of the Image*, especially "Are Some Things Unrepresentable?," 109–138.

79. Han, *Sonyŏni onda*, 78.

80. Han, *Sonyŏni onda*, 79.

81. Han, *Sonyŏni onda*, 99–100.

82. Han, *Sonyŏni onda*, 101.

83. Han, *Sonyŏni onda*, 103. It is worth pointing out that neither of the theatrical adoptions of Han's novel—one put on in South Korea, the other in Poland—allow Tongho to appear on the stage. He remains an absent cause, one that is never there yet perpetually arriving. In this way, the staging of the novel is consistent with the formal constraints it establishes for itself, resisting a simplistic mimetic representation of Kwangju and the idea of witness testimony as the foundation establishing the historical truth of the event.

84. "불가능한 대화"; "들리지 않는 타자의 목소리." Kim here is writing specifically about Han's novel *Nun han songi ka nongnŭn tongan* (Kim Yŏngch'an, "Kot'ong kwa munhak, kot'ong ŭi munhak," 298).

85. Kim Yŏngch'an, "Kot'ong kwa munhak, kot'ong ŭi munhak," 302.

86. Han, *Sonyŏni onda*, 102–103.

87. Kim Yŏngch'an, "Kot'ong kwa munhak, kot'ong ŭi munhak," 306.

88. Han, *Sonyŏni onda*, 143.

89. Han, *Sonyŏni onda*, 162.

90. Han, *Sonyŏni onda*, 166–167.

91. Han, *Sonyŏni onda*, 53.

92. Han, *Sonyŏni onda*, 85.

93. Han, *Sonyŏni onda*, 119.

94. Cho Y., "'Kwangju' rŭl hyŏnjaehwa hanŭn il," 129.

95. Han, *Sonyŏni onda*, 108, 139.

96. Han, *Sonyŏni onda*, 167.

97. Han, *Sonyŏni onda*, 174.

98. Han, *Sonyŏni onda*, 143–144.

99. "그것은 언어를 통한 전달 능력의 한계 나타낼 뿐이다" (Cho Sŏnghŭi, "Han Kang ŭi *Sonyŏni onda* wa Hollok'osŭt'ŭ munhak," 14). See Jean Améry, *At the Mind's Limits: Contemplations by a Survivor on Auschwitz and Its Realities*, trans. Sidney Rosenfeld and Stella P. Rosenfeld (Bloomington: Indiana University Press, 1980), 33, where he writes: "It would be totally senseless to try and describe here the pain that was inflicted on me. . . . One comparison would only stand for the other, and in the end we would be hoaxed by turn on the hopeless merry-go-round of figurative speech. The pain was what it was. Beyond that there is

184   *2. Displacing the Common Sense of Trauma*

nothing to say. Qualities of feeling are as incomparable as they are indescribable. They mark the limit of the capacity of language to communicate."

100. Han, *Sonyŏni onda*, 161.

101. Han, *Sonyŏni onda*, 108.

102. Han, *Sonyŏni onda*, 132; my emphasis.

103. Han, *Sonyŏni onda*, 133.

104. Rancière, *The Future of the Image*, 126. In some ways, Rancière's argument here is specific to his theory of regimes of art, with the "aesthetic regime" removing any inherent limits to representation that might have set "conditions defining the properties that subjects of representation must possess to permit an adequate submission of the visible to the sayable" in a previous regime, meaning that "there is no longer a language or form which is appropriate to a subject, whatever it might be" (Rancière, *The Future of the Image*, 136–137). Consequently, all language is available to the representation of any and all subjects, including extreme experiences.

105. Rancière, *The Future of the Image*, 129–130.

106. Cho Y., " 'Kwangju' rŭl hyŏnjaehwa hanŭn il," 105.

107. Freud, *Beyond the Pleasure Principle*, 12.

108. Rothberg, *Traumatic Realism*, 162.

109. Cho Y., " 'Kwangju' rŭl hyŏnjaehwa hanŭn il," 105.

110. Sŏ, "Kwangju ŭi poksu rŭl kkumkkunŭn il," 6.

111. The security headquarters building was acquired by the city of Kwangju in 2014 from the Ministry of National Defense, and there are plans to preserve the site as part of a historical memorial.

112. Hwang Chŏnga, " 'Kyŏl ŭl kŏsŭllŏ yŏksa rŭl solchil' hanŭn munhak," 72–73, 76; cited in Cho Sŏnghŭi, "Han Kang ŭi *Sonyŏni onda* wa Hollok'osŭt'ŭ munhak," 11.

113. Han, *Sonyŏni onda*, 199–200.

114. Han, *Sonyŏni onda*, 205.

115. Han, *Sonyŏni onda*, 203.

116. Han, *Sonyŏni onda*, 203–204.

117. Kim Yŏngch'an, "Kot'ong kwa munhak, kot'ong ŭi munhak," 310.

118. Cho Sŏnghŭi, "Han Kang ŭi *Sonyŏni onda* wa Hollok'osŭt'ŭ munhak," 7.

119. Rothberg, *Traumatic Realism*, 13.

120. Jacques Rancière, *The Edges of Fiction*, trans. Steve Corcoran (Cambridge: Polity Press, 2020), 9.

121. Agamben, *Remnants of Auschwitz*, 12. Agamben here is introducing the "aporia of history" in a far more complex way than my simple use of the quotation reveals. Yet it states perfectly what Han achieves with *Boy*: a principled

insistence on truth and comprehension over a political expediency that would make of Kwangju nothing but a verifiable fact.

122. Kim Yŏngch'an, "Kot'ong kwa munhak, kot'ong ŭi munhak," 293; see also Cho Sŏnghŭi, "Han Kang ŭi *Sonyŏni onda* wa Hollok'osŭt'ŭ munhak," 7–8, where the novel testifies to the "true memory" (*chinsilhan kiŏk*) of Kwangju against ongoing distortion (*waegok*) and slander (*p'yŏmhwe*).

123. LaCapra, *Writing History, Writing Trauma*, 46.

124. LaCapra, *Writing History, Writing Trauma*, xxii.

125. LaCapra, *Writing History, Writing Trauma*, 3.

126. Han, *Sonyŏni onda*, 118.

127. Han, *Sonyŏni onda*, 117.

128. Marc Nichanian, *The Historiographic Perversion*, trans. Gil Anidjar (New York: Columbia University Press, 2009), 17.

129. Nichanian, *The Historiographic Perversion*, 8.

130. Nichanian, *The Historiographic Perversion*, 122.

131. Nichanian, *The Historiographic Perversion*, 15.

132. Nichanian, *The Historiographic Perversion*, 64.

133. Nichanian, *The Historiographic Perversion*, 72; emphasis in the original.

134. Nichanian, *The Historiographic Perversion*, 68–69.

135. Rancière, *The Future of the Image*, 129.

136. Han, *Sonyŏni onda*, 202–203.

137. Allan Sekula, "Reading an Archive: Photography Between Labour and Capital," in *Visual Culture: The Reader*, ed. Jessica Evans and Stuart Hall (London: SAGE, 1999), 186.

138. Allan Sekula, Reading an Archive," 184.

139. Allan Sekula, Reading an Archive," 187; emphasis in the original.

140. Jacques Rancière, *Disagreement: Politics and Philosophy*, trans. Julie Rose (Minneapolis: University of Minnesota Press, 1999), 29–30.

141. Saidiya V. Hartman, *Scenes of Subjection: Terror, Slavery, and Self-Making in Nineteenth-Century America* (New York: Oxford University Press, 1997), 11. Hartman is paraphrasing Michel Foucault, *The Archaeology of Knowledge*, trans. A. M. Sheridan Smith (New York: Vintage, 1972), 130–131.

142. Butler, *Excitable Speech*, 140–141.

143. Rothberg, *Traumatic Realism*, 80. This is precisely what happens in the epilogue—the narrator remembers coming across a photo book from Kwangju when she was ten years old. She recalls that when she saw a photograph of horrible damage to a woman's face, "some tender part inside me, that I hadn't known existed, was broken without a sound" (Han, *Sonyŏni onda*, 199). What is narrated to us is the memory of a traumatic encounter with a photograph of an

event—we are doubly removed from the event itself; trauma arises in the linkage between present and past.

144. See Jean Laplanche, *Essays on Otherness* (London: Routledge, 1999), 157–161.

145. Jean Laplanche and J.-B. Pontalis, *The Language of Psycho-Analysis*, trans. Donald Nicholson-Smith (New York: Norton, 1973), 112.

146. Dominique Scarfone, "A Brief Introduction to the Work of Jean Laplanche," *International Journal of Psychoanalysis* 94 (2013): 554. Scarfone is citing Sigmund Freud, "Letter 52 (December 6, 1896)," in *Pre-Psycho-Analytic Publications and Unpublished Drafts (1886–1899)*, vol. 1 of *The Standard Edition of the Complete Psychological Works of Sigmund Freud*, trans. and ed. James Strachey (London: Hogarth Press, 1966), 235. See also Laplanche, *Essays on Otherness*, 154.

147. John Fletcher, "Introduction: Psychoanalysis and the Question of the Other," in Laplanche, *Essays on Otherness*, 13.

148. "Translation is compulsory because the content of the message is that which is spun by the web of relations of tenderness, affection, attachment, but also, at times, of passion and violence. Regardless of the emotional charge, the only way the tie can endure beyond death, beyond the loss of the object, of the other, is as a message. A message that remains only partially translated because its enigmatic part was transmitted unconsciously by the lost object. The enigma, Laplanche explains, is an enigma for the transmitter himself" (Scarfone, "A Brief Introduction to the Work of Jean Laplanche," 94).

149. Laplanche, *Essays on Otherness*, 158. See also Jean Laplanche, "Psychoanalysis as Anti-hermeneutics," trans. Luke Thurston, *Radical Philosophy* 79 (September/October 1996), 11; emphasis in the original. Here meaning is not contained entirely in the original, traumatic event; the "message" of the event is "compromised" and the determining power of the "facts" of the event fail to explain the present.

150. See Scarfone, "A Brief Introduction to the Work of Jean Laplanche," 562, where he cites Laplanche, *Essays on Otherness*, 250.

151. LaCapra, *Writing History, Writing Trauma*, xiv–xv, 21.

152. Scarfone, "A Brief Introduction to the Work of Jean Laplanche," 563.

153. Rothberg, *Traumatic Realism*, 78–79.

154. Laplanche and Pontalis, *The Language of Psycho-Analysis*, 112.

155. Scarfone, "A Brief Introduction to the Work of Jean Laplanche," 554.

156. Rothberg, *Tramatic Realism*, 131.

157. Gerasimos Kolaitis and Miranda Olff, "Psychotraumatology in Greece," *European Journal of Psychotraumatology* 8 (2017), 1.

158. This layering of images reminds me of Zbigniew Libera's "Positives" series from the early 2000s. "We are always dealing with remembered images of

things, not the things themselves," the artist wrote. "I wanted to use this mechanism of seeing and remembering, to touch on the phenomenon of after-image. This is in fact how we perceive these ["positive"] photographs—flashbacks of the cruel original images pierce through the innocent scenes" (Ewa Gorządek, "Positives—Zbigniew Libera," trans. Bozhana Nikolova, Culture.pl, March 2015, https://culture.pl/en/work/positives-zbigniew-libera).

159. Ch'oe Yun, *Chŏgi sori ŏpsi hanjŏm kkotnip i chigo* [There a petal silently falls], *Munhak kwa sahoe* [Literature and society] 1, no. 2 (1988): 730–788.

160. Ch'oe Yun, *There a Petal Silently Falls*, trans. Bruce and Ju-Chan Fulton, in *There a Petal Silently Falls: Three Stories by Ch'oe Yun* (New York: Columbia University Press, 2008), 3.

161. Im is quoted in Cho Y., " 'Kwangju' rŭl hyŏnjaehwa hanŭn il," 103.

162. Cho Y., " 'Kwangju' rŭl hyŏnjaehwa hanŭn il," 111.

163. Jacques Rancière, *Aesthetics and Its Discontents*, trans. Steven Corcoran (Cambridge: Polity Press, 2009), 24.

164. Rancière, *Disagreement*, 28.

165. Rancière, *Disagreement*, 28–29.

166. "5.18에 대해 말할 수 있는 자격이 따로 있다면 그것은 아직 5·18정신이 만개하지 않았다는 것입니다"; my emphasis. The "youngster" is most likely Pak Ŭnhyŏn, speaking at the November 19, 2019, "New Methods for Future Generations to Remember 5.18" forum at the May 18 Democratization Movement Archives (http://www.518.org/sub.php?PID=0201&action=Read&idx=1627). As part of her presentation, Pak asked: "누가 5·18에 대해 말할 수 있는 자격을 가졌을까요?" (Who has the qualification to be able to speak of 5.18?).

167. Jacques Rancière, *The Politics of Literature*, trans. Julie Rose (Cambridge: Polity, 2011), 83.

168. Rancière, *Disagreement*, 104–105.

169. "5.18 kinyŏmsik: Mun Chaein Taet'ongryŏng kinyŏmsa chŏnmun (2020)."

170. "5.18 kinyŏmsik: Mun Chaein Taet'ongryŏng kinyŏmsa chŏnmun (2019)."

171. Han, *Sonyŏni onda*, 69.

172. Han, *Sonyŏni onda*, 96.

173. Han, *Sonyŏni onda*, 97.

174. Rancière, *The Edges of Fiction*, 110.

175. Nichanian, *The Historiographic Perversion*, 123.

176. Walter Benjamin, *Illuminations: Essays and Reflections* (New York: Schocken, 1969), 255.

177. "훼손된 것, 훼손되지 말았어야 했던 것의 다른 이름" (Han, *Sonyŏni onda*, 202–207). Cho Sŏnghŭi mentions this passage in "Han Kang ŭi *Sonyŏni onda* wa Hollok'osŭt'ŭ munhak," 8.

188   2. *Displacing the Common Sense of Trauma*

178. See Rancière, *The Edges of Fiction*, 129.

179. Han, *Sonyŏni onda*, 214.

3. FABRICATING THE REAL

1. Douglas Gabriel, "Reality Effects for a Dangerous Age: Projecting North Korean Youth on the International Screen," *Situations* 13, no. 2 (2020): 70.

2. David Shields, *Reality Hunger: A Manifesto* (New York: Knopf, 2010).

3. Yeonmi Park, "What I Learned About Freedom After Escaping North Korea," TED Talk, September 26, 2019, YouTube video, 10:48, https://www.youtube.com/watch?v=mLzTo-y8Efo.

4. Marc Nichanian, *The Historiographic Perversion*, trans. Gil Anidjar (New York: Columbia University Press, 2009), 85.

5. Nichanian, *The Historiographic Perversion*, 8.

6. Nichanian, *The Historiographic Perversion*, 108–109.

7. Nichanian, *The Historiographic Perversion*, 27.

8. Judith Butler, *Excitable Speech: The Politics of the Performative* (New York: Routledge, 1997), 140–141.

9. Christine Hong, "War by Other Means: The Violence of North Korean Human Rights," *Asia-Pacific Journal: Japan Focus* 12, no. 2 (March 2014): 18.

10. "*The Orphan Master's Son*: A Novel," https://www.randomhousebooks.com/books/212862/.

11. "The 2013 Pulitzer Prize Winner in Fiction: *The Orphan Master's Son*, by Adam Johnson (Random House)," https://www.pulitzer.org/winners/adam-johnson.

12. Don George, "New Book Roundups," *National Geographic*, January 6, 2012, https://www.nationalgeographic.com/travel/article/ruins-of-us.

13. Michiko Kakutani, "A North Korean Soldier Finds His 'Casablanca,'" review of *The Orphan Master's Son*, by Adam Johnson, *New York Times*, January 12, 2012, https://www.nytimes.com/2012/01/13/books/the-orphan-masters-son-by-adam-johnson-review.html.

14. David Ignatius, review of *The Orphan Master's Son*, by Adam Johnson, *Washington Post*, January 9, 2012, https://www.washingtonpost.com/entertainment/books/book-review-the-orphan-masters-son-by-david-ignatius/2012/01/02/gIQAIZWZmP_story.html.

15. Thomas Gaughan, review of *The Orphan Master's Son*, *Booklist*, https://www.booklistonline.com/The-Orphan-Master-s-Son-Adam-Johnson/pid=5075833.

16. "*The Orphan Master's Son*," *Publishers Weekly*, January 2012, https://www.publishersweekly.com/978–0-8129-9279-3.

17. Barbara Demick, "A Spot-On Depiction of North Korea," review of *The Orphan Master's Son*, by Adam Johnson, *Guardian*, February 17, 2012, https://www.theguardian.com/books/2012/feb/17/orphan-masters-son-adam-johnson-review.

18. Ignatius, review of *The Orphan Master's Son*.

19. Hayden White, "The Fictions of Factual Representation," in *The Literature of Fact*, ed. Angus Fletcher (New York: Columbia University Press, 1976), 22.

20. Hong, "War by Other Means," 6.

21. Jacques Rancière, *Disagreement: Politics and Philosophy*, trans. Julie Rose (Minneapolis: University of Minnesota Press, 1999), 102.

22. Rancière, *Disagreement*, 30.

23. It is here, with the loss of the "relevance of speech," that Arendt locates the loss of human rights, a "fundamental deprivation . . . manifested first and above all in the deprivation of a place in the world which makes opinions significant and actions effective." In this sense, refugees are deprived "not of freedom, but of the right to action; not of the right to think whatever they please, but of the right to opinion" (Hannah Arendt, *The Origins of Totalitarianism* [New York: Harcourt Brace Jovanovich, 1973], 296–297).

24. Jacques Rancière, "Politics, Identification, and Subjectivization," *October* 61 (Summer 1992): 62.

25. Rancière, *Disagreement*, 29.

26. Rancière, "Politics, Identification, and Subjectivization," 61.

27. Adam Johnson, *The Orphan Master's Son* (New York: Random House, 2012), 379.

28. Jacques Rancière, *The Flesh of Words: The Politics of Writing*, trans. Charlotte Mandell (Stanford, CA: Stanford University Press, 2004), 103. See also Luka Arsenjuk for an extremely cogent summary of this argument: "The written word—the 'orphan word' Plato calls it—is always a supplementary element in relation to the communal order. It can liberate itself from a situation in which the roles of the proper addresser and the addressee, as well as the limits of what is sayable, are strictly determined. The written word can be appropriated by anyone. Unlike the individual utterance of the spoken word which is tied to 'the logic of the proper,' the written word, unexpected and inexhaustible, presents a certain 'wandering excess' in relation to the world of carefully distributed roles, tasks and the speech that is understood as properly belonging to the individuals and groups that are seen as performing these roles and tasks within the communal order. This excess of words over the existing distribution of the common that establishes the communal order represents the egalitarian power of language—which Rancière calls literarity—the ability to disturb the existing circuits of words, meanings and places of enunciation" (Luka

Arsenjuk, "On Jacques Rancière," *Eurozine*, March 1, 2007, https://www.eurozine.com/on-jacques-ranciere/. First published in *Fronesis* 19–20 [2005]).

29. Nichanian, *The Historiographic Perversion*, 94.

30. Davide Panagia, "Dissenting Words: A Conversation with Jacques Rancière," *Diacritics* 30, no. 2 (Summer 2000): 115.

31. Johnson, *The Orphan Master's Son*, 39–40.

32. Johnson, *The Orphan Master's Son*, 230, 330.

33. Johnson, *The Orphan Master's Son*, 184.

34. Adam Johnson, "Fortune Smiles," in *Fortune Smiles* (New York: Random House, 2015), 254.

35. Johnson, "Fortune Smiles," 251.

36. Johnson, "Fortune Smiles," 252.

37. Johnson, "Fortune Smiles," 252.

38. Johnson, "Fortune Smiles," 257.

39. Johnson, "Fortune Smiles," 261.

40. Johnson, "Fortune Smiles," 300.

41. Johnson, "Fortune Smiles," 252–253.

42. Johnson, "Fortune Smiles," 279.

43. Johnson, "Fortune Smiles," 256.

44. Johnson, "Fortune Smiles," 289.

45. Johnson, "Fortune Smiles," 262.

46. Johnson, "Fortune Smiles," 265.

47. Johnson, "Fortune Smiles," 266.

48. Johnson, "Fortune Smiles," 256.

49. Johnson, "Fortune Smiles," 290–291.

50. Hong, "War by Other Means," 1.

51. Hong, "War by Other Means," 6.

52. Hong, "War by Other Means," 18.

53. Wendy Brown, "'The Most We Can Hope For . . .': Human Rights and the Politics of Fatalism," *South Atlantic Quarterly* 103, no. 2/3 (Spring/Summer 2004): 455.

54. Brown, "'The Most We Can Hope For . . .,'" 456.

55. Brown, "'The Most We Can Hope For . . .,'" 453.

56. Slavoj Žižek, "Against Human Rights," *New Left Review* 34 (July/August 2005): 128.

57. Rancière, *Disagreement*, 126.

58. Rancière, *Disagreement*, 126–127. The critique of "cultural purism and the obsession with authenticity" provides the starting point for Soo Yeon Kim's review of Johnson's novel *The Orphan Master's Son*, opening with Lionel Shriver's assertion of "the right to write fiction, inauthentic by definition." See

3. Fabricating the Real 191

Soo Yeon Kim, "Cultural Appropriation, or the Right to Write Fiction: Narrating North Korea in Adam Johnson's *The Orphan Master's Son*," *Foreign Literature Studies* 73 (February 2019): 94.

59. Rancière, *Disagreement*, 127.

60. Johnson, "Fortune Smiles," 256.

61. Johnson, "Fortune Smiles," 277–278.

62. Hong, "War by Other Means," 18. Johnson concurs: "Few things about North Korea are verifiable (beyond satellite images and the testimonies of defectors)." North Korea is thus seemingly "a realm in which the imaginative reach of literary fiction is our best tool to discover the human dimension of such an elusive society" ("A Conversation Between Adam Johnson and David Ebershoff," in Johnson, *The Orphan Master's Son*, 453).

63. Hong, "War by Other Means," 18.

64. Hong, "War by Other Means," 6.

65. Giorgio Agamben, *Remnants of Auschwitz: The Witness and the Archive*, trans. Daniel Heller-Roazen (New York: Zone Books, 1999), 17.

66. Nichanian, *The Historiographic Perversion*, 97.

67. Nichanian, *The Historiographic Perversion*, 120–121. "I have felt shame, therefore, each time testimony was exhibited, presented, offered as proof," Nichanian goes on. "Each time, we were, we had to be so many living proofs of our own death."

68. Rancière, *Disagreement*, 112; Jacques Rancière, *The Lost Thread: The Democracy of Modern Fiction*, trans. Steven Corcoran (London: Bloomsbury Academic, 2017), 67.

69. Theodore Hughes, "'North Koreans' and Other Virtual Subjects: Kim Yeongha, Hwang Seok-yeong, and National Division in the Age of Posthumanism," *Review of Korean Studies* 11, no. 1 (March 2008): 115.

70. Rancière, *The Lost Thread*, 66.

71. See Hal Foster, "Obscene, Abject, Traumatic," *October* 78 (Autumn 1996): 106–124.

72. Rancière, *Disagreement*, 102–104.

73. Kellen Hoxworth, "Performative Correctness; or, the Subject of Performance and Politics," *Journal of Dramatic Theory and Criticism* 35, no. 2 (Spring 2021): 107.

74. John Cussen, "On the Call to Dismiss North Korean Defectors' Memoirs and on Their Dark American Alternative," *Korean Studies* 40 (2016): 140–141.

75. Hoxworth, "Performative Correctness," 108.

76. Hoxworth, "Performative Correctness," 110.

77. Blaine Harden, *Escape from Camp 14: One Man's Remarkable Odyssey from North Korea to Freedom in the West* (London: Pan Books, 2015), viii, ix.

78. Harden, *Escape from Camp 14*, viii, ix, xi.

79. Harden, *Escape from Camp 14*, xiii.

80. Žižek, "Against Human Rights," 128.

81. Rancière, *Disagreement*, 102.

82. Rancière, *Disagreement*, 104.

83. Rey Chow, *Writing Diaspora: Tactics of Intervention in Contemporary Cultural Studies* (Bloomington: Indiana University Press, 1993), 111. While the quotation is taken out of context—Chow is discussing minority discourse in relation to the status of the topic of women in the field of Chinese studies—her focus is similarly on the construction of discourse and the establishment of "the difference that separates those who speak and those who are spoken of/for" (114).

84. See John Power, "North Korea: Defectors and Their Skeptics," *The Diplomat*, October 29, 2014, https://thediplomat.com/2014/10/north-korea-defectors -and-their-skeptics/.

85. Mary Ann Jolley, "The Strange Tale of Yeonmi Park," *The Diplomat*, December 10, 2014, https://thediplomat.com/2014/12/the-strange-tale-of-yeonmi -park.

86. Yeonmi Park, *In Order to Live: A North Korean Girl's Journey to Freedom* (New York: Penguin, 2015), 4.

87. See Cussen, "On the Call to Dismiss North Korean Defectors' Memoirs"; Power, "North Korea: Defectors and Their Skeptics"; and Jolley, "The Strange Tale of Yeonmi Park."

88. Nichanian, *The Historiographic Perversion*, 7.

89. Nichanian, *The Historiographic Perversion*, 28.

90. Roland Barthes, *The Rustle of Language*, trans. Richard Howard (Berkeley: University of California Press, 1989), 147.

91. Barthes, *The Rustle of Language*, 146.

92. Barthes, *The Rustle of Language*, 148; my emphasis.

93. Barthes, *The Rustle of Language*, 147; emphasis in the original.

94. Barthes, *The Rustle of Language*, 146.

95. *Oxford Dictionary of English*, ed. Angus Stevenson (Oxford: Oxford University Press, 2010), 626, s.v. "factive."

96. Park, *In Order to* Live, 51.

97. Park, *In Order to* Live, 113.

98. Even with statements such as "I was amazed that Leonardo DiCaprio and Kate Winslet were willing to die for love, not just for the regime, as we were" (Park, *In Order to Live*, 53), the factive works to produce a sense of truth, with the narrator's willingness to "die . . . for the regime" bolstered by its proximity to the tragic romantic plot of *Titanic*. The factive logic of the memoir form works seamlessly with that of the fictional narrative of the feature film.

3. Fabricating the Real 193

99. Rancière, *Disagreement*, 126–127.

100. Here we have only to look at the objections raised to Park's statements on the popular South Korean television show *Now on My Way to Meet You*, where Park points to photos of her family wearing clothes imported from Japan and carrying Chanel bags, describes the famine of the 1990s as "nothing special . . . because I have so much fun playing with my friends," hiking and swimming, and claims that her family never endured starvation or struggled to find food. Jolley also raises questions regarding aspects of Park's testimony that the escapee appears to refute elsewhere, including whether or not both parents were with her when she crossed the border into China, whether or not she buried her father by herself following his death, whether or not she was stripped daily in a detention center in Mongolia, and even whether or not she climbed mountains to get to the border during the escape. ("Hyesan," Jolley tells us, "where Park was living is right on the river that divides the two countries and there are no mountains to cross.") The point is that there is no interest whatsoever in gathering facts from Park's testimony regarding the topography of North Korea or the punitive practices at Mongolian detention centers. The outrage here is not due to the uncertainty of the facts, but rather the suggestion that Park did not *suffer* as much as she had suggested elsewhere. In this suffering lies the authenticity of the one framed in human rights discourse as a victim; her words may refer only to this degree of suffering that qualifies her to speak, and she is silenced when her speech suggests that such suffering did not take place to the degree demanded or expected.

101. Jacques Rancière, "Who Is the Subject of the Rights of Man?," *South Atlantic Quarterly* 103, no. 2/3 (Spring/Summer 2004): 306. In this sense, we can consider the anxiety regarding the hackneyed plot of escapee narratives to Žižek's discussion of the "pornographic." Pornography traditionally respects the prohibition against showing real intimacy, Žižek writes: "the narrative which provided the frame for repeated sexual encounters was as a rule ridiculously non-realistic, stereotypical, stupidly comical," filled with "one-dimensional types" (Slavoj Žižek, *The Fright of Real Tears: Krzysztof Kieślowski Between Theory and Post-Theory* [London: British Film Institute, 2001], 76). We know that it is not real, that the actors are not actually engaged, and it is this that makes the "showing everything" enjoyable rather than what it would be otherwise, an atrocious intrusion into intimacy. Similarly, the stereotypical plots of escapee narratives, the predictable dialogue, events, and so on are precisely what shields the reader from the horrifying intimacy, the "too close to the scene," of their stories. In this sense, Johnson's fiction is transgressive in that it integrates the "hardcore" into a literary narrative, not the enjoyment permitted by the *too good to be real* but an exposure that is *all too real* despite its overt fictionality.

102. Rancière, *Disagreement*, 37.

103. Rancière, "Who Is the Subject of the Rights of Man?," 304.

104. Hoxworth, "Performative Correctness," 107.

105. Hoxworth, "Performative Correctness," 111.

106. Gabriel, "Reality Effects for a Dangerous Age," 71–72.

107. Gabriel, "Reality Effects for a Dangerous Age," 83.

108. Gabriel, "Reality Effects for a Dangerous Age," 85.

109. Vitaly Mansky, "Real'noe kino" [Real cinema], http://manski-doc.com /page134648.html; cited in Gabriel, "Reality Effects for a Dangerous Age," 86.

110. Mansky is quoted in Carmen Gray, "Russian Film Exposes the Workings of North Korea's Propaganda Machine: *Under the Sun* Shows Behind-the-Scenes Coercion by Government Minders Trying to Construct and Image of a 'Normal' Family," *Guardian*, December 3, 2015, https://www.theguardian.com /world/2015/dec/02/north-korea-under-the-sun-vitaly-mansky-film.

111. "We Will Not Forget," *Arirang Meari*, May 19, 2016; cited in Gabriel, "Reality Effects for a Dangerous Age," 89.

112. Gabriel, "Reality Effects for a Dangerous Age," 91.

113. Žižek, *The Fright of Real Tears*, 75; emphasis in the original.

114. Žižek, *The Fright of Real Tears*, 75; emphasis in the original.

115. Žižek, *The Fright of Real Tears*, 72.

116. Rancière, *Disagreement*, 104.

117. Johnson, *The Orphan Master's Son*, 140.

118. Johnson, *The Orphan Master's Son*, 175.

119. Johnson, *The Orphan Master's Son*, 3.

120. Johnson, *The Orphan Master's Son*, 4.

121. Johnson, *The Orphan Master's Son*, 4.

122. See Philippe Lejeune, *On Autobiography*, ed. Paul Eakin, trans. Katherine Leary (Minneapolis: University of Minnesota Press, 1989), especially 3–30.

123. "How can narrative embody life in words and at the same time respect what we cannot know? How does one listen for the groans and cries, the indecipherable songs, the crackle of fire in the cane fields, the laments for the dead, and the shouts of victory, and then assign words to all of it?" Saidiya Hartman, "Venus in Two Acts," *Small Axe* 12, no. 2 (June 2008): 3.

124. Hartman, "Venus in Two Acts," 4.

125. Johnson, *The Orphan Master's Son*, 146.

126. Johnson, *The Orphan Master's Son*, 210.

127. Johnson, *The Orphan Master's Son*, 315.

128. Johnson, *The Orphan Master's Son*, 181.

129. Johnson, *The Orphan Master's Son*, 316.

130. Johnson, *The Orphan Master's Son*, 316–317.

3. Fabricating the Real   195

131. Johnson, *The Orphan Master's Son*, 188.

132. Johnson, *The Orphan Master's Son*, 316.

133. Johnson, *The Orphan Master's Son*, 184.

134. Hartman, "Venus in Two Acts," 4.

135. Johnson, *The Orphan Master's Son*, 204.

136. Johnson, *The Orphan Master's Son*, 187.

137. Johnson, *The Orphan Master's Son*, 379.

138. Johnson, *The Orphan Master's Son*, 406.

139. Johnson, *The Orphan Master's Son*, 443.

140. Johnson, *The Orphan Master's Son*, 294.

141. Johnson, *The Orphan Master's Son*, 443.

142. Johnson, *The Orphan Master's Son*, 425.

143. Johnson, *The Orphan Master's Son*, 184.

144. Johnson, *The Orphan Master's Son*, 73.

145. Johnson, *The Orphan Master's Son*, 91.

146. Johnson, *The Orphan Master's Son*, 342.

147. Johnson, *The Orphan Master's Son*, 306.

148. Johnson, *The Orphan Master's Son*, 185.

149. Johnson, *The Orphan Master's Son*, 121–122.

150. Johnson, *The Orphan Master's Son*, 153.

151. Johnson, *The Orphan Master's Son*, 393.

152. Johnson, *The Orphan Master's Son*, 384.

153. Johnson, *The Orphan Master's Son*, 242–243.

154. Johnson, *The Orphan Master's Son*, 382.

155. Johnson, *The Orphan Master's Son*, 253.

156. Johnson, *The Orphan Master's Son*, 258.

157. Rancière, "Who Is the Subject of the Rights of Man?," 306.

158. Johnson, *The Orphan Master's Son*, 421.

159. Johnson, *The Orphan Master's Son*, 418.

160. Johnson, *The Orphan Master's Son*, 83.

161. Johnson, *The Orphan Master's Son*, 85.

162. Johnson, *The Orphan Master's Son*, 88.

163. Johnson, *The Orphan Master's Son*, 89.

164. Johnson, *The Orphan Master's Son*, 75.

165. Johnson, *The Orphan Master's Son*, 90.

166. Johnson, *The Orphan Master's Son*, 342.

167. Johnson, *The Orphan Master's Son*, 435.

168. Johnson, *The Orphan Master's Son*, 328, 438.

169. Johnson, *The Orphan Master's Son*, 438.

170. Johnson, *The Orphan Master's Son*, 363.

171. Rancière, *The Flesh of Words*, 102.

172. Johnson, *The Orphan Master's Son*, 437.

173. Johnson, *The Orphan Master's Son*, 399.

174. Rancière, *The Flesh of Words*, 102.

175. Johnson, *The Orphan Master's Son*, 207–208.

176. Johnson, *The Orphan Master's Son*, 427–428.

177. Butler, *Excitable Speech*, 144.

178. Butler, *Excitable Speech*, 144–145.

179. Rancière, *Disagreement*, 36–37.

180. Johnson, *The Orphan Master's Son*, 155.

181. "What am I doing?" the protagonist asks at one point. "There's no name for it," he is told. "There's no name because no one's ever done it before" (Johnson, *The Orphan Master's Son*, 249).

182. The point is not "to create credible characters, situations, and connections between events, because in a way they are real, so you don't have to prove that they are possible. . . . The question is not, 'Is it real?,' but: 'What kind of reality is at play here?'" (Stoffel Debuysere, "On the Borders of Fiction: A Conversation with Jacques Rancière," *Sabzian*, September 20, 2017, https://www.sabzian.be/article/on-the-borders-of-fiction).

183. Jonardon Ganeri, *Virtual Subjects, Fugitive Selves: Fernando Pessoa and His Philosophy* (Oxford: Oxford University Press, 2020), 96.

184. Johnson, "Fortune Smiles," 301.

185. Rancière, *The Flesh of Words*, 102.

4. DISTURBING SENSIBILITY

1. Jacques Rancière, *The Flesh of Words: The Politics of Writing*, trans. Charlotte Mandell (Stanford, CA: Stanford University Press, 2004), 102.

2. Rancière, *The Flesh of Words*, 103–104.

3. Jacques Rancière, *The Names of History: On the Poetics of Knowledge*, trans. Hassan Melehy (Minneapolis: University of Minnesota Press, 1994), 84.

4. Jörg Schweinitz, *Film and Stereotype: A Challenge for Cinema and Theory*, trans. Laura Schleussner (New York: Columbia University Press, 2011), 90; emphasis in the original.

5. Naoki Sakai, "Introduction: Nationality and the Politics of the 'Mother Tongue,'" in *Deconstructing Nationality*, ed. Naoki Sakai, Brett de Bary, and Iyotani Toshio (Ithaca, NY: East Asia Program, 2005), 3.

6. Sakai, "Introduction," 6.

7. See Georges Canguilhem, *The Normal and the Pathological*, trans. Carolyn R. Fawcett (New York: Zone Books, 1991), 115.

8. On the reification of the patient, see Kathryn Hunter, *Doctors' Stories: The Narrative Structure of Medical Knowledge* (Princeton, NJ: Princeton University Press, 1991), 132–138.

9. Jacques Rancière, *The Lost Thread: The Democracy of Modern Fiction*, trans. Steven Corcoran (London: Bloomsbury Academic, 2017), xxxiii.

10. Jacques Rancière, *Aesthetics and Its Discontents*, trans. Steven Corcoran (Cambridge: Polity Press, 2009), 24.

11. Rancière, *Aesthetics and Its Discontents*, 24.

12. David Palumbo-Liu, *The Deliverance of Others: Reading Literature in a Global Age* (Durham, NC: Duke University Press, 2012), 2.

13. Palumbo-Liu, *The Deliverance of Others*, 3.

14. Palumbo-Liu, *The Deliverance of Others*, 5.

15. Henri Lefebvre, *State, Space, World: Selected Essays*, ed. Neil Brenner and Stuart Elden, trans. Gerald Moore, Neil Brenner, and Stuart Elden (Minneapolis: University of Minnesota Press, 2009), 278.

16. Lefebvre, *State, Space, World*, 285.

17. Here we can consider the significance of the films in terms of their capacity to suggest the impossible, as representations of what Žižek calls a "true act" that is impossible prior to its enactment, but that in enactment changes the very field of possible action. The authentic act is an "enacted utopia," living as though utopia were already here, but is also a *criminal* act, in violation of the law. See Slavoj Žižek, "Lenin's Choice," in *Revolution at the Gates*, ed. Žižek (London: Verso, 2002), 259; cited in Tere Vadén, "Žižek's Phenomenology of the Subject: Transcendental or Materialist?," *International Journal of Žižek Studies* 2, no. 2 (2008): 10. Or, as Hakim Bey puts it, the revolutionary act is to "act as if you were already free." See Hakim Bey, *T.A.Z.: The Temporary Autonomous Zone: Ontological Anarchy, Poetic Terrorism* (New York: Autonomedia, 2004), 21.

18. Theodor W. Adorno, *Aesthetic Theory*, trans. and ed. Robert Hullot-Kentor (Minneapolis: University of Minnesota Press, 1997), 233.

19. Jacques Rancière, "How Does Architecture Distribute the Sensible?" Architecture Exchange, Cooper Union, November 16, 2019, YouTube video, 1:42:34, https://www.youtube.com/watch?v=7NcWthWJflw.

20. Gabriel Rockhill, "Translator's Introduction: Jacques Rancière's Politics of Perception," in Jacques Rancière, *The Politics of Aesthetics: The Distribution of the Sensible*, trans. Gabriel Rockhill (London: Continuum, 2004), 3.

21. Slavoj Žižek, "The Lesson of Rancière," in Rancière, *The Politics of Aesthetics*, 77.

22. Rockhill, "Translator's Introduction," 3.

23. Lefebvre, *State, Space, World*, 278.

24. Rancière, "How Does Architecture Distribute the Sensible?": "The utopist must then play the part of a super-architect, who invents the well-partitioned space suitable for people who don't hold a place."

25. See Sigmund Freud, "Transference," in *Introductory Letters on Psycho-Analysis (Part 3) (1916–1917)*, vol. 16 of *The Standard Edition of the Complete Psychological Works of Sigmund Freud*, trans. and ed. James Strachey (London: Hogarth Press, 1963), 431–447.

26. Sigmund Freud, "Remembering, Repeating and Working-Through," in *Case History of Schreber, Papers on Technique and Other Works (1911–1913)*, vol. 12 of *The Standard Edition of the Complete Psychological Works of Sigmund Freud*, trans. and ed. James Strachey (London: Hogarth Press, 1958), 154; emphasis mine.

27. Palumbo-Liu, *The Deliverance of Others*, x.

28. Palumbo-Liu, *The Deliverance of Others*, 14.

29. Palumbo-Liu, *The Deliverance of Others*, 10.

30. Jacques Rancière, *Disagreement: Politics and Philosophy*, trans. Julie Rose (Minneapolis: University of Minnesota Press, 1999), 104, 11.

31. The final visual overlap involves the removal of director Pak Ch'anuk's name from a wall-mounted nametag holder and its replacement with Yŏnggun's, inaugurating the remainder of the film, which takes place in the asylum, and further blurring the distinction between the real and fantasy.

32. "There are 'blind fields' whenever language fails us, whenever there is a surfeit or redundancy in a metalanguage (discourse about discourse, signifiers floating far from their signifieds). . . . The blinding is the luminous source (knowledge or ideology) that projects a beam of light, that illuminates *elsewhere*. The blinded is our dazed stare, as well as the region left in shadow. On the one hand a path is opened to exploration; on the other there is an enclosure to break out of, a consecration to transgress" (Henri Lefebvre, *The Urban Revolution*, trans. Robert Bononno [Minneapolis: University of Minnesota Press, 2003], 31).

33. "Reification goes beyond the defensible, useful 'translation' of the patient into a case to the summary reduction of that case to a diagnostic label. The physician—or the philosophy of medicine—that fails to recognize the inalienability of the patient's story and the experience it represents will offer little resistance other than mere etiquette to reification" (Hunter, *Doctors' Stories*, 136).

34. See Julie Hepworth, *The Social Construction of Anorexia Nervosa* (London: Sage, 1999), especially 1–6.

35. Simona Giordano, *Understanding Eating Disorders* (Oxford: Clarendon Press, 2005), 40.

36. Hunter, *Doctors' Stories*, 119.

4. Disturbing Sensibility 199

37. Though *Cyborg* also contains a moment of a-nationalism: when Yŏnggun emerges from EST, the psychiatrist asks her her name, and then who the president is, to ascertain her awareness, her retention of memory, her mental health. Yŏnggun cannot answer regarding the president—instead, she draws the doctor down to her, smiles, and whispers, "But I didn't know in the first place."

38. Rancière, *The Flesh of Words*, 103–104.

39. Rancière, *Aesthetics and Its Discontents*, 24.

40. Tamar Jeffers McDonald, *Romantic Comedy* (London: Wallflower Press, 2007), 9.

41. "In my view, a cure is impossible" (Kim Young-jin, *Korean Film Directors: Park Chan-wook* [Seoul: KOFIC, 2007], 117).

42. Karin Siegl, *The Robinsonade Tradition in Robert Michael Ballantyne's "The Coral Island" and William Golding's "The Lord of the Flies"* (Lewiston, NY: Mellen, 1996), 8; cited in Verena Schörkhuber, "*Robinson Crusoe* Goes Postcolonial: Re-Writings of the Crusoe Myth by Derek Walcott and J. M. Coetzee," MPhil diss. (University of Vienna, 2009), 4.

43. Janet Bertsch, *Storytelling in the Works of Bunyan, Grimmelshausen, Defoe and Schnabel* (Columbia, SC: Camden House, 2004), 79; cited in Schörkhuber, "*Robinson Crusoe* Goes Postcolonial," 4.

44. Carl Fisher, "The Robinsonade: An Intercultural History of an Idea," in *Approaches to Teaching Defoe's "Robinson Crusoe,"* ed. Maximillian E. Novak and Carl Fisher (New York: Modern Language Association of America, 2005), 130; cited in Sophia Nikoleishvili, "The Many Faces of Daniel Defoe's 'Robinson Crusoe': Examining the Crusoe Myth in Film and on Television" (PhD diss., University of Missouri, 2007), 3.

45. My thanks to Anne McKnight for pointing out these connections.

46. Edward Said, *The World, the Text, and the Critic* (Cambridge, MA: Harvard University Press, 1983), 135; emphasis in the original.

47. This is a wonderful reversal of the cynical Robinsonade, exemplified by Huxley's Dr. MacPhail: "whether we shall be able to persuade you people to follow our example, or whether we shall even be able to preserve our tiny oasis of humanity in the midst of your world-wide wilderness of monkeys—that, alas . . . is another question" (Aldous Huxley, *Island* [New York: Harper and Row, 1962], 134). Here instead it is a matter of preserving a tiny oasis of wilderness within the civilized city, while retaining the values assigned in Huxley's text—the city becomes an alien landscape while human relations are formed through the connection of encampments within that worldwide space.

48. "그냥 희망을 버려 그리고 힘 냅시다!" (Give up hope [of losing your fantasy, of being normal, of being cured] but give it all you've got [continue living, living in and with the fantasy, in a way that allows you to survive]!).

49. Palumbo-Liu, *The Deliverance of Others*, 24.

50. Rancière, *The Flesh of Words*, 102.

51. Rancière, *Disagreement*, 37.

52. Palumbo-Liu, *The Deliverance of Others*, 5.

53. Palumbo-Liu, *The Deliverance of Others*, xii.

54. In the sense of the character of the asset manager in DeLillo's *Cosmopolis*, who, when confronted with street protests against capitalist injustice outside his limousine window, notes that their resistance itself is a product of the market. "There is nowhere they can go to be on the outside," he tell us. "There is no outside." See Don DeLillo, *Cosmopolis* (New York: Scribner, 2003), 90.

55. Rancière, *Disagreement*, 36.

56. Lefebvre, *The Urban Revolution*, 38–39.

57. Lefebvre, *State, Space, World*, 40.

58. Lefebvre, *State, Space, World*, 285.

59. "The future illuminates the past, the virtual allows us to examine and situate the realized" (Lefebvre, *The Urban Revolution*, 23).

60. Rockhill, "Translator's Introduction," 3.

61. Constantinos A. Doxiadis, "Man's Movement and His Settlements," *Ekistics* 29, no. 174 (May 1970): 298.

62. Constantinos A. Doxiadis, "Ecumenopolis, World-City of Tomorrow," in *The Ecology of Many: An Ecosystem Approach*, ed. Robert Leo Smith (New York: Harper and Row, 1972), 161.

63. Here see Ulf Hannerz's treatment of the "global ecumene," where he retains the division between global and local along a center-periphery model. Ulf Hannerz, "Cosmopolitans and Locals in World Culture," *Theory, Culture, Society* 7 (1990): 237–251; and Ulf Hannerz, "Notes on the Global Ecumene," *Public Culture* 1, no. 2 (Spring 1989): 66–75.

64. Doxiadis, "Man's Movement," 313–314.

65. Gregory Jusdanis, *Belated Modernity and Aesthetic Culture: Inventing National Literature* (Minneapolis: University of Minnesota Press, 1991), 2–9.

66. Lefebvre, *The Urban Revolution*, 3. For Lefebvre, this "virtual object" is itself planetary society, the "global city" (Lefebvre, *The Urban Revolution*, 17).

67. See Slavoj Žižek, *The Parallax View* (Cambridge, MA: MIT Press, 2006), 17. A better figure might be Lefebvre's when he writes: "Theory opens the road, clears a new way; practice takes it, it *produces* the route and the space" (Lefebvre, *State, Space, World*, 288).

68. Peter Hallward, *Absolutely Postcolonial: Writing Between the Singular and the Specific* (Manchester: Manchester University Press, 2001), 37.

4. Disturbing Sensibility   201

CONCLUSION

1. Jacques Rancière, *Disagreement: Politics and Philosophy*, trans. Julie Rose (Minneapolis: University of Minnesota Press, 1999), 28.
2. Jacques Rancière, *The Lost Thread: The Democracy of Modern Fiction*, trans. Steven Corcoran (London: Bloomsbury Academic, 2017), 66.
3. Saidiya V. Hartman, *Scenes of Subjection: Terror, Slavery, and Self-Making in Nineteenth-Century America* (New York: Oxford University Press, 1997), 11.
4. Judith Butler, *Excitable Speech: The Politics of the Performative* (New York: Routledge, 1997), 140.
5. Rancière, *The Lost Thread*, 67; Rancière, *Disagreement*, 112.
6. Marc Nichanian, *The Historiographic Perversion*, trans. Gil Anidjar (New York: Columbia University Press, 2009), 112.
7. See Mark M. Anderson, "The Edge of Darkness: On W. G. Sebald," *October* 106 (Autumn 2003): 102–121.
8. The Korean translation of Sebald's book has this as "기억은 최후의 것 마저 파괴하지 않은가" (Doesn't memory destroy even the last thing?).
9. W. G. Sebald, *On the Natural History of Destruction*, trans. Anthea Bell (New York: Modern Library, 2003), 75.
10. Sebald, *On the Natural History of Destruction*, 25.
11. Sebald, *On the Natural History of Destruction*, 80.
12. Sebald, *On the Natural History of Destruction*, 83.
13. Sebald, *On the Natural History of Destruction*, 92.
14. Sebald, *On the Natural History of Destruction*, 92.
15. Sebald, *On the Natural History of Destruction*, 70.
16. The epigraph to the second story in *The Emigrants* reads: "There is a mist that no eye can dispel."
17. Sebald, *On the Natural History of Destruction*, 98.
18. Roland Barthes, *The Rustle of Language*, trans. Richard Howard (Berkeley: University of California Press, 1989), 4.
19. Han Kang, *Sonyŏni onda* [A boy is coming] (Seoul: Ch'angbi, 2018), 152.
20. What, after all, is the patient asked after undergoing electroshock therapy? "What is your name?" "What year is it?" "Who is the president?" A common understanding of the identity of the subject, a shared point in time, and knowledge of the political present signal a return to normative health. Yet *Cyborg* ends with a scene of failed translation, an inability to receive a clear message on the "purpose of life," and an inexplicable night spent on a mountaintop. In *A Boy Is Coming*, we have the silent performance, the indistinct photograph, the refusal to testify; *Castaway* ends with the unanswered question, "Who are you?"; and *The Orphan Master's Son*—despite the work of the "autopilot," the

self-modulating torture device that also runs electricity through the body of the incarcerated—likewise refuses from first to last to identify its protagonist, to assign a name by which we can finally understand the subject's place in a human rights order.

21. Sebald, *On the Natural History of Destruction*, 25.

22. From Moon's social media comments on the thirty-fourth anniversary of the 1987 June Democratic Uprising and the commencement of construction of the Democratic and Human Rights Memorial Hall, quoted in "Yet Namyŏngdong punsil e minju-inkwŏn kidong sewŏ kukka p'ongnyŏki dŭlŏsŏji mot'hage hal kŏt" [Setting up pillars of democracy and human rights at old Namyŏngdong branch office to prevent the recurrence of state violence in our country], *Kyŏnghyang sinmun* [Kyunghyang news], June 10, 2021, https://m.khan.co.kr /politics/president/article/202106102150025.

23. Jacques Rancière, "Politics, Identification, and Subjectivization," *October* 61 (Summer 1992): 62.

24. Theodor W. Adorno, *Aesthetic Theory*, trans. and ed. Robert Hullot-Kentor (Minneapolis: University of Minnesota Press, 1997), 233.

25. Rancière, *Disagreement*, 29–30.

26. See Jean-Jacques Lecercle, "Storming Language," *Crisis and Critique* 5, no. 2 (November 2018): 205–216.

27. Joan Scott, "The Evidence of Experience," *Critical Inquiry* 17, no. 4 (Summer 1991): 793. "Treating the emergence of a new identity as a discursive event," Scott writes, "is not to introduce a new form of linguistic determinism, nor to deprive subjects of agency. It is to refuse a separation between 'experience' and language and to insist instead on the productive quality of discourse."

28. There is perhaps no greater example of the potential of literature to set forth a dispute about the "rules of speakability" and to disrupt the limits of sensible discourse established in the process of foreclosure than Cho Sehŭi's series of linked short stories titled *Nanjangi ka ssoaollin chagŭn kong* [A dwarf launches a little ball] (Seoul: Isŏng kwa him, 2000). Here is a text that, as critic Kim Pyŏngik wrote, puts forward "the one displaced from the existing social structure" who has "lost the right to be human," uprooted in the processes of industrialization and urbanization in late 1970s South Korea, an "alien" or "space traveler" who has no place on the surface of the earth (Kim Pyŏngik, "Nanjangi, hogŭn sooe chipdan ŭi ŏnŏ" [The dwarf, or, the language of the alienated], *Munhak kwa chisŏng* [Literature and intellect] [Spring 1977]: 63–64). Yet, as Kim writes in a 1978 essay, in the "uncrossable abyss" between the worlds of the haves and the have-nots, the laborers and the consumers—a spatial rupture understood as an ethical rupture—we find a "confrontation of coexisting worlds" in a single text (Kim Pyŏngik, "Taeripjŏk segyegwan kwa mihak" [Aesthetics and the

oppositional worldview], in Cho Sehǔi, *Nanjangi*, 322–326). This is a confrontation adjudicated not in the realm of content, where the impossibility of coexistence is demonstrated again and again as a "situation that cannot be spoken" (Kim P., "Taeripjŏk segyegwan kwa mihak," 326; citing Cho Sehǔi, *Nanjangi*, 175). Rather, it is in the *form* of the text—through its famous use of simple sentences with no connectives, a failure to distinguish grammatically between past and present, the absence of any gap between objective and subjective depiction, and so on—all techniques that allow the language of Cho's work to stand as a formal demonstration of the failure of explanatory power of language and to undermine clear-cut classificatory categories of (abstract, aesthetic) "modernism" or (materialist, empirical) "realism." For more on Cho's fiction, see Youngju Ryu, *Writers of the Winter Republic: Literature and Resistance in Park Chung Hee's Korea* (Honolulu: University of Hawai'i Press, 2016), 99–135.

29. Rey Chow, *Writing Diaspora: Tactics of Intervention in Contemporary Cultural Studies* (Bloomington: Indiana University Press, 1993), 28.

30. Butler, *Excitable Speech*, 146–147.

31. Butler, *Excitable Speech*, 140.

32. Chow, *Writing Diaspora*, 111.

33. See Nichanian, *The Historiographic Perversion*, 112.

34. Jacques Lacan, *Les écrits techniques de Freud* [Freud's papers on technique], vol. 1 of *Le séminaire* [The seminar] (Paris: Seuil, 1975), 87–88; cited in Shoshana Felman, "Introduction to Claude Lanzmann's Speech," in *Trauma: Explorations in Memory*, ed. Cathy Caruth (Baltimore, MD: Johns Hopkins University Press), 203–204. "Not understanding is not a deficit," as Rancière puts it. "It is an interruption in the dominant mode of the process of production of meaning that incessantly rationalizes the work of destruction" (Jacques Rancière, *The Edges of Fiction*, trans. Steve Corcoran [Cambridge: Polity Press, 2020], 124).

35. "The act of transmitting is the only thing that matters, and no intelligibility, that is to say no true knowledge, preexists the process of transmission" (Claude Lanzmann, "Hier is Kein Warum" [There is no why here], in *Au sujet de Shoah: Le film de Claude Lanzmann* [On the Shoah: The film by Claude Lanzmann], ed. Bernard Cuau, Michel Deguy, and Claude Lanzmann [Paris: Belin, 1990], 279; cited by Felman, "Introduction to Claude Lanzmann's Speech," 204).

36. Nichanian, *The Historiographic Perversion*, 28.

37. "The task of writing the impossible" is "not the fanciful or the utopian but 'histories rendered unreal and fantastic'" (Saidiya Hartman, "Venus in Two Acts," *Small Axe* 12, no. 2 [June 2008]: 14; citing Stephan Palmié, *Wizards and Scientists: Explorations in Afro-Cuban Modernity and Tradition* [Durham, NC: Duke University Press, 2002], 97).

38. Rancière, *Disagreement*, 28–29.

39. See Jacques Rancière, *The Names of History: On the Poetics of Knowledge*, trans. Hassan Melehy (Minneapolis: University of Minnesota Press, 1994), 88–103.

40. I write "so-called" because this silencing can also be detected in the euphemism "comfort women." Agamben points out that a euphemism, a term "that cannot be uttered for reasons of modesty or civility," stems from *euphemein*, originally meaning "to observe religious silence." His point is that historical disaster must not become "unsayable" lest it take on the sense of "adoring in silence," as with a god (Giorgio Agamben, *Remnants of Auschwitz: The Witness and the Archive*, trans. Daniel Heller-Roazen [New York: Zone Books, 1999], 32–33). "So-called," then, not because there is any doubt about the matter, but to call attention to the fact that this is a euphemism, which itself may work to silence, and to the colonial origin of the term (*ianfu*) that continues to operate largely unchallenged in the present, and because the term has come to function as a point of political decision, a "call" that calls attention to but also calls to account.

41. Agamben, *Remnants of Auschwitz*, 17.

42. The primary reference to Agamben's work in South Korean scholarship dealing with testimony, particularly in literary studies, is the phrase "lacuna of testimony." Han Kang's 2014 Kwangju novel *A Boy Is Coming*, for instance, is often read as a *discursus* on the limits of testimony, or even the impossibility of testimony in the case of events that eradicate their witnesses.

43. Agamben, *Remnants of Auschwitz*, 26.

44. *I Can Speak* was released in 2017, on the tenth anniversary of the passage of H.R. 121, which called upon Japan to acknowledge and apologize for the military's sexual enslavement of women during the 1930s and 1940s.

45. "내가 바로 증거예요."

46. Nichanian, *The Historiographic Perversion*, 8.

47. Nichanian, *The Historiographic Perversion*, 85.

48. Nichanian, *The Historiographic Perversion*, 97.

49. Nichanian, *The Historiographic Perversion*, 120–121.

50. Theodore Hughes, "'North Koreans' and Other Virtual Subjects: Kim Yeong-ha, Hwang Seok-yeong, and National Division in the Age of Posthumanism," *Review of Korean Studies* 11, no. 1 (March 2008): 115.

51. A translation of Kim's novel was published in 2020. See Kim Soom, *One Left*, trans. Bruce Fulton and Ju-Chan Fulton (Seattle: University of Washington Press, 2020).

52. In a sense, the problem of the edition notice with Johnson's *The Orphan Master's Son*—in which "real-life figures" appear speaking fictional words—is reversed, with fictional characters speaking "real words."

53. "어떤 말로도 자신의 고통을 설명할 수 없다" (Kim Sum, *Hanmyŏng* [One person] [Seoul: Hyŏndae munhak, 2016], 237).

54. Kim, *Hanmyŏng*, 236.

55. Kim, *Hanmyŏng*, 238.

56. Nichanian, *The Historiographic Perversion*, 17.

57. Nichanian, *The Historiographic Perversion*, 94.

58. Kim, *Hanmyŏng*, 258.

59. Jie-Hyun Lim, "Victimhood Nationalism and History Reconciliation in East Asia," *History Compass* 8, no. 1 (2010): 1.

60. Kim, *Hanmyŏng*, 263n130, 268n316.

61. Agamben, *Remnants of Auschwitz*, 32–33.

62. Gilles Deleuze and Félix Guattari, *Kafka: Toward a Minor Literature*, trans. Dana Polan (Minneapolis: University of Minnesota Press, 1986), 48.

63. Nichanian, *The Historiographic Perversion*, 94.

64. Agamben, *Remnants of Auschwitz*, 144.

Bibliography

"5.18 kinyŏmsik: Mun Chaein Taet'ongryŏng kinyŏmsa chŏnmun (2019)" [Full text of President Moon Jae-in's commemorative speech on the anniversary of May 18 (2019)]. https://www1.president.go.kr/articles/6318.

"5.18 kinyŏmsik: Mun Chaein Taet'ongryŏng kinyŏmsa chŏnmun (2020)" [Full text of President Moon Jae-in's commemorative speech on the anniversary of May 18 (2020)]. https://www1.president.go.kr/articles/8639.

"The 2013 Pulitzer Prize Winner in Fiction: *The Orphan Master's Son*, by Adam Johnson (Random House)." https://www.pulitzer.org/winners/adam-johnson.

Adorno, Theodor W. *Aesthetic Theory*. Trans. and ed. Robert Hullot-Kentor. Minneapolis: University of Minnesota Press, 1997.

Agamben, Giorgio. *Remnants of Auschwitz: The Witness and the Archive*. Trans. Daniel Heller-Roazen. New York: Zone Books, 1999.

Améry, Jean. *At the Mind's Limits: Contemplations by a Survivor on Auschwitz and Its Realities*. Trans. Sidney Rosenfeld and Stella P. Rosenfeld. Bloomington: Indiana University Press, 1980.

Anderson, Mark M. "The Edge of Darkness: On W. G. Sebald." *October* 106 (Autumn 2003): 102–121.

Arendt, Hannah. *The Origins of Totalitarianism*. New York: Harcourt Brace Jovanovich, 1973.

Arsenjuk, Luka. "On Jacques Rancière." *Eurozine*, March 1, 2007. https://www.eurozine.com/on-jacques-ranciere/.

Barthes, Roland. *The Rustle of Language*. Trans. Richard Howard. Berkeley: University of California Press, 1989.

Benjamin, Walter. *Illuminations: Essays and Reflections*. New York: Schocken, 1969.

Bertsch, Janet. *Storytelling in the Works of Bunyan, Grimmelshausen, Defoe and Schnabel*. Columbia, SC: Camden House, 2004.

Bey, Hakim. *T.A.Z.: The Temporary Autonomous Zone: Ontological Anarchy, Poetic Terrorism*. New York: Autonomedia, 2004.

Brown, Wendy. "Freedom's Silences." In *Censorship and Silencing: Practices of Cultural Regulation*, ed. Robert Post, 313–327. Los Angeles: Getty Research Institute, 1998.

——. "'The Most We Can Hope For . . .' : Human Rights and the Politics of Fatalism." *South Atlantic Quarterly* 103, no. 2/3 (Spring/Summer 2004): 451–463.

Butler, Judith. *Excitable Speech: The Politics of the Performative*. New York: Routledge, 1997.

——. *Precarious Life: The Powers of Mourning and Violence*. London: Verso, 2004.

Canguilhem, Georges. *The Normal and the Pathological*. Trans. Carolyn R. Fawcett. New York: Zone Books, 1991.

Caruth, Cathy. *Unclaimed Experience: Trauma, Narrative, and History*. Baltimore, MD: Johns Hopkins University Press, 1996.

Chakrabarty, Dipesh. *Provincializing Europe: Postcolonial Thought and Historical Difference*. Princeton, NJ: Princeton University Press, 2000.

Chin Ŭnyŏng. "Kamgakjŏgin kŏt ŭi punbae: 2000 nyŏndae ŭi si e taehayŏ" [The distribution of the sensible: On the poetry of the 2000s]. *Ch'angjak kwa pip'yŏng* [Creation and criticism] 36, no. 4 (2008): 67–84.

Cho Sehŭi. *Nanjangi ka ssoaollin chagŭn kong* [A dwarf launches a little ball]. Seoul: Isŏng kwa him, 2000.

Cho Sŏnghŭi. "Han Kang ŭi *Sonyŏni onda* wa Hollok'osŭt'ŭ munhak: Kot'ong wa ch'iyok ŭi chŭngŏn kwa wŏnhan ŭi yulli rŭl chungsim ŭro" [Han Kang's *A Boy Is Coming* and Holocaust literature: With a focus on the testimony of suffering and shame and the ethics of resentment]. *Segye munhak pigyo yŏngu* [Comparative world literature studies] 62 (Spring 2018): 5–28.

Cho Yŏnjŏng. "'Kwangju' rŭl hyŏnjaehwa hanŭn il: Kwŏn Yŏsŏn ŭi *Legat'o* (2012) wa Han Kang ŭi *Sonyŏni onda* (2014) rŭl chungsim ŭro" [The task of the making present of "Kwangju": With a focus on Kwŏn Yŏsŏn's *Legato* (2012) and Han Kang's *A Boy Is Coming* (2014)]. *Taejung sŏsa yŏngu* [Journal of popular narrative] 20, no. 3 (December 2014): 101–138.

Ch'oe Yun. *Chŏgi sori ŏpsi hanjŏm kkotnip i chigo* [There a petal silently falls]. *Munhak kwa sahoe* [Literature and society] 1, no. 2 (1988): 730–788.

——. *There a Petal Silently Falls*. In *There a Petal Silently Falls: Three Stories by Ch'oe Yun*, trans. Bruce and Ju-Chan Fulton, 1–78. New York: Columbia University Press, 2008.

Choi, Jung-woon. "The Formation of an 'Absolute Community.'" In *Contentious Kwangju: The May 18 Uprising in Korea's Past and Present*, ed. Gi-Wook Shin and Kyung Moon Hwang, 3–10. Lanham, MD: Rowman and Littlefield, 2003.

——. "The Kwangju People's Uprising: The Formation of Absolute Community." *Korea Journal* 39, no. 4 (Summer 1999): 238–282.

Chŏng Pyŏnggi. "Yŏnghwa *Pyŏnhoin* ŭi sŏnt'aek kwa nurak kŭrigo konggam ŭi chŏngch'ihak—konggam ŭi posusŏng kwa minjujuŭi ŭi posusŏng" [Conservative empathy and conservative democracy: Selection and omission in *The Attorney* and the politics of empathy]. *Kyŏngje wa sahoe* [Economy and society] 106 (2015): 271–295.

Choo, Hae Yeon. *Decentering Citizenship: Gender, Labor, and Migrant Rights in South Korea*. Stanford, CA: Stanford University Press, 2016.

Chow, Rey. *Not Like a Native Speaker: On Languaging as a Postcolonial Experience*. New York: Columbia University Press, 2014.

——. *Writing Diaspora: Tactics of Intervention in Contemporary Cultural Studies*. Bloomington: Indiana University Press, 1993.

Cussen, John. "On the Call to Dismiss North Korean Defectors' Memoirs and on Their Dark American Alternative." *Korean Studies* 40 (2016): 140–157.

de Certeau, Michel. *La prise de parole* [The capture of language]. Paris: Seuil, 1994.

Debuysere, Stoffel. "On the Borders of Fiction: A Conversation with Jacques Rancière." *Sabzian*, September 20, 2017. https://www.sabzian.be/article/on-the-borders-of-fiction.

Deleuze, Gilles, and Félix Guattari. *Kafka: Toward a Minor Literature*. Trans. Dana Polan. Minneapolis: University of Minnesota Press, 1986.

DeLillo, Don. *Cosmopolis*. New York: Scribner, 2003.

Demick, Barbara. "A Spot-On Depiction of North Korea." Review of *The Orphan Master's Son*, by Adam Johnson. *Guardian*, February 17, 2012. https://www.theguardian.com/books/2012/feb/17/orphan-masters-son-adam-johnson-review.

Doxiadis, Constantinos A. "Ecumenopolis, World-City of Tomorrow." In *The Ecology of Many: An Ecosystem Approach*, ed. Robert Leo Smith, 154–162. New York: Harper and Row, 1972.

——. "Man's Movement and His Settlements." *Ekistics* 29, no. 174 (May 1970): 296–321.

Felman, Shoshana. "Introduction to Claude Lanzmann's Speech." In *Trauma: Explorations in Memory*, ed. Cathy Caruth, 201–204. Baltimore, MD: Johns Hopkins University Press, 1995.

Felman, Shoshana, and Dori Laub. *Testimony: Crises of Witnessing in Literature, Psychoanalysis, and History*. New York: Routledge, 1992.

Fisher, Carl. "The Robinsonade: An Intercultural History of an Idea." In *Approaches to Teaching Defoe's* Robinson Crusoe, ed. Maximillian E. Novak and Carl Fisher, 129–139. New York: Modern Language Association of America, 2005.

Fletcher, John. "Introduction: Psychoanalysis and the Question of the Other." In *Essays on Otherness*, by Jean Laplanche, 1–51. London: Routledge, 1999.

Foster, Hal. "Obscene, Abject, Traumatic." *October* 78 (Autumn 1996): 106–124.

Foucault, Michel. *The Archaeology of Knowledge*. Trans. A. M. Sheridan Smith. New York: Vintage, 1972.

Fraser, Nancy. "The Politics of Framing: An Interview with Nancy Fraser." Interviewed by Kate Nash and Vikki Bell. *Theory, Culture and Society* 24, no. 4 (2007): 73–86.

Freud, Sigmund. *Beyond the Pleasure Principle*. Trans. and ed. James Strachey. New York: W.W. Norton, 1961.

——. "Letter 52 (December 6, 1896)." In *Pre-Psycho-Analytic Publications and Unpublished Drafts (1886–1899)*, 233–239. Vol. 1 of *The Standard Edition of the Complete Psychological Works of Sigmund Freud*, trans. and ed. James Strachey. London: Hogarth Press, 1966.

——. "Remembering, Repeating and Working-Through." In *Case History of Schreber, Papers on Technique and Other Works (1911–1913)*, 147–156. Vol. 12 of *The Standard Edition of the Complete Psychological Works of Sigmund Freud*, trans. and ed. James Strachey. London: Hogarth Press, 1958.

——. "Screen Memories." In *Early Psycho-Analytic Publications (1893–1899)*, 301–322. Vol. 3 of *The Standard Edition of the Complete Psychological Works of Sigmund Freud*, ed. James Strachey. London: Hogarth Press, 1962.

——. "Transference." In *Introductory Letters on Psycho-Analysis (Part 3) (1916–1917)*, 431–447. Vol. 16 of *The Standard Edition of the Complete Psychological Works of Sigmund Freud*, trans. and ed. James Strachey. London: Hogarth Press, 1963.

Frow, John. *Genre*. London: Routledge, 2015 [2006].

Gabriel, Douglas. "Reality Effects for a Dangerous Age: Projecting North Korean Youth on the International Screen." *Situations* 13, no. 2 (2020): 69–95.

Ganeri, Jonardon. *Virtual Subjects, Fugitive Selves: Fernando Pessoa and His Philosophy*. Oxford: Oxford University Press, 2020.

Gaughan, Thomas. Review of *The Orphan Master's Son*. *Booklist*. https://www.booklistonline.com/The-Orphan-Master-s-Son-Adam-Johnson/pid=5075833.

George, Don. "New Book Roundups." *National Geographic*, January 6, 2012. https://www.nationalgeographic.com/travel/article/ruins-of-us.

Gilroy, Paul. *The Black Atlantic: Modernity and Double Consciousness*. Cambridge, MA: Harvard University Press, 1993.

Giltrow, Janet. "Meta-Genre." In *The Rhetoric and Ideology of Genre: Strategies for Stability and Change*, ed. Richard Coe, Lorelei Lingard, and Tatiana Teslenko, 187–205. Creskill, NJ: Hampton Press, 2002.

Giordano, Simona. *Understanding Eating Disorders*. Oxford: Clarendon Press, 2005.

Gorządek, Ewa. "Positives—Zbigniew Libera." Trans. Bozhana Nikolova. Culture.pl, March 2015. https://culture.pl/en/work/positives-zbigniew-libera.

Gray, Carmen. "Russian Film Exposes the Workings of North Korea's Propaganda Machine: *Under the Sun* Shows Behind-the-Scenes Coercion by Government Minders Trying to Construct and Image of a 'Normal' Family." *Guardian*, December 3, 2015. https://www.theguardian.com/world/2015/dec/02/north-korea -under-the-sun-vitaly-mansky-film.

Hallward, Peter. *Absolutely Postcolonial: Writing Between the Singular and the Specific*. Manchester: Manchester University Press, 2001.

Han Kang. *Human Acts*. Trans. Deborah Smith. London: Portobello Books, 2016.

——. *Sonyŏni onda* [A boy is coming]. Seoul: Ch'angbi, 2018.

Hannerz, Ulf. "Cosmopolitans and Locals in World Culture." *Theory, Culture, Society* 7 (1990): 237–251.

——. "Notes on the Global Ecumene." *Public Culture* 1, no. 2 (Spring 1989): 66–75.

Harden, Blaine. *Escape from Camp 14: One Man's Remarkable Odyssey from North Korea to Freedom in the West*. London: Pan Books, 2015.

Hartman, Saidiya V. *Scenes of Subjection: Terror, Slavery, and Self-Making in Nineteenth-Century America*. New York: Oxford University Press, 1997.

——. "Venus in Two Acts." *Small Axe* 12, no. 2 (June 2008): 1–14.

Hepworth, Julie. *The Social Construction of Anorexia Nervosa*. London: Sage, 1999.

Hong, Christine. "War by Other Means: The Violence of North Korean Human Rights." *Asia-Pacific Journal: Japan Focus* 12, no. 2 (March 2014): 1–29.

Hoxworth, Kellen. "Performative Correctness; or, the Subject of Performance and Politics." *Journal of Dramatic Theory and Criticism* 35, no. 2 (Spring 2021): 107–112.

Hughes, Theodore. "'North Koreans' and Other Virtual Subjects: Kim Yeong-ha, Hwang Seok-yeong, and National Division in the Age of Posthumanism." *Review of Korean Studies* 11, no. 1 (March 2008): 99–117.

Hunter, Kathryn. *Doctors' Stories: The Narrative Structure of Medical Knowledge*. Princeton, NJ: Princeton University Press, 1991.

Hutton, Christopher. *Linguistics and the Third Reich: Mother-Tongue Fascism, Race and the Science of Language*. London: Routledge, 1999.

Huxley, Aldous. *Island*. New York: Harper and Row, 1962.

Hwang Chŏnga. "'Kyŏl ŭl kŏsŭllŏ yŏksa rŭl solchil' hanŭn munhak: Pam ŭi nun kwa Sonyŏni onda" [Literature that "brushes history against the grain": The Eye of Night and A Boy Is Coming]. *An kwa pak* [Inside/outside] 38 (May 2015): 58–81.

Hwang, Chongyŏn. "A Postmodern Turn in Korean Literature." *Korea Journal* 47, no. 1 (2007): 5–7.

Hwang Hodŏk. "Nŏmŭn kŏsi anida—kukkyŏng kwa munhak" [Not crossed—state borders and literature]. *Munhak tongne* [Literary community] 13, no. 4 (2006): 418–434.

Ignatius, David. Review of *The Orphan Master's Son*, by Adam Johnson. *Washington Post*, January 9, 2012. https://www.washingtonpost.com/entertainment /books/book-review-the-orphan-masters-son-by-david-ignatius/2012/01/02 /gIQAIZWZmP_story.html.

Johnson, Adam. "Fortune Smiles." In *Fortune Smiles*, 247–301. New York: Random House, 2015.

——. *The Orphan Master's Son*. New York: Random House, 2012.

Jolley, Mary Ann. "The Strange Tale of Yeonmi Park." *The Diplomat*, December 10, 2014. https://thediplomat.com/2014/12/the-strange-tale-of-yeonmi-park/.

Jusdanis, Gregory. *Belated Modernity and Aesthetic Culture: Inventing National Literature*. Minneapolis: University of Minnesota Press, 1991.

Kakutani, Michiko. "A North Korean Soldier Finds His 'Casablanca.'" Review of *The Orphan Master's Son*, by Adam Johnson. *New York Times*, January 12, 2012. https://www.nytimes.com/2012/01/13/books/the-orphan-masters-son-by-adam -johnson-review.html.

Kang Chingu. "Hanguk sosŏl e nat'anan ijunodongja ŭi chaehyŏn yangsang" [Aspects of the representation of migrant laborers in Korean fiction]. *Ŏmun nonjip* [Journal of language and literature] 41 (2009): 241–266.

Kang Yŏngsuk. "Brown Tears." In *New Writing from Korea*, vol. 1, 132–151. Seoul: Korean Literature Translation Institute, 2008.

——. *Ppalgang sok ŭi kŏmjŏng e taehayŏ* [On the black in the red]. Seoul: Munhak tongne, 2009.

Kim Chaeyŏng. "Elephant." In *New Writing from Korea*, vol. 1, 182–208. Seoul: Korean Literature Translation Institute, 2008.

——. *K'okkiri* [Elephant]. Silch'ŏn munhaksa, 2005.

Kim Hyŏnsŏk, dir. *Ai k'aen sŭp'ik'ŭ* [I can speak]. Seoul: Myung Films, See Sun, 2017.

Kim Insuk. "Pada wa nabi" [Sea and butterfly]. *Silch'ŏn munhak* [Praxis literature] (2002): 257–290.

——. "Sea and Butterfly." In *New Writing from Korea*, vol. 1, 152–181. Seoul: Korean Literature Translation Institute, 2008.

Kim Pyŏngik. "Nanjangi, hogŭn sooe chipdan ŭi ŏnŏ" [The dwarf, or, the language of the alienated]. *Munhak kwa chisŏng* [Literature and intellect] (Spring 1977): 63–64.

——. "Taeripjŏk segyegwan kwa mihak" [Aesthetics and the oppositional world-view]. In *Nanjangi ka ssoaollin chagŭn kong* [A dwarf launches a little ball], by Cho Sehŭi, 319–336. Seoul: Isŏng kwa him, 2000.

Kim Sangbong. "Ŭngdap ŭrosŏŭi yŏksa: 5.18 ŭl saenggakham" [History as response: Thoughts on May 18]. *Minjujuŭi wa ingwŏn* [Democracy and Human Rights] 6, no. 2 (2006): 139–156.

Kim, Soo Yeon. "Cultural Appropriation, or the Right to Write Fiction: Narrating North Korea in Adam Johnson's *The Orphan Master's Son.*" *Foreign Literature Studies* 73 (February 2019): 93–114.

Kim Soom [Kim Sum]. *One Left.* Trans. Bruce Fulton and Ju-Chan Fulton. Seattle: University of Washington Press, 2020.

Kim Sum. *Hanmyŏng* [One person]. Seoul: Hyŏndae munhak, 2016.

Kim Yŏngch'an. "Kot'ong kwa munhak, kot'ong ŭi munhak: Han Kang ŭi *Sonyŏni onda* wa *Nun han songi ka nongnŭn tongan* ŭl chungsim ŭro" [Suffering and lit-erature, literature of suffering: With a focus on Han Kang's *A Boy Is Coming* and *While a Snowflake Melts*]. *Urimalgŭl* [Our speech and writing] 72 (March 2017): 291–314.

Kim Yŏnsu, "Sarang i anin tarŭn mallonŭn sŏlmyŏng hal su opnŭn" [It cannot be explained in words other than love]. *Ch'angjak kwa pip'yŏng* [Creation and criti-cism] 165 (Autumn 2014): 312–332.

Kim Yosŏp. "Yŏksa ŭi nun kwa mal haejiji anŭn sonyŏn: Cho Kapsang ŭi *Pam ŭi nun* kwa Han Kang ŭi *Sonyŏni onda* e taehayŏ" [The eye of history and the unspoken boy: On Cho Kapsang's *The Eye of Night* and Han Kang's *A Boy Is Coming*]. *Ch'angjak kwa pipy'ŏng* [Creation and criticism] 43, no. 3 (2015): 458–482.

Kim, Young-jin. *Korean Film Directors: Park Chan-wook.* Seoul: KOFIC, 2007.

Kolaitis, Gerasimos, and Miranda Olff. "Psychotraumatology in Greece." *European Journal of Psychotraumatology* 8 (2017): 1–4.

Lacan, Jacques. *Les écrits techniques de Freud* [Freud's papers on technique]. Vol. 1 of *Le séminaire* [The seminar]. Paris: Seuil, 1975.

LaCapra, Dominick. *History and Its Limits: Human, Animal, Violence.* Ithaca, NY: Cornell University Press, 2009.

——. *Writing History, Writing Trauma.* Baltimore, MD: Johns Hopkins University Press, 2014.

Lanzmann, Claude. "Hier is Kein Warum" [There is no why here]. In *Au sujet de Shoah: Le film de Claude Lanzmann* [On the Shoah: The film by Claude Lan-zmann], ed. Bernard Cuau, Michel Deguy, and Claude Lanzmann. Paris: Belin, 1990.

——. "The Obscenity of Understanding: An Evening with Claude Lanzmann." In *Trauma: Explorations in Memory*, ed. Cathy Caruth, 204–220. Baltimore, MD: Johns Hopkins University Press, 1995.

Laplanche, Jean. *Essays on Otherness*. London: Routledge, 1999.

——. "Psychoanalysis as Anti-hermeneutics." Trans. Luke Thurston. *Radical Philosophy* 79 (September/October 1996): 7–12.

Laplanche, Jean, and J.-B. Pontalis. *The Language of Psycho-Analysis*. Trans. Donald Nicholson-Smith. New York: Norton, 1973.

Lecercle, Jean-Jacques. "Storming Language." *Crisis and Critique* 5, no. 2 (November 2018): 205–216.

Lee, Ji-Eun. "(Dis)embodiment of Memory: Gender, Memory, and Ethics in *Human Acts* by Han Kang." In *Routledge Companion to Korean Literature*, ed. Heekyoung Cho, 357–370. New York: Routledge, 2022.

Lee, Jin-kyung. "Immigrant Subempire, Migrant Labor Activism, and Multiculturalism in Contemporary South Korea." In *The Routledge Handbook of Korean Culture and Society*, ed. Youna Kim, 149–161. London: Routledge, 2017.

Lefebvre, Henri. *State, Space, World: Selected Essays*. Ed. Neil Brenner and Stuart Elden. Trans. Gerald Moore, Neil Brenner, and Stuart Elden. Minneapolis: University of Minnesota Press, 2009.

——. *The Urban Revolution*. Trans. Robert Bononno. Minneapolis: University of Minnesota Press, 2003.

Lejeune, Philippe. *On Autobiography*. Ed. Paul Eakin. Trans. Katherine Leary. Minneapolis: University of Minnesota Press, 1989.

Lim, Jie-Hyun. "Victimhood Nationalism and History Reconciliation in East Asia." *History Compass* 8, no. 1 (2010): 1–10.

Lim, Timothy. "Rethinking Belongingness in Korea: Transnational Migration, 'Migrant Marriages' and the Politics of Multiculturalism." *Pacific Affairs* 83, no. 1 (2010): 51–71.

McDonald, Tamar Jeffers. *Romantic Comedy*. London: Wallflower Press, 2007.

Miller, Gavin. "Literary Narrative as Soteriology in the Work of Kurt Vonnegut and Alasdair Gray." *Journal of Narrative Theory* 31, no. 1 (Fall 2001): 299–323.

Mun Kwangyu, "Yŏksa wa sŏnbi chŏngsin ŭi sohwan kŭrigo chinsil ŭi him—Yang Wusŏk ŭi *Pyŏnhoin*" [Summoning history and the spirit of the classical scholar, and the power of truth: Yang Wusŏk's *The Attorney*]. *Hyŏndae yŏnghwa yŏngu* [Contemporary film research] 10, no. 1 (2014): 69–93.

Nancy, Jean-Luc. *The Ground of the Image*. Trans. Jeff Fort. New York: Fordham University Press, 2005.

——. *The Inoperative Community*. Ed. Peter Connor. Trans. Peter Connor, Lisa Garbus, Michael Holland, and Simona Sawhney. Minneapolis: University of Minnesota Press, 1991.

Nichanian, Marc. *The Historiographic Perversion*. Trans. Gil Anidjar. New York: Columbia University Press, 2009.

Nikoleishvili, Sophia. "The Many Faces of Daniel Defoe's *Robinson Crusoe*: Examining the Crusoe Myth in Film and on Television." PhD diss., University of Missouri, 2007.

"*The Orphan Master's Son*: A Novel." https://www.randomhousebooks.com/books/212862/.

"*The Orphan Master's Son.*" *Publishers Weekly.* January 2012. https://www.publishersweekly.com/978-0-8129-9279-3.

Oxford Dictionary of English. Ed. Angus Stevenson. Oxford: Oxford University Press, 2010.

Pak Ch'anuk, dir. *Ssaibogŭjiman kwaench'ana* [I'm a cyborg, but that's OK]. Seoul: CJ Entertainment, 2006.

Palmié, Stephan. *Wizards and Scientists: Explorations in Afro-Cuban Modernity and Tradition.* Durham, NC: Duke University Press, 2002.

Palumbo-Liu, David. *The Deliverance of Others: Reading Literature in a Global Age.* Durham, NC: Duke University Press, 2012.

Panagia, Davide. "Dissenting Words: A Conversation with Jacques Rancière." *Diacritics* 30, no. 2 (Summer 2000): 113–126.

Park, Yeonmi. *In Order to Live: A North Korean Girl's Journey to Freedom.* New York: Penguin, 2015.

——. "What I Learned About Freedom After Escaping North Korea." TED Talk. September 26, 2019. YouTube video, 10:48. https://www.youtube.com/watch?v=mLzTo-y8Efo.

Park, Young-A, Do-hoon Lee, and Keith B. Wagner. "Changing Representations of the Urban Poor in Korean Independent Cinema: *Minjung* Heroes, Atomized Paupers, and New Possibilities." *Quarterly Review of Film and Video* 34, no. 4 (2017): 361–378.

Perkins, David. *Is Literary History Possible?* Baltimore, MD: Johns Hopkins University Press, 1992.

Power, John. "North Korea: Defectors and Their Skeptics." *The Diplomat*, October 29, 2014. https://thediplomat.com/2014/10/north-korea-defectors-and-their-skeptics/.

Rancière, Jacques. *Aesthetics and Its Discontents.* Trans. Steven Corcoran. Cambridge: Polity Press, 2009.

——. *Disagreement: Politics and Philosophy.* Trans. Julie Rose. Minneapolis: University of Minnesota Press, 1999.

——. *The Edges of Fiction.* Trans. Steve Corcoran. Cambridge: Polity Press, 2020.

——. *The Flesh of Words: The Politics of Writing.* Trans. Charlotte Mandell. Stanford, CA: Stanford University Press, 2004.

——. *The Future of the Image.* Trans. Gregory Elliott. London: Verso, 2007.

——. "How Does Architecture Distribute the Sensible?" Architecture Exchange, Cooper Union, November 16, 2019. YouTube video, 1:42:34. https://www.youtube.com/watch?v=7NcWthWJflw.

——. *The Lost Thread: The Democracy of Modern Fiction.* Trans. Steven Corcoran. London: Bloomsbury Academic, 2017.

——. *The Names of History: On the Poetics of Knowledge.* Trans. Hassan Melehy. Minneapolis: University of Minnesota Press, 1994.

——. "Politics, Identification, and Subjectivization." *October* 61 (Summer 1992): 58–64.

——. *The Politics of Aesthetics: The Distribution of the Sensible.* Trans. Gabriel Rockhill. London: Continuum, 2004.

——. *The Politics of Literature.* Trans. Julie Rose. Cambridge: Polity, 2011.

——. "Who Is the Subject of the Rights of Man?" *South Atlantic Quarterly* 103, no. 2/3 (Spring/Summer 2004): 297–310.

Root, Michael. "The Narrative Structure of Soteriology." *Modern Theology* 2, no. 2 (January 1986): 145–158.

Rothberg, Michael. *Traumatic Realism: The Demands of Holocaust Representation.* Minneapolis: University of Minnesota Press, 2000.

Ryu, Youngju. *Writers of the Winter Republic: Literature and Resistance in Park Chung Hee's Korea.* Honolulu: University of Hawai'i Press, 2016.

Said, Edward. *Orientalism.* New York: Vintage, 1979.

——. *The World, the Text, and the Critic.* Cambridge, MA: Harvard University Press, 1983.

Sakai, Naoki. "Introduction: Nationality and the Politics of the 'Mother Tongue.'" In *Deconstructing Nationality*, ed. Naoki Sakai, Brett de Bary, and Iyotani Toshio, 1–38. Ithaca, NY: East Asia Program, 2005.

——. *Translation and Subjectivity: On Japan and Cultural Nationalism.* Minneapolis: University of Minnesota Press, 1997.

Sakai, Naoki, Brett de Bary, and Iyotani Toshio, eds. *Deconstructing Nationality.* Ithaca, NY: East Asia Program, Cornell University, 2005.

Scarfone, Dominique. "A Brief Introduction to the Work of Jean Laplanche." *International Journal of Psychoanalysis* 94 (2013): 545–566.

Schörkhuber, Verena. "*Robinson Crusoe* Goes Postcolonial: Re-Writings of the Crusoe Myth by Derek Walcott and J. M. Coetzee." MPhil diss., University of Vienna, 2009.

Schweinitz, Jörg. *Film and Stereotype: A Challenge for Cinema and Theory.* Trans. Laura Schleussner. New York: Columbia University Press, 2011 [2006].

Scott, Joan. "The Evidence of Experience." *Critical Inquiry* 17, no. 4 (Summer 1991): 773–797.

Sebald, W. G. *The Emigrants.* Trans. Michael Hulse. New York: New Directions, 1996.

——. *On the Natural History of Destruction*. Trans. Anthea Bell. New York: Modern Library, 2003.

Sekula, Allan. "Reading an Archive: Photography Between Labour and Capital." In *Visual Culture: The Reader*, ed. Jessica Evans and Stuart Hall, 181–192. London: SAGE, 1999.

Shields, David. *Reality Hunger: A Manifesto*. New York: Knopf, 2010.

Siegl, Karin. *The Robinsonade Tradition in Robert Michael Ballantyne's "The Coral Island" and William Golding's "The Lord of the Flies."* Lewiston, NY: Mellen, 1996.

Sŏ Yŏngch'ae. "Kwangju ŭi poksu rŭl kkumkkunŭn il: Kim Kyŏnguk kwa Yi Haegyŏng ŭi changp'yŏn ŭl chungsim ŭro" [The work of dreaming the dream of Kwangju's vengeance: With a focus on the long fiction of Kim Kyŏnguk and Yi Haegyŏng]. *Munhak tongne* [Literary community] 78 (2014): 1–23.

"Sosŏlga Han Kang, *Sonyŏni onda* ro It'alia Mallap'arŭt'e munhaksang susang" [Author Han Kang awarded the Malaparte Prize for *A Boy Is Coming*]. *Hangyŏre* [Hankyoreh], October 2, 2017. http://www.hani.co.kr/arti/culture/culture_general/813384.html.

Su Kyŏng. "Hwansang sosŏl losŏŭi Hanguk ijumunhak" [Korean immigrant literature as fantasy fiction]. Seminar on Memory and Migration, Kyumun Research Institute, Seoul, Korea, May 19, 2017.

Todorov, Tzvetan. *Genres in Discourse*. Cambridge: Cambridge University Press, 1990 [1978].

Tynyanov, Yury. "On Literary Evolution." In *Readings in Russian Poetics: Formalist and Structuralist Views*, ed. Ladislav Matejka and Krystyna Pomorska, 66–78. Champaign, IL: Dalkey Archive Press, 2002 [1927].

Vadén, Tere. "Žižek's Phenomenology of the Subject: Transcendental or Materialist?" *International Journal of Žižek Studies* 2, no. 2 (2008): 1–17.

Weheliye, Alexander G. *Habeas Viscus: Racializing Assemblages, Biopolitics, and Black Feminist Theories of the Human*. Durham, NC: Duke University Press, 2014.

White, Hayden. "The Fictions of Factual Representation." In *The Literature of Fact*, ed. Angus Fletcher, 21–44. New York: Columbia University Press, 1976.

Whitney, William D. *Language and the Study of Language: Twelve Lectures on the Principles of Linguistic Science*. London: Trübner, 1867.

Yang Usŏk, dir. *Pyŏnhoin* [The attorney]. Seoul: Withus Films, 2013.

"Yet Namyŏngdong punsil e minju-inkwŏn kidong sewŏ kukka p'ongnyŏki dŭlŏsŏji mot'hage hal kŏt" [Setting up pillars of democracy and human rights at old Namyŏngdong branch office to prevent the recurrence of state violence in our country]. *Kyŏnghyang sinmunn* [Kyunghyang news], June 10, 2021. https://m.khan.co.kr/politics/president/article/202106102150025.

Yi Haejun, dir. *Kimssi p'yoryugi* [Castaway on the Moon]. Seoul: CJ Entertainment, 2009.

Yi Kyŏngjae. "2000 nyŏndae tamunhwa sosŏl yŏngu: Hangugin kwa ijumin ŭi kwangye yangsang ŭl chungsim ŭro" [A study of multicultural fiction of the 2000s: On aspects of the relationship between Koreans and migrants]. *Hanguk hyŏndae munhak yŏngu* [Modern Korean literature] 40 (2013): 249–287.

Yi Suk. "Yesulga ŭi sahoejŏk ch'aengmu: P'ongnyŏk ŭi kiŏk kwa ingan ŭi ponjil— Han Kang ŭi *Sonyŏni onda* rŭl chungsim ŭro (2014)" [The social responsibility of the artist: The memory of violence and the essence of the human—with a focus on Han Kang's *A Boy Is Coming* (2014)]. *Hyŏndae munhak iron* [Journal of modern literary theory] 60 (2015): 439–462.

Yŏn Namgyŏng. "2000 nyŏndae Hanguk sosŏl ŭi ijumin chaehyŏn yŏngu— chŏnjiguhwa, minjok kukka, ijumin ŭi kwangye rŭl chungsim ŭro" [Representing the migrant in Korean fiction of the 2000s—with a focus on the relationship between globalization, the ethnic-national state, and the migrant]. *Kugŏ kungmunhak* [National literature and language] 165 (2013): 63–85.

——. "Hanguk hyŏndae sosŏl e nat'ansan chŏpgyŏng chidae wa kusŏngdoen chŏngch'esŏng" [The borderland and the construction of identity in recent Korean fiction]. *Hyŏndae sosŏl yŏngu* [Modern fiction] 52 (2013): 253–281.

——. *T'algyŏnggye sayu wa sŏsa ŭi yulli: Hanguk munhak kwa iju* [Post-border reason and the ethics of narrative: Korean literature and migration]. Seoul: Ihwa yŏja taehakkyo ch'ulp'an munhwawŏn, 2017.

Yuk Chŏnghak. "Ch'ŏnman kwangaek tolp'a yŏnghwa *Pyŏnhoin* ŭi munhwasahoejŏk ŭimi" [Surpassing the ten million viewer mark: The sociocultural significance of *The Attorney*]. *Kanguk ent'ŏt'einmŏnt'ŭ sanŏp hakhoe nonmunji* [Journal of the Association of the Korean Entertainment Industry] 9, no. 1 (2015): 23–33.

Žižek, Slavoj. "Against Human Rights." *New Left Review* 34 (July/August 2005): 115–131.

——. *The Fright of Real Tears: Krzysztof Kieślowski Between Theory and Post-Theory*. London: British Film Institute, 2001.

——. "Lenin's Choice." In *Revolution at the Gates*, ed. Slavoj Žižek, 167–336. London: Verso, 2002.

——. *The Parallax View*. Cambridge, MA: MIT Press, 2006.

Index

Adorno, Theodor, 152, 157, 173n30
afterward-ness of trauma, 75–83
Anderson, Mark, 154
art, politics of, 7–9, 23–24, 50, 89, 152, 161
Attorney, The (2013), 1–6
authenticity, 24–25, 29, 35, 72, 85, 89–90, 102, 104, 108, 114, 120–21, 150, 162, 191n58, 194n100
authoritarianism, 3, 6, 21, 46, 80, 82
autobiographical narrative, 61, 71, 85, 109, 120, 153

biographical narrative, 3–4, 6, 12, 19, 61, 71, 85, 109, 113–20
bodily speech, 97, 164
borderland (chŏpgyŏng chidae), 30
boundary/boundaries: common sense and, 10; communication across, 35, 42–43, 72, 135; of community, 9, 16, 77; elimination or transgression, 34; intelligible language and, 23, 29; realism *vs.* fantasy, 141; speech and, 10, 12–16, 25–26, 39, 89, 96, 153–61;

transgression of, 34, 125–28, 142, 147–49; trauma and, 79, 89; truth *vs.* reality, 18
Boy Is Coming, A (Han Kang): absence and loss, 56–60; absent witness in, 60–65; historical imperative, 69–75, 84–85; introduction to, 16–17, 22, 45–51; limits of testimony, 65–69, 96–97; multiple narrative perspectives, 51–56; understanding trauma, 75–83
Brown, Wendy, 24, 94, 183n64
"Brown Tears" (Kang Yŏngsuk), 37–40
Butler, Judith, 10–11, 24, 57–58

Candlelight Revolution (2016–2017), 47
Castaway on the Moon (2009). *See Kimssi p'yoryugi*
Ch'oe Yun, 79
Chŏng Pyŏnggi, 2–3
Cho Sŏnghŭi, 62, 67
Cho Yŏnjŏng, 46, 66, 68
civilized humanity, 18, 23, 97, 163–65

comfort women narratives, 12–13, 23, 161–68

common sense, 8, 10–11, 16, 22, 23, 45, 50, 55–56, 78, 82, 119, 123–24, 156–57

communication: absolute, 45, 57, 70, 80–81; at a distance, 125, 131–32, 133; fantasy of, 33, 35, 37, 42; limits of, 67, 69; obligatory, 18, 86; translingual, 29, 33, 42; transparent, 29, 33, 40, 153

communism, 1–2

community: absolute, 45, 57, 70, 80–81; (ethnic-)national, 13, 33–34, 82, 126–27, 167; language and, 15, 40, 56; literature and, 15, 26; postnational, 15, 130; trauma and, 4, 49, 51, 56, 58–60, 73

compulsory discursivity, 13, 23, 24–26, 43, 97, 153–54, 160–63

compulsory testimony, 12, 17

confessional narratives, 3–4, 12, 17–19, 22, 85–86, 107–11, 117, 120, 153, 156

conventional narratives, 12, 58, 70, 76

crimes against humanity, 94–96

Cussen, John, 98

death camps, 24

defector narratives, 13, 93, 97–104, 153

Deliverance of Others, The (Palumbo-Liu), 135–36

Demick, Barbara, 18

democratization, 3–4, 6, 45–48, 82

dignity, 32, 50

documentary: defector narratives in, 100–103; identity and, 120–21; realism in, 22, 74, 83, 90, 106, 121, 168; *Under the Sun*, 104–5; testimony in, 3, 85–86, 101; torture in, 3; trauma in, 79–80; truth in, 121, 163, 166

doubling, 113

"Elephant" (Kim Chaeyŏng), 34–37, 42

emancipation narratives, 86, 96, 120

empathy *(tongsimjŏng)*, 134–35

enigmatic message, 17, 45, 76–79, 81

escapee narratives, 12, 17–19, 84–106

Escape from Camp 14: One Man's Remarkable Odyssey from North Korea to Freedom in the West (Harden), 99

ethnic nationalism, 14, 21–22, 27, 29–30, 33–42, 127, 155

euphemisms, 167–68

exclusion, politics of, 12

facticity, 4, 23, 100–103, 156, 161, 168

factuality, 4, 18, 47–48, 101–2, 162–63

fluency of speech, 34–40

foreclosure, 5, 10, 12, 22–23, 26, 76, 104, 119, 156, 159, 166

"Fortune Smiles" (Johnson), 92–104, 121

Foster, Hal, 98

founding trauma, 22, 49–51, 58–59, 83, 155

framing, 10, 21, 41, 101, 119, 127

Fraser, Nancy, 10

Gabriel, Douglas, 104–5

generic norms, 3, 17, 19, 22–23, 123. *See also* transgression of generic norms

globality, 127, 147

globalization, 127, 150

Hanawŏn resettlement center, 13, 92, 95

Han Kang, 16–17, 22

Hanmyŏng (Kim Sum), 165–67

happy ending convention, 143–44, 146–47, 167

Harden, Blaine, 99

hereditary trauma, 75, 81

historical trauma. *See* Kwangju uprising

historical truth, 3–4, 7–8, 47–48, 58, 74, 80–83

historiographic imperative, 4, 69–75, 83, 86, 88, 109, 157

historiographic stranglehold, 74, 163

Hughes, Theodore, 97

Human Acts (2016). *See A Boy Is Coming*

humanity/humanitarianism: civilized humanity, 18, 23, 97, 163–65; crimes against, 94–96; of migrant laborer, 15, 27, 31, 36, 57; role of, 94–95

human rights: *The Attorney,* 1–6; bodily speech and, 164; comfort women narratives, 12–13, 23, 161–68; compulsory discursivity and, 153; escapee narratives and, 12, 17–19, 84–106; international politics of, 13, 23, 161–62; logic of, 90–108; performative correctness and, 119–21; possible speech and, 117, 124, 156; suffering narratives, 119–20; trauma narrative and, 167

Hwang Chŏnga, 62, 71

Hwang Chongyŏn, 41

Hwang Hodŏk, 30

hyperintelligibility, 33

hyperrealism, 22

I Can Speak (Ai k'aen sŭp'ik'ŭ) (2017), 162–67

identity: of community, 59; demand for, 86–87, 95, 98, 138, 161; denial of, 89–91, 131–32, 156; documentary truth and, 120–21; ecumenical sense of, 125; ethnic/racial identity, 35–39; historical trauma and, 48–49, 57; individual identity, 41; of language,

56, 76; narrative modes of, 10–12, 20, 23, 26; national identity, 12, 15, 30, 39, 42, 46, 53, 55, 58, 83, 126–27, 167; of political art, 50; political identity, 35; possibilized speech and, 164; question of, 136–39, 142, 147–50, 157; realism and, 25, 128, 153; space and, 23; of speech, 42, 84, 166; torture and, 110, 164–65; transcription and, 91; transgression of, 121, 124–25, 129; uncertainty around, 106–8, 110–12

I'm a Cyborg, but That's OK (2006). *See Ssaibogŭjiman kwaench'ana*

Im Ch'ŏru, 57, 80

impossibilization of impossible speech, 11, 25, 43, 49, 93, 99, 104, 168

impossible speech: defined, 160–61; impossibilization of, 11, 25, 43, 49, 93, 99, 104, 168; introduction to, 1–6; overview of, 9–26; politics of art and, 7–9, 23–24, 50, 89, 152, 161; possibilized speech *vs.,* 84, 155–61, 164; representation of, 27, 29, 43, 96, 111, 124, 152, 158–61, 169; silence and, 12, 93–96, 103, 117, 143, 146, 154–57, 167–68. *See also* speech

In Order to Live: A North Korean Girl's Journey to Freedom (Park), 84, 100

international human rights, 13, 23, 100, 161–62

intimate spaces, 87

involuntary speech, 11, 18, 86, 89, 102–3

Johnson, Adam, 17–18, 84, 87–91, 104–20, 124, 156

Jolley, Mary Ann, 100–101, 103

Kang Chingu, 30–31, 35, 38

Kang Yŏngsuk, 14–15, 27, 29, 37–40

Kieślowski, Krzysztof, 106
Kim Chaeyŏng, 14–15, 27–29, 34–37
Kim Hyŏnsŏk, 162–67
Kim Insuk, 14–15, 27–28
Kimssi p'yoryugi (Castaway on the Moon) (2009): identity in, 136–39; introduction to, 19–22, 123–29; place in, 135–42; politics of the possible, 124, 147–51; space in, 125–35, 156–57
Kim Sum, 165–67
Kim Yŏngch'an, 62, 64
Kim Yosŏp, 62
Kwangju Democratization Movement, 45–47
Kwangju uprising (1980), 9, 12, 16–17, 24, 119, 153, 155–56. *See also A Boy Is Coming*

LaCapra, Dominick, 16, 48–49, 56
Lanzmann, Claude, 160, 204n35
Lefebvre, Henri, 124–25, 149
literarity, 90, 190n28
literary text, politics of, 4, 12, 24–26, 32, 45, 50, 89, 101
literature, politics of, 1–6, 8, 25, 169
logic of naming, 86, 89, 109–11, 159
logic of story, 86, 109, 111–19
logic of torture, 84, 97, 102, 106, 110, 164
logic of trauma, 16, 83, 99

manifest impasse, 86, 90
Mansky, Vitaly, 104–5
marginal spaces, 30
meaningless waste (*ŭimi ŏpnŭn somo*), 82
memorialization/memorization of trauma, 3–6, 154

migrant labor fiction in South Korea: fluency of speech, 34–40; introduction to, 9, 14–15, 27–29; limits of, 29–34; migrant marriages, 14, 28; return of the real, 21, 27–29, 40–44; transnational migration, 14, 28; urban poverty and, 27, 34
migrant marriages, 14, 28
minjung (common people), 21, 35–36, 119
modern realism, 101
monolingualism, 12, 15, 22–23, 119, 155, 157
Moon Jae-in, 12, 43, 45–47, 80–81, 119
mother tongue, 15, 29, 33, 35, 38, 40, 42
mourning, 48, 53–54, 56–58, 78
multiculturalism, 14–15, 28–31, 42–43

narrative form, 3–4, 6, 12, 85–86
national identity, 12, 15, 30, 39, 42, 46, 53, 55, 58, 83, 126–27, 167
National Intelligence Service, 13
National Security Law, 1–2
native speaker, 35
neoliberalization, 3, 9, 16, 82, 94
Nichanian, Marc, 45, 85, 101, 163; coordinates of the fact, 4, 74–75, 86
nonsensical speech, 12–13

obscenity of understanding, 160
obstinate silence, 33
One Left (2020). See *Hanmyŏng*
ontological realism, 18, 22
Orientalism, 18
Orphan Master's Son, The (Johnson): introduction to, 17–18; logic of naming, 86, 89, 109–11, 159; logic of story, 86, 109, 111–19; performative correctness, 104, 108, 119–22; realism and, 87–91, 104–19; space in, 157

222 *Index*

orphan utterance, 90, 124

Oshagan, Hagop, 97

Pak Ch'anuk, 19, 123

Palumbo-Liu, David, 135–36

Park, Yeonmi, 84, 100

Park Chung Hee, 2, 46–47

Park Geun-hye, 2, 46–47, 49–50

people *(kungmin)*, 2

Peppermint Candy (Pakha sat'ang) (film), 69

performative correctness, 98, 104, 108, 119–22

place, role of, 8, 135–42, 159–60

political activity, 9, 88

political art, 7–8, 50, 85, 159

political identity, 35

political subjectivization, 25, 89, 94

politics: of art, 7–9, 23–24, 50, 89, 152, 161; of exclusion, 12; of literary text, 4, 12, 24–26, 32, 45, 50, 89, 101; of literature, 1–6, 8, 25, 169; of the possible, 124, 147–51; of representation, 10, 14, 27, 29; of space, 41

possibilized speech, 84, 155–61, 164

the possible, politics of, 124, 147–51

postmodernism, 15, 41

privileging of language, 13, 25, 55, 157

propriety of speaking, 14, 96, 159

protests/protestors, 4, 46–47, 52–55, 132, 135, 138, 141–42

psychological autopsy *(simni pugŏm)*, 65–69

Purim affair, 1, 6

Pusan-Masan protests (1979), 47

radical communicability, 15, 43

radical potential, 10, 81, 161

rambling speech, 11

Rancière, Jacques, 7–9, 25, 32, 41, 68, 80, 89, 90, 95, 128, 152–53, 157–58

real cinema, 105

realism: in documentary, 22, 74, 83, 90, 106, 121, 168; euphemism and, 167–68; fantasy and, 22, 141; hyperrealism, 22; identity and, 25, 128, 153; modern realism, 101; ontological realism, 18, 22; *The Orphan Master's Son* and, 87–91, 104–19; privileging of, 25; traumatic realism, 22

realist insult, 74, 85, 88, 163

realist shame, 66, 70, 74, 153, 166

real-life scenes, 106, 111

redemption narratives, 21, 126, 131, 146–48

referential illusion, 102

religious silence, 205n40

representation, politics of, 10, 14, 27, 29

representation of speech, 7, 15, 44

resistant politics, 3

return of the real in South Korean fiction, 21, 27–29, 40–44

rhetorical behavior, 22

Roh Moo-hyun, 1, 3

romance narratives, 130, 143–45, 153

Rothberg, Michael, 22, 45

Sakai, Naoki, 35

salvation narratives, 4–6, 12, 19, 21, 123–26, 131

"Sea and Butterfly" (Pada wa nabi) (Kim Insuk), 27–28, 33, 37, 42

sensibility: boundaries of, 43; distribution of, 41, 129; in film, 20–21, 124–29, 148–51; identity and, 157; in novels, 58, 119; shift in, 32; speech and, 43, 49, 152

Shin Dong-hyuk, 99–100

Index 223

silence: breaking of, 2, 5–7, 24, 106, 117, 119–20, 155, 164; civilized humanity and, 23; as communication, 40; in film, 3–7, 126; impossible speech and, 12, 93–96, 103, 117, 143, 146, 154–57, 167–68; logic of identification, 89; of migrant laborers, 29, 43, 49–50, 64; obstinate silence, 33; politics of, 2, 61–62, 161, 164; realist insult and, 85; religious, 205n40; stubborn silence, 15; testimony and, 68; trauma and, 24

silent speech, 32, 65, 158

social support systems, 9

Sonyŏni onda (Han Kang). *See A Boy Is Coming*

soteriological narratives, 6, 8, 19, 123, 131, 146

Sŏ Yŏngch'ae, 60

space: blank spaces, 52, 65, 73; in film, 20–21, 125–35, 157; of general visibility, 166–68; identity and, 23; intimate spaces, 87; marginal spaces, 30; politics of, 41; transgression of generic norms, 22, 123–42, 148–50, 156–57; trauma and, 59, 73; unknowable space, 120

speech: bodily speech, 97, 164; boundaries and, 10, 12–16, 25–26, 39, 89, 96, 153–61; euphemisms and, 167–68; in film, 20; fluency of, 34–40; identity of, 42, 84, 166; involuntary, 11, 18, 86, 89, 102–3; nonsensical speech, 12–13; outside established discourse, 11; possibilization of, 84, 155–61, 164; rambling, 11; representation of, 7, 15, 44; sensibility and, 43, 49, 152; silent speech, 32, 65, 158. *See also* impossible speech

Spring Day (Pomnal) (Im Ch'ŏru), 57, 80

Ssaibogŭjiman kwaench'ana (I'm a Cyborg, but That's OK) (2006): identity in, 139–41; introduction to, 19–22, 123–29; linguistic malleability in, 141; place in, 135–42; politics of the possible, 124, 147–51; space in, 125–35, 156–57

subjective memory, 50, 60

suffering narratives, 119–20, 154

Su Kyŏng, 40

survival narratives, 66, 131, 137, 144–46

Syngman Rhee, 47

testimony: in *A Boy Is Coming* (Han Kang), 65–69, 96–97; compulsory, 12, 17; in documentary, 3, 85–86, 101; with given narrative, 106; limits of, 65–69; silence and, 68; transformation of, 101–3, 153

There a Petal Silently Falls (Ch'oe Yun), 79

tie of blood, 15, 27, 34, 42–43, 153, 157

tie of language, 15, 27, 34, 43, 153

torture: in documentary, 3; in film, 3–4, 164; identity and, 110, 164–65; logic of, 84, 97, 102, 106, 110, 164

totalitarianism, 18, 87–89, 108, 117, 119–20

transference, 125, 128, 133–35, 141

transformation narratives, 3, 6, 57, 101, 123, 130, 137, 148–49, 153, 160

transgression: of boundaries, 34, 125–28, 142, 147–49; of identity, 121, 124–25, 129; violent inclusion, 10–11; of voices and idioms, 14

transgression of generic norms: introduction to, 123–29; politics of the possible, 124, 147–51; role of place in, 135–42; role of space in, 22,

224 *Index*

123–42, 148–50, 156–57; transference and, 125, 128, 133–35, 141
transnational migration, 14, 28
trauma: afterward-ness of, 75–83; as basis for community, 4, 49, 51, 56, 58–60, 73; boundaries and, 79, 89; in *A Boy Is Coming*, 75–83; in documentary, 79–80; hereditary trauma, 75, 81; human rights and, 167; identity and, 48–49, 57; logic of, 16, 83, 99; melancholic reproduction of, 25; memorialization/memorization of, 3–6, 154; as piercing, 70, 78–79, 156, 167; realism and, 22; silence and, 24; space and, 59, 73
traumatropism, 16, 45, 48, 50–51, 59, 73, 75, 79, 83
true memory, 49–50, 72
truth in documentary, 121, 163, 166

Under the Sun (2015), 104–5
unintelligibility, 15, 24, 29, 33, 40–41, 50, 58, 75, 78, 157
universal humanity, 31–32
unknowable space, 120
urban poverty, 27, 34

victimhood narratives, 16, 22, 46–48, 61, 68, 160, 166–67
violent inclusion, 10–11

White, Hayden, 32

Yi Ch'angdong, 69
Yi Haejun, 19, 123
Yi Kyŏngjae, 31–32, 39
Yŏn Namgyŏng, 30–31, 35–36

Žižek, Slavoj, 106

Index 225

Printed in the USA
CPSIA information can be obtained
at www.ICGtesting.com
JSHW081514031224
74705JS00001B/8